Literacy

Literacy
An introduction

RANDAL HOLME

EDINBURGH UNIVERSITY PRESS

© Randal Holme, 2004

Edinburgh University Press Ltd
22 George Square, Edinburgh

Typeset in 10/12 Times New Roman
by Servis Filmsetting Ltd, Manchester, and
printed and bound in Great Britain by
The Cromwell Press Ltd, Trowbridge, Wilts

A CIP record for this book is available from the British Library

ISBN 0 7486 1688 8 (hardback)
ISBN 0 7486 1689 6 (paperback)

The right of Randal Holme
to be identified as author of this work
has been asserted in accordance with
the Copyright, Designs and Patents Act 1988.

Published with the support of the Edinburgh University Scholarly
Publishing Initiatives Fund.

Contents

List of figures   xi

Introduction   1
    The elusive nature of literacy   1
    Analogical literacies   1
    The socio-economic nature of literacy   3
    Literacy's use of sign-systems   4
    Literacy's use of language   5
    Literacy and mind   6
    The many-fold nature of literacy   6

PART I: THE SOCIO-ECONOMIC NATURE OF LITERACY

Chapter 1 Functional Literacy   11
    Introduction   11
    Literacy and economy   11
    Functionality and social change: the literacy campaign   13
    Functionality and economy   15
    Functionality and development economics   15
    Functional literacy in the developed world   17
    Functional literacy and social exclusion   19
    Problems with the idea of a functional literacy   21
    Problems with functional literacy: the economic impact   21
    How do we construct literacy according to what it allows us to do?   27
    The problem of treating literacy as a set of competencies: the need
       for a cultural literacy   30
    Conclusions   33

Chapter 2 Critical Literacy   36
    Introduction   36
    Two tenets of post-modernism   37
    Post-modernism and minority movements   37

Who we are shapes how we see: we have no final vocabulary   39
Critical discourse analysis   44
Systemic functional linguistics   45
Metaphor and critical literacy   49
Towards a participatory pedagogy   52
Critical literacy in practice   54
Difficulties with critical literacy   57
If 'there is nothing outside the text', how do we know anything?   58
Problems with the concept of criticality   59
Conclusions   61

Chapter 3 From Literacy to Literacies   64
Introduction   64
Social practice: literacy practice   65
The practice as a context of use   67
The variety and history of literacy practices   70
Conclusions   77

Chapter 4 Literacy and Language Choice   80
Introduction   80
Why there is a language choice   80
Responding to the language-choice question   83
Attitudes to language   83
Bilingualism and biliteracy   87
How the use of languages is predicated upon economic, political
   and military power relationships   89
Conclusions   92

PART II: SIGN

Chapter 5 Understanding Sign   99
Introduction   99
The nature of sign   100
Different kinds of sign   101
Signs and the development of pre-writing   104
Symbol interpretation: categories and prototype theory   104
Symbol manipulation: the importance of metonymy   107
Metonymy and indexical signs   108
Conclusions   109

Chapter 6 Writing   111
Introduction   111
Writing systems   111
The alphabet   111

The syllabary   113
Distinguishing syllabaries from alphabets   114
The Chinese writing system: a morphosyllabic script?   117
Writing and non-writing: semasiographic systems   121
Conventional and iconic semasiographic systems: the role of
    metonymy in visual meaning representation   124
Conclusions   132

Chapter 7 Writing through Time   135
Introduction   135
From accidental to motivated sign-creation   135
Early writing systems   137
The evolution of the alphabet   142
Conclusions   143

Chapter 8 The Nature of Writing   145
Introduction   145
Writing systems as technological solutions   145
Successful writing systems must represent speech   146
The question of phonocentrism and the centrality of writing   148
Conclusions   149

PART III: THE LANGUAGE OF LITERACY

Chapter 9 Basic Differences between Speech and Writing   153
Introduction   153
Personal vs. interpersonal   154
Monologue vs. dialogue   156
Durable vs. ephemeral   159
Contextualised vs. decontextualised   160
Scannable vs. linearly accessible   163
Planned/highly structured vs. spontaneous/loosely structured   163
Syntactically complex vs. syntactically simple   167
Concerned with past and future not the present   168
Formal vs. informal   169
Expository- and argument-oriented vs. event- and narrative-oriented 170
Abstract vs. concrete   172
Syntactically and morphologically complete   174
Conclusions   176

Chapter 10 Dimensions of Difference between Spoken and Written Language 178
Introduction   178
What is a dimension of difference?   178
Narrative vs. non-narrative concerns   179

Explicit vs. situation-dependent reference   180
Persuasion   180
Higher lexical varieties   180
Informational elaboration under strict, real-time conditions   181
Conclusions   181

Chapter 11 Written Language in Context   183
Introduction   183
Understanding genre   183
Grammatical metaphor as an expression of how register and
    genre affect text   186
Looking at text   191
Conclusions   193

PART IV: LITERACY AS MIND

Chapter 12 Social Practice and a Socio-historical Theory of Mind 197
Introduction   197
A socio-historical construction of mind   198
The zone of proximal development   201
Conclusions   203

Chapter 13 Great Divide Theory   205
Introduction   205
The historical Great Divide   205
The psychological Great Divide   210
Literacy practices and Vygotsky's view of mind   214
Scaffolding with literacy practices   216
Conclusions   219

Chapter 14 Literacy and Patterns of Mind   220
Introduction   220
Frame theory   220
Script theory   222
Schema theory and narrative frames   222
Genre, schema and literacy practice   223
Image schema   224
Conclusions   231

PART V: CONCLUSIONS

Chapter 15 The Social Nature of Literacy   235
Introduction   235
Literacy as skill, practice and socio-economic function   235

Contents

Participatory appraisal: the model in practice   237
Text as a forum of the literacy practice   238
Conclusions   239

Glossary   240
References   249
Index   262

List of figures

3.1 The configuration of literacies   ·   67
6.1 The Hiragana syllabary   114
6.2 The trilateral root in Arabic (DeFranus 1989: 172)   115
6.3 'I ate': an illustration of the rebus principle   118
6.4 The evolution of the Chinese character for horse 'mǎ' (Halliday 1979)   118
6.5 The difference between texts that represent meaning and texts that represent language   123
6.6 Graphic extensions of alphabetic text   127
6.7 Blend use in totem creation: the centaur (derived from Fauconnier and Turner 2002)   130
6.8 Rebus as a cognitive blend   131
7.1 The use of metaphor and metonymy in the interpretation of accidental signs   137
7.2 The abstraction of cuneiform signs (Halliday 1979)   139
7.3 Egyptian determinatives (Collier and Manley 1998)   140
7.4 Consonantal hieroglyphs (Collier and Manley 1998)   140
7.5 The derivation of the letter m   143
9.1 A continuum of difference between speech and writing   177
11.1 Martin's model of genre (based on Martin 1997)   185
11.2 History genres and their proximity to spoken forms (based on Coffin 1997)   187
11.3 Literacy and context configuring grammatical metaphor   190
12.1 Vygotsky's two-channel model of psychological development   200
12.2 Vygotsky's zone of proximal development   202
13.1 Accommodating a social practice view of literacy within a socio-historical model of mind   216
14.1 Genre as an attribute of practice and frame   224
14.2 Exploiting a metaphor of spatial connection *circa* 1530 (by permission of the British Library)   228

14.3 Geneaology, spatial metaphor and lineage as an ascending
order: 'the house of wisdom' (by permission of the British
Library)   229
14.4 Literacy's many dimensions: the tree diagram shows a sentence
at four levels of analysis   230

Introduction

The elusive nature of literacy

When asked to define literacy, students will often say that it refers to the practice of reading and writing. Others will think more about the adjective, 'literate', and say how it means 'an ability to read and write' or 'the knowledge of reading and writing'. Because such interpretations are generally suggested without hesitation or great thought, it seems safe to say that most people who can read or write have a fairly clear idea of what literacy is. But when we look more closely at any definition of a practice or a state of knowledge it can become harder to discover what we really mean. For example, if we were to operate with the definition that 'literacy is the knowledge of reading and writing', we might want to ask several further questions:

1. How much does one have to know about reading and writing to be literate?
2. What does it really mean to read and to write?

Each of these questions raises further problems. We might ask whether we are illiterate if we make an occasional spelling mistake or fail to use an accepted form of written grammar in a sentence such as 'He ain't coming home'. When considering the meaning of reading and writing, we might question whether 'reading' means being able to understand road signs, differential equations or texts with multiple graphic insertions. And the problem does not end here.

Analogical literacies

Understanding the nature of literacy is made more complicated by how the term's frame of reference is extended by analogy. We therefore talk about *analogical literacies* (Wiley 1996). These use the term literacy to refer to meanings that are similar to its original sense in some basic ways but different in others. For example, a core feature of literacy's meaning is 'a knowledge', often of the basic skills, of 'reading and writing'. Now we use the term to refer simply to basic knowledge as in 'computer literacy'. Though even more confusingly, computer literacy is also bound up with reading and writing skills. Some other extensions related to this idea of basic or survival knowledge are: 'historical literacy', 'emotional literacy', 'citizenship literacy', 'artistic literacy', 'scientific literacy' and 'geographical literacy'.

'Literate' may also be used on its own to refer to people who are well read in a given literacy culture. In the English-speaking world, it may refer to people who command a more extensive, and often Latinate, vocabulary, producing sentences such as 'I received a book' instead of 'I got a book'. In the United Kingdom, the recent introduction of a National Literacy Strategy (NLS) has extended the meaning of literacy in other ways. The NLS asserts that literacy 'unites the important skills of reading and writing' and that 'speaking and listening' are also part of the Literacy Framework (DFEE 1998). The strategy elaborates that 'good oral work enhances pupils' understanding of language in both oral and written forms and of the way language can be used to communicate' (ibid.). Clearly there are two quite major assumptions about the nature of literacy that underpin this view.

First is the idea that literacy is somehow associated with a different, more elaborate and effective use of language. To be literate is no longer about just being able to read and write; it is about speaking and understanding the more elaborate forms of language that literacy has allowed us to create. De Temple and Snow (2001: 56) take this one step further, concluding that their definition of literacy does not 'place' books at its centre so much as 'conversations about books'. Second is the assumption that structured speaking and listening promote the successful use of written language, and that successful oral communication is fostered by contact with the written word.

A further development of this idea is that if literacy includes our ability to talk about books, then it may also be implicated in the enhancement of the thinking processes that underlie such talk. Literacy then comes to suggest a capacity to talk and, hence, to think about complicated issues and abstract problems. Literacy thus assumes a variety of spin-off activities and benefits from the core skills of reading and writing. Although few now contest these benefits, we should remember that people have not always been so sure about them. The Ancient Greeks had many concerns about the effects of literacy. Plato, for example, worried that the artful nature of writing would corrupt the integrity of language, interfering with the clarity of its representation of the human soul (Derrida 1997: 34).

The concept of a *visual literacy* adds further confusion because it makes us think harder about the perceptual area in which reading must first operate. Visual literacy is about the ability to interpret diagrams and pictures. At first sight this might seem to be an odd usage since when we see a picture of a 'dog' we think we know whether it is a good likeness or not. But even quite basic acts of image recognition may be based upon our having imbibed cultural traditions of learning. Pictures employ perspective to give the illusion of three-dimensional space. Representative artists commonly use perspective, increasing the size of an object in order to make it appear closer to us. Another different perception would be that size is associated with the importance of what is being represented, not with its proximity to us. Certainly, the inhabitants of the Byzantine Empire would have seen pictures that way when they made their representations of Christ larger than any other figure in a picture. More radically, it has been claimed that when illiterates in Madagascar were shown simple representations of objects they were often 'image-blind', seeing the picture 'not as a representation of reality but as an object in itself' or a collection of 'lines' (UNESCO 1973: 36). These people lived in communities that were almost totally deprived of visual images. How we perceive a picture is a product of our being literate in the visual conventions that operate at a given time. Pictorial representations depend upon the use of conventions that we have absorbed from birth and in which we are made literate by the fact of growing up in a visually-oriented culture.

Few would disagree that to understand visual information as graphs or timetables is part of the modern concept of being literate. Yet visual literacy may also be a precursor to literacy. This is not just showing picture books to children before they can read. The French national curriculum advocates that the year before letters are introduced should be spent in the visual literacy tasks of shape recognition and discrimination. These tasks are called *pre-reading* (prélecture). Visual literacy is therefore bound up with literacy both as its precursor and as a set of component skills.

There are many other extensions of literacy that we could discuss. My key point is that whether these refer to computers, pictures or emotions, they are not just different ways of using the same word, literacy, they also reveal how broad and ubiquitous the topic has become. Even when we confine our concept of literacy to activities associated with reading and writing, it is not open to easy definition. I will now think more about quite where these complexities lie.

The socio-economic nature of literacy

Reading and writing are about the interpretation of language or meanings when these are realised as visual signs. A sign is something we hear, see, touch or smell and which refers 'to something other than' itself (Johansen and Larsen 2002: 1). The creation and interpretation of such signs is inescapably a social activity. Generally, we convey meanings as signs so that others can interpret them. Of course, we write shopping lists and secret diaries only to ourselves. But shopping lists are exchanged for goods in the social forum of the supermarket, while diary writers are not so much engaged in lonely monologue as operating a socially sanctioned method of reflecting upon their life and its problems. Literacy is therefore inescapably a social phenomenon.

A core function of society is economic. Literacy's social function cannot be separated from the economic advantage that it clearly confers upon the societies that make use of it. Educational economists are interested in how literacy may or may not affect economic performance. The concept of 'functional literacy' is finally about whether an individual has the literacy they need to fulfil a given socio-economic role. In placing literacy in society, I will also be examining it within the economy of which it is a part.

In Part I, therefore, I will examine the socio-economic nature of literacy. I will look at how we can see literacy as simply an ability to accomplish certain socio-economic objectives such as reading an instruction manual, enjoying a newspaper or completing a tax return. I will consider how a lack of literacy may make us socially dysfunctional in a society where it is assumed that everybody can read and write. I will also ask whether literacy should not also be about achieving a higher level of understanding of the social forces to which we are subject. I will discuss whether the responsibility of literacy teachers goes further than simply helping their students to consume a written instruction, extending towards asking why that instruction was given at all.

A culture consists of certain smaller communities that are identifiable by how they practise certain skills. For example, trades-people and artisans perform certain job skills. The way that carpenters shape wood or hunters catch their quarry will make the practices that start to give a culture its identity. However, social practices go far beyond these job skills. They embrace the types of interactions that we have when we work or play and the way we may or may not defer to older or more senior people. They arise from religious rituals and numerous uses of language. In Part I, I will examine what is meant by these practices. I will consider how our idea of literacy can itself be developed when we understand it as a collection of such social practices, such as exchanging text messages or reading novels, rather than as some single, overarching activity in which we all participate.

A view of society as separate social groups using literacy in different ways must also provoke thought about how society also includes cultural and linguistic minorities who use different languages, and the different ways of using literacy that these involve. Part I will therefore also think about the question of the languages in which literacy should be delivered.

Literacy's use of sign-systems

Literacy deals with activities that emerge from the processes of encoding and decoding language and meanings as visual signs. The nature of these processes, whether they are perceived as operating in language, mind, society, economy or across history, cannot but be affected by the type of sign-system in which they must finally reside. For example, the iconic or pictographic writing systems of the Incas in pre-Columbian Mexico did not represent a language in the precise sense of setting out a particular form of words. The same signs could be interpreted differently by different readers and might be decoded into different forms of words. Such systems posit a very different concept of reading from any which would be common today. The literacy that resulted would also be very different.

Part II of this book will therefore accomplish the second objective of understanding more about literacy's sign systems. This study will carry us into a discussion about the nature and history of writing and its relationship to other visual sign systems. It will also steer us towards an examination of the different types of writing systems in use in the world today and how they are constructed.

Literacy's use of language

If literacy is partly a visual sign system it is also bound up with an even more complex use of sign: namely, language. It should be clear to any user of written language that when we write we do not produce the same kind of language as when we speak. This is obvious in the case of an academic essay but it is also the case in a rapid exchange of messages between mobile phones. The latter practice forces important changes in our approach to writing and may sometimes seem to unfold like a spoken conversation. Yet, the representation of language and meaning on a mobile phone is effort-intensive in a way speech is not, certainly more so than speaking or using a larger keyboard. This forces us to search for ways to economise on effort at the level of the signs that are used. The result is a revival of methods of meaning construction that would have been familiar to some of our ancient forebears.

It has been argued that this need for language to reorganise itself to fit a different system of representation was one of the very early effects of literacy (e.g. Derrida 1997, Foucault 1974, Petterson 1996). Yet exactly how literacy re-engineers or repackages language remains a subject of intense debate. One effect is in language standardisation. Developing a set way to use a language with an idea of what is correct and what is not is very much a product of literacy. In the early medieval world, when literacy was not widespread, the vast majority of people spent their lives without going far from the village where they were born. It did not matter greatly if the dialect spoken by one community was not fully intelligible to people who lived in another community that was not very far away. There was no great reason for even adjoining groups to communicate with each other. Writing carried language across time and space in a manner that had never been possible before. If the message of one community can be carried into another, then there is a need for it to be understood. In fifteenth- and sixteenth-century England this created a great pressure to standardise the way English was used. This standardised form of English was itself a type of dialect, or *grapholect*, because of its development as a written form. The grapholect is also why literacy educators need to be aware of how the acquisition of literacy is about acquiring a way of using language.

Part III of this book will therefore look at the question of literacy and language, and the extent to which literacy promotes different methods of language use. We will look at how the concepts of a genre or text-type and of register can help us to understand how the written medium will adjust its way of using language according to different contexts and circumstances. We will ask if the field of corpus linguistics with its related techniques of computer analysis can help us construct the differences between spoken and written usage as these are based upon data derived from how people actually speak and write. Such data will tell us about the real as opposed to hypothetical differences between spoken and written English.

Literacy and mind

A study of literacy will also be too limited in scope if it perceives itself simply as a system of communicative exchange that has no reference to how it impacts upon the minds that communicate. If a social context exerts an effect on language, it must be through the medium of the mind by which it is produced. Even if literacy is seen purely as set of socio-linguistic practices, we cannot deny these a mental existence.

My last area of enquiry, therefore, will be about literacy as a mental construct. A reference to the mental existence of literacy may also tempt us towards some thought about the nature of reading and writing, as these are processes of mind. The question of how we read and the related area of reading disabilities has formed a huge area of psychological inquiry, spawning a significant literature. Writing processes have also become the subject of growing interest. These topics would require another book. In Part III, my focus will not be here upon how we accomplish and acquire the literacy skills of reading and writing. I will consider literacy itself as a form of mental organisation, asking whether or not being literate can help us to conduct other cognitive operations such as the production of logical argument.

The many-fold nature of literacy

These, then, will be the four core themes of this book:

1. Literacy: in society and economy
2. Literacy as sign
3. Literacy as language
4. Literacy as mind

Some scholars argue that literacy should be viewed in a particular way, as an economic function or as a social practice. Whilst giving credence to many of these views, our larger conclusion will be that a singular outlook impoverishes the nature of this subject.

After the development of quantum physics in the first half of the twentieth century, light came to be seen as having a dual nature. It was waves or particles according to the method by which it was captured. If a common feature of the physical universe can be perceived as having a two-fold nature, then it may not be stretching our imagination to allow an abstract phenomenon such as literacy to take some of the different forms that we can reasonably ascribe to it. Literacy can then hold those forms at one and the same time, revealing its complex nature. This many-fold nature of this literacy is what we will now explore.

Part I

The Socio-Economic Nature of Literacy

1 Functional Literacy

Introduction

Seeing literacy as the mastery of a set of skills can mean that this mastery is never attained. There is always a way in which a person can be more skilled, or a better reader and writer. The indeterminate nature of what being literate means was clearly acknowledged in a UNESCO report:

> Literacy is a characteristic acquired by individuals in varying degrees from just above none to an indeterminate upper level. Some individuals are more or less literate than others but it is really not possible to speak of illiterate and literate persons as two distinct categories. (UNESCO 1957)

One way to decide what it means to be literate is by asking what we want literacy for. Somebody who wants to be a lawyer needs a different kind of literacy from somebody who wants to be a soldier. Literacy is then no longer a fixed set of competencies that everyone in basic education is struggling to acquire. It means having the level of reading and writing that allows you to follow your chosen career path and to do what society requires of you. The concept of a *functional literacy* is then born.

This chapter will explore that concept. It will examine the literacy function as economic and social. It will also look at the concept of literacy 'dysfunctionality' by looking at the link between literacy and criminality. Finally, it will look at problems with the idea of functionality.

Literacy and economy

We are now quite used to thinking about education as being linked to the economic performance of both the individual and their society. The post-industrial emphasis upon a 'knowledge economy' creates further justification for this increasing investment because it treats learning itself as a commodity that can be sold or exchanged for goods. Post-industrial societies turn from making things to manufacturing knowledge. A parallel concept is that of *human capital*, where a nation invests in its population in order to make them more skilled and more productive. In the subject of development economics, the concept of *diminishing marginal productivity* states that if you use more and more of a *variable factor* such as labour upon the fixed amount of another factor such as land, then you will achieve a diminishing return (Todaro 2000: 54). In order to counter this, we must enhance the value of that variable factor. A key variable factor is labour and we can increase its value through education and training. Thus three farmers will get proportionately less from a given plot of land than two with the same level of agricultural skills. A way to counter this is for a country to invest in its human capital by raising the level of their skills. Such an investment may improve the productivity of an individual, increasing the amount of wealth they produce.

To ensure that education plays a role in the value-enhancement of labour, we can examine formal and informal education much in the way that we look at other industrial processes. Education and training then become a means to *add value* to the students who are 'its products' just as manufacturing increases the worth of raw materials by turning them into usable goods. If we see education and training as being about adding value to 'the variable' that is a workforce, then we need to ask if the knowledge we teach can translate into work or social skills that will make students more productive. Functional literacy consists of some of the *basic skills* that the individual needs to fulfil their economic and social potential. The concept of functional literacy should therefore be associated with that of education and training as adding value through training in basic skills.

A more traditional or humanist view of education would find this insistence on a link between learning and socio-economic benefit surprising, not to say distasteful. Education was not about finding better ways to do something else, it was about the development of self or a process of becoming a complete and right-thinking person. Such a view has fashioned our approach to education since classical times. Plato held that education was about the achievement of 'discipline, courage, generosity, greatness of mind' and other similar virtues (Plato 1974). Until more recently, educational debate was not about ways to enable the student to be more socially or economically productive. It was about the type of person the learner would become.

Others disputed the link between literacy education and wealth production on economic grounds. Some eighteenth- and early nineteenth-century commentators perceived a negative association between successful education and a successful economy, arguing that a well-educated labouring class would be functionally detrimental. There was a concern that an ability to read and write might create difficulties if servants could read their master's or mistress's letters (Graff 1991: 174).

Enlightenment philosophy also linked eighteenth-century ideas of literacy education to socio-economic function. However, this was most often based on the belief that a 'properly educated people would understand' and so 'accept their place in society' (Graff 1991: 178). Adam Smith, generally recognised as a founder of the discipline of economics, was less concerned about maintaining the status quo and more interested in understanding how nations achieved prosperity. He considered it economically beneficial for all citizens to learn the skills of reading, writing and counting (ibid.). In 1848, the Chief Superintendent of Education for Upper Canada, Egerton Ryerson, made a clear statement about the functional nature of literacy education when he declared that 'education' was 'designed to prepare us for the duties of life'. Later, he elaborated that a 'mechanic' would be 'a member of society' and as such 'should know how to read and write' (Graff 1981: 232).

The military provided another forum where it was thought an individual's education might be linked to how good they were at what they did. Shipboard schools were common in the British Navy of the eighteenth century. The Navy always had difficulty recruiting men and was often a refuge for the least advantaged and hence least educated in society. Literacy education was part of life on many warships, even if this provision was inconsistent, ad hoc and not clearly linked to the successful operation of what was, by the standards of the time, a complicated technology. Significantly, the case for greater investment in education was also pressed by military anxieties during the late nineteenth century. During the 1870s, the rapid victories of Prussia over France in the Franco-Prussian war were commonly attributed to the effectiveness of Prussian schoolrooms (Cipolla 1969). The modern concept of a functional literacy may itself have evolved in the US Army, which in 1942 had to introduce literacy education after deferring the draft for 433,000 people because they could not understand basic written instructions.

Functionality and social change: the literacy campaign

Our notion of a literacy 'function' should not always be grounded in economy. The Organisation for Economic Co-operation and Development (OECD) has come to understand functionality more broadly. It is about the individual's use of 'printed and written information in society to achieve' their 'goals' (1997). These 'goals' have traditionally been seen as both social and economic. We need literacy to work and to make the informed judgements that participation in a democratic society requires. This understanding of the social importance of literacy was not new either, even though its incorporation into a concept of functionality was. Both the Romans and Greeks saw literacy as a condition of full civic participation and, hence, of citizenship itself. The Protestant reformation that swept through Europe in the sixteenth and seventeenth centuries made literacy into a religious duty. Literacy enabled the individual to read the scriptures, which were now translated from Latin into their mother tongue. In Catholic doctrine, the Church interpreted the Word of God to humanity. For

Protestants, the individual had a duty to receive that Word themselves. They had to read it in the scripture. We could now assess such a literacy as functional, in the sense of being a skill they acquired to undertake a specifiable function, albeit a socio-religious one.

In the literacy campaign we encounter another social dimension of functionality and perhaps some of the concept's limitations also. Functionality as a goal of literacy can seem socially conservative. It suggests that we are preparing people to fulfil a given social role and that this role and the society that confers it upon us are not factors we can change. Yet when we are becoming literate in order to fulfil a socio-economic objective, this objective could be part of a wider movement for social change.

Movements that advocate the spread of literacy generally do so with a strong sense of its socio-economic purpose. One of the world's first great literacy campaigns had religion as its purpose. Under the direction of the Lutheran Church, and often without any significant development in formal schooling, the reading levels of seventeenth- and eighteenth-century Sweden rose at an extraordinary rate. In the mid-seventeenth century, less than 50 per cent of the Swedish population could read. By about 1740, after an astonishing and almost unparalleled effort, this literacy level had increased to over 90 per cent (Johannson 1981).

In the nineteenth century the literacy goal was politicised. Socialist and Marxist thinkers stressed the political education of the individual. Marx and Engels' *Communist Manifesto* of 1848 held that home education was a form of parental exploitation that replicated the exploitative socio-economic structure of capitalism. Mass or 'social education' would therefore have to replace it in order to make people aware of the relationship of capital and labour (Marx 1848). Literacy education is now perceived as a vehicle for wider social re-engineering. Individual literacy functions are subsumed into a larger agenda of social change. To this end, Lenin, the leader of the Russian Revolution, advocated the establishment of 'industrial armies' in order to begin a 'literacy battle' (1913). 'Urban' and 'rural working people' were to co-operate in order to assist 'the cultural development of villages' (Lenin 1918).

The communist revolutions of China, Cuba and Nicaragua tried to reverse the cities' impoverishment of the countryside by mobilising the educated urban population to bring mass literacy to the peasantry. In the 1980s, for example, the Nicaraguan Sandinista National Liberation Front embarked upon a 'crusade' to eradicate illiteracy and raise revolutionary consciousness by allowing people access to the appropriate literature (Grigsby 1985: 66, cited in Rassoul 1999). They organised university and secondary-school students into brigades (*brigidista*) under the command of a teacher (ibid.). Such campaigns appear to have enjoyed some success, with levels of literacy in communist and ex-communist societies being higher than their economic performance would normally warrant. Towards the end of the twentieth century, this may have led UNESCO to adopt the rhetoric of a global campaign when they argued that literacy had become 'a fundamental human right' which would contribute 'to the liberation of man' (Rassoul 1999: 86). Borrowing the rhetoric of its success-ful campaign to eradicate the smallpox virus, UNESCO set out its intention to 'eradicate' illiteracy by the year 2000 (International Bureau of Education 1990). The metaphors of war and Lenin's 'literacy battle' were discarded for those of the illiteracy epidemic, of medicine, nutrition and human rights.

A concept of functionality questions a romantic humanism where the first goal of education is to widen horizons and foster individual development. It also sits uneasily with a concept of social hierarchy where the many must labour in ignorance so that they can maintain the quest for knowledge of the few. In this sense we can link a concept of functionality to the politicisation of literacy in the campaign and its mass mobilisation for human capacity-building. Yet, finally, functionality is less about social revolution than about fostering an expansion in socio-economic activity through individual capacity development. It is not about changing the status quo.

Functionality and economy

It should therefore be clear that when governments and organisations like UNESCO adopted a functional view of literacy in the 1950s, they were making a new appeal to a quite long intellectual tradition. What was different was the clarity with which the idea of functionality was linked to the concept of economy and society that had started to emerge. This linkage between lit-eracy, society and economy was made in two distinct but related areas:

1. In development economics and aid project design: in the search for ways to help the people of less developed countries to achieve greater prosperity, better health and greater self-fulfilment.
2. In the social, economic and educational problems of developed countries: in searching for ways to:
   • ensure a fuller participation in society by all a nation's citizens;
   • secure a future where prosperity was dependent on new 'knowledge-intensive' industries (industries that require the workforce to have high levels of skills and knowledge so that they could impart high added value to a product).

I will now look at functional literacy in these two areas.

Functionality and development economics

In the immediate post-war decades, 1950–1970, the large number of newly independent but industrially underdeveloped nations raised the question of how to accelerate economic development. Economic development was seen as a measure of how technology was used and produced. Development was also a measure of the effectiveness of the administration through which that technology was deployed in a given state. Literacy was seen as underpinning the effective implementation of technology and administration. Since the highest illiteracy rates are still found in the developing world, 50 per cent in South Asia for example, as opposed to 1 per cent and 2.5 per cent in North America and Europe respectively (Todaro 2000: 331), some elements of this thinking remain. This divide is further accentuated when figures for men and women are examined. For example, female adult literacy among all Less Developed Countries (LDCs) is 71 per cent of the figure achieved by men (ibid.: 334). The development gap was finally a knowledge and gender gap which had to be rectified through education.

For the governments of newly independent states, development was seen as a goal of independence. For the first president of Tanzania, Julius Nyerere, the urgency of this task meant education could not wait for a new generation of educated children to grow up and enter the workplace. Education had to begin with adults so that it would have 'an impact now' (Rassoul 1999: 106–7). Then as now, literacy was the skill on which the construction of formal education depended. A student who could not read or write could not study. Literacy was also a life-skill upon which future vocational and non-vocational learning was thought to depend. If an educated population was seen as essential to economic development, then literacy underpinned its achievement.

Functional literacy reached out of the educational arena and brought about improvements in 'productivity', thus increasing 'wages' and 'raising standards of living' (UNESCO 1972: 29). A further impact would be upon Gross National Product (GNP), with a related improvement in economic self-sufficiency and a decline in import dependency. Thus 'literacy and other forms of training should be linked horizontally to other types of social interventions and institutions to which individuals have daily access' (Wagner and Puchner 1992). Literacy was a feature of a larger developmental package. It was there in order to allow economic and social development to occur.

These literacy objectives therefore had to be identified or provided by the goals of the larger development project that literacy education was designed to facilitate. Thus the project designer had to begin by identifying different sets of objectives. These were characterised as 'economic', 'technico-occupational' (what would be done to reach the economic objective, e.g. improve fruit production to increase fruit exports) and socio-economic (how social organisation might have to change in order to accommodate new management techniques) (UNESCO 1973).

Functional literacy was 'treated as part of a continuum', not as a separate phenomenon. It was a continuum that led to functional education and through that to the better performance of tasks that could result in sustainable economic improvement (Shrestha 1997). There was also a growing awareness that the link between literacy and individual functionality can be less direct. Thus, it was recognised that one of the best ways to keep children in school in LCDs was by involving their mothers in literacy programmes. The children of literate mothers were more likely to complete their education (Eisemon et al. 1998). Functionality thus extended to an enhancement of the skills of parenthood. Functional literacy has also been broadened into a larger concept of 'health literacy'. Literacy was about achieving 'the cognitive and social skills which determine the motivation and abilities of individuals' 'to understand and use information to promote and maintain good health' (Nutbeam 1998).

Functional literacy in the developed world

Development economists and aid project designers seized upon the concept of functional literacy because it seemed to identify a remediable cause of poverty and underdevelopment. Yet we should not forget that the idea was formulated in order to help remedy the problem of poor literacy in the developed world as this affected the US Army in 1942. Furthermore, while interest in the functional concept declined among aid project designers working in the developing world, it became an increasingly important feature of the education debate that was taking place in developed economies. This was for two reasons, one related to the now familiar problem of deciding what being literate really means, the other to an agenda of wider socio-economic change.

The problem of literacy measurement is intensified in a developed economy where schooling, though sometimes resulting in educational failure, is at least universal. Functional literacy sees its component skills as spread out along a continuum. There are not two contrary states, literate and illiterate. Functional literacy recognises that people will master the skills of literacy to different degrees. Functional illiteracy occurs when the ability to read and write is not sufficient for an individual to engage in society, work effectively and pursue their life-style choices. At first sight, functional literacy therefore offers the educational economist different gradations of skills deficiency which are useful if we are to assess the literacy deficits of societies where it is unusual to meet people who are illiterate in an absolute sense. For example, we can talk of people whose literacy is so low that they cannot do anything but the most menial work. Then there are others whose poor level of literacy means that they perform certain job tasks badly. While both these categories constitute a serious economic problem, neither would be defined as illiterate in the sense of being unable to sign their names.

Functional literacy seems to have the advantage of assessing reading and writing skills according to a community's socio-economic needs. For example, an apprentice plumber now needs to do more than read a few words and decipher numbers. This is partly because plumbing is about more than just fitting pipes. Innovations in heating technology mean that a boiler will come with increasingly complicated installation instructions. These instructions will combine specialised texts and diagrams.

A concept of functional literacy asks whether a trades-person has the skills to understand material that is essential to their successful job performance. It suggests literacy does not imply the fixed level of competence that an individual should attain when leaving primary school. It must contain within it a capacity to ensure its future development so that individuals can keep pace with new technologies and the types of literacy demands that these make. Because it extends beyond reading and writing, functional literacy also enables us to take on board the question of visual literacy and diagram interpretation. It is extensible into health literacy as this permits understanding of how to stay safe at work and adopt a more sustainable life-style.

Economic change in developed countries also encouraged policy-makers to see literacy education as a form of human capital investment. Throughout the nineteenth and early twentieth centuries manufacturing had replaced agriculture as the main type of employment for the people of Western Europe and the United States. New industries demanded new industrial skills, particularly in metal working, but their accompanying need was for a large workforce which could learn limited work routines and tolerate high levels of boredom. Failures in literacy education may have partly been concealed by the fact that the ability to read and write was not always central to employment or successful job performance in such an economy.

Across Europe and the United States, the closure of mines and factories in the latter half of the twentieth century broke the link between schooling and employment within a given community. Basic education could not be seen as a gateway to employment when there were no visible employment prospects within a given area. For some individuals, a sense of literacy's irrelevance to their diminished economic prospects may also have been compounded by the rise of new audio-visual media and a consequent decline in the perceived need for recreational reading.

Globalisation, and the accompanying relocation of manufacturing employment to developing nations, contributed to the underdevelopment of certain regions within the United States, Europe and Japan. Competition from low-wage economies has also forced manufacturers to make their workforce more productive. The ability to acquire new skills or to extend old ones has become vital to the maintenance of a successful manufacturing base. Levels of literacy and numeracy underpin such human capital development. The concentration of new jobs in the high-tech and service industries of the knowledge economy has further exaggerated our sense of a gap between those who have basic skills that are strong enough to let them be trained for employment in a modern economy and those who do not.

A need for constant re-education and retraining gives literacy a larger dimension of functional significance. It is one of the instruments of re-education. In the UK, the Basic Skills Agency, charged with ensuring higher levels of basic education among British adults, defined literacy as 'the ability to read, write, and speak at a level necessary to *function* at work and in society in general' (Literacy Trust 2001). In 1993 a Gallup survey conducted in the UK also stressed the link between literacy and its function when it estimated the damage caused to the UK economy by problems with basic skills education at £4.8 billion a year. Such educational under-achievement was held to result in problems 'with quality control, lost orders, poor communications and constraints on internal promotions' (Kempa 1993).

This awareness of the functional nature of literacy has contributed to something of a panic about educational deficiencies. For example, in 2001, Britain's *Observer* newspaper carried the headline that literacy levels in the UK were worse than in 1912. This judgement was based upon a school inspectors' report which put the number of 15–21-year-olds unable to read and write at 2 per cent as opposed to the contemporary 15 per cent rate of functional illiteracy in 2001 (McVeigh 2001). However, assertions about the deteriorating literacy levels of developed nations are often suspect. A concept of functionality makes clear that the nature of literacy has changed because what we need it for has changed also. Even if we replicate the testing procedures used in earlier years – 1914, for example – then compare contemporary results with those of that time, this may not tell us much. A 1914 test might stress an ability to recognise incorrect spellings, a skill that may be less central to functional literacy in the age of the spell-checker. More important in contemporary literacy might be the ability to understand and reproduce information in graphic form, skills which would not have figured in 1914.

Functional literacy and social exclusion

Whether or not the measures talking of a decline in national literacy standards are correct, the linkage of these standards to a function or external criterion has stressed their importance. Literacy unlocks both the school curriculum and vocational training. Functional illiteracy has become part of an index of social exclusion. It has been associated with poorer employment prospects, malaise, poorer health, higher rates of criminality and re-offending by convicted criminals, younger parenthood and an increased likelihood of having children with learning problems (Bynner 2001, Dalglish 1982).

The link to deprived or socially excluded sections of developed country populations is best expressed by figures showing a high concentration of illiterates in certain areas of the UK. For example, in one deprived inner city area, Sparkbrook, in the city of Birmingham, 36.4 per cent of the population were defined as functionally illiterate; they were unable to understand written instructions, labelling for parcels, recipes and timetables (Literacy Trust 2001).

Of the measures that relate poor functional literacy to social exclusion, one of the best researched, and the most telling, deals with criminality. Such an interest is not new. The great nineteenth-century penal reformer, Elizabeth Fry (1780–1845), founded a school for the children of the female inmates of London's notorious Newgate prison, while introducing bible reading to accompany other 'improving' activities such as needlework. Across nineteenth-century Europe there was a developing consensus that literacy should be used as the medium for a moral education that would ensure greater social cohesion (Graff 1991: 262).

In the US, UK and Canada, prisoners are more likely to be illiterate than non-prisoners even if that correlation cannot support the belief that illiteracy is a cause of criminality (Palfrey 1974). For example, in the UK, Dalglish (1982) examined a cross-section of offenders who were either on probation or in penal institutions. On a scale corresponding to UNESCO's standard for functional illiteracy, 48–60 per cent of Dalglish's sample were functionally illiterate, with the proportion varying according to the strictness of the literacy measures that were applied (ibid.: 23). Figures for the population as a whole would be 15–20 per cent. Numerous studies completed in other countries support this view; see, for example, Roberts and Coffey (1976) and Hills and Karcz (1990) in the United States, as well as Ross (1978) in Canada.

There is obviously no sense in which those who have poor literacy are destined to penal servitude or will have an underdeveloped sense of social responsibility. We cannot assert that illiteracy is a cause of criminality because functional illiteracy is more common among prisoners than among the population at large. These studies are correlative only, indicating a positive statistical relationship between two phenomena, but pointing only to the possibility of a causal connection. There are also other factors that complicate this type of connection. For example, it could be that the embryonic criminal personality is less likely to tolerate schooling. The early problems with socialisation that may lead towards later criminal behaviour may also impede the acquisition of literacy.

One way to investigate the plausibility of that link is to look at another related area, the rate of *recidivism*. Recidivism refers to the return to prison of released prisoners after they commit further crimes. If prisoners who had improved their functional literacy in prison proved less likely to commit offences when released, then this would be a clearer link between a higher level of literacy skills and the ability to stay out of prison. The evidence here is more mixed and the probability is that literacy training needs to be integrated with the development of other skills. To have a lasting impact on criminal behaviour, functional literacy must be linked to the more elaborate forms of educational achievement for which it is a springboard.

Dalglish observed how poor literacy had resulted in poor community awareness (1982: 33) and that when literacy education was accompanied by discussion related to job applications and form filling, or used to promote cooking and dressmaking, educational programmes achieved a greater impact. Discussing Canadian programmes, such as that of the notorious Matsqui Penitentiary in British Columbia, Ross and Mckay reported on the achievement of a 38 per cent drop in recidivism when students undertook advanced courses in the humanities (Ross and McKay 1979). Even more impressive was a reduction in recidivism from 53 per cent to 6 per cent among the female inmates of another institution after they had received training in what might now be called emotional literacy, or in their ability to help each other with personal problems and conflict resolution (ibid.). A tentative conclusion might be that literacy is not itself functional in the sense of promoting our adoption of a law-abiding social role. It does, however, combine with other factors, such as the achievement of a higher level of education and training, to bring about greater social cohesion and economic growth.

Problems with the idea of a functional literacy

Broadly, functional literacy is based upon three core assumptions:

1. Literacy has an economic impact (if it does not, it has no economic function).
2. Literacy can be measured according to what it allows us to do.
3. A literacy shaped by the socio-economic opportunities that it affords us is a necessary and sufficient educational goal.

All of these assumptions are open to question if we are to explore the validity of the larger functional literacy concept. I will now explore each in turn.

Problems with functional literacy: the economic impact

Defining literacy according to its socio-economic function makes an assumption about the positive impact of literacy on the larger economy. If literacy does not have a significant socio-economic impact, then this would question the premise that it is a set of skills that enable an individual to function better in the socio-economic arena. We will therefore have to examine the nature of this impact more closely.

Those who link literacy and education to economic development should first look at the spread of literacy in the West and how this is related to the industrialisation of society. A straightforward causal relationship between the spread of literacy and economic growth would be indicated most clearly by an increase in the literate population when industrialisation spread through nineteenth-century Europe and North America. The evidence here is not convincing. Although literacy began to approach contemporary levels over the course of the nineteenth century, the relationship between 'literacy', 'work', 'occupation' and earnings was then, as now, an 'imprecise' and 'complex' one (Graff 1981: 233). The complexity of this relationship between literacy levels and socio-economic activity can be shown by Graff's study of 135 illiterates in Hamilton, Kingston and London, Canada. This sample was comprised of skilled artisans, with forty-four holding positions of higher rank. One cannot know how their lack of literacy impeded their daily existence, but it does not seem to have stopped them attaining a comfortable social position. By contrast, in a lower social strata, labourers, servants and seemstresses, for example, one can find quite high rates of literacy. Among female servants illiteracy was as low as 5 per cent, yet there is no evidence that this helped to lift them up the occupational ladder. Literacy cannot be identified as one of the major consistent factors which determined occupational status. The factors that do determine occupational status are gender, race and ethnic background, with women, blacks and Irish Catholics occupying the lower strata (ibid.: 234–6).

Graff's conclusion as to the complex and difficult relationship between an individual's literacy and their socio-economic function is supported by another study of England in the period 1750–1850 (Schofield 1981). Schofield concludes that literacy was widespread in nineteenth-century England, with evidence of higher earnings among literate people and an active literate culture among the working class. However, there does not seem to have been a growing perception that literacy education was a means through which to purchase a better future for one's children. What children studied and the time they spent in school was 'dependent on the occupation of their parents' (ibid.: 212). Even more relevant is how 'male illiteracy remained constant until the decade 1805–1815' despite this being a time when some of the foundations of the world's first industrial revolution were being put in place (ibid.: 212). This does not point to a strong causal link between levels of literacy and productivity at the time.

The probability is that an increase in literacy rates is as much a product of economic development as a cause. There does not seem to be much historical evidence for an easy causal connection between improving literacy and increasing economic growth. A society that is becoming more technologically innovative will start to make greater demands on the educational levels of some members of its workforce. The extent to which this will happen must depend on the types of innovation that are taking place and the type of community that is instigating them. Setting the new steam printing presses of the nineteenth century was obviously a craft steeped in a literacy tradition, yet the qualities needed to tend steam-powered looms largely involved an ability to remain alert during hours of repetitive operations. As our example of Sweden's literacy development showed, Scandinavia pioneered mass literacy after the Reformation, yet it is difficult to identify a clear economic benefit from this early emphasis on education. As Sandberg (1979) observes, 'the driving force' behind Scandinavia's economic growth in the nineteenth century remained 'the international processes of trade, migration and capital flows'. The literacy effect is less significant after these other, much larger effects have been accounted for (Vincent 2000: 83–4).

Although some occupations may encourage higher levels of literacy than others, a larger momentum may be created by literacy's social role. In any society, the plain fact that more people are becoming literate will create a larger need for literacy. One way to understand society is as a collection of *communities of practice*, a concept employed by ethnographers or anthropologists to examine how communities are created by their sharing of skills and activities (e.g Chaiklin and Lave 1993). Some communities of practice will have higher literacy demands than others and these will also change with time. For example, Graff (1991: 234–5) discusses how in the period 1660–1780, the commercialisation of agriculture in England meant that literacy became an increasingly important part of the 'nexus of exchange'. A greater number of literate farmers increased the pressure on the others to become literate, creating a greater functional literacy requirement. By contrast, rates of illiteracy among labourers and servants remained high throughout that period.

As more communities of practice develop a literacy requirement, not just to achieve more efficient work habits but also to ensure a greater cohesion and a more powerful sense of identity, so society as a whole develops a literacy culture to which people are expected to belong. A literate society makes the *modus operandi* of the illiterate inefficient even if, for some, that society's own paper-based practices are cumbersome and arcane. Even where the spread of literacy does not create greater prosperity for a society as a whole, it may do much to ensure the marginalisation and continuing impoverishment of its illiterate members.

One current view is that economic change in developed countries has created two tiers of literacy need. Howell and Wolf (1992) see a pressure to deskill the middle range of occupations, as these are categorised by earnings. The numerous clerks, book-keepers and secretaries who staffed private and public bureaucracies during the first half of the twentieth century typified a middle-income stratum whose high level of literacy and numeracy was a job requirement. By the end of the millennium, these job functions had largely been computerised. One assumption is that computerisation requires new and even more advanced forms of literacy, but another outlook is that it deskills clerical work by reducing it to set routines such as data entry (Perie et al.1999). According to this last opinion, a high level of literacy has become less central to the communities of practice of middle-income earners. At the same time, there has been no increase in the demand for literacy among the many occupations for which it always had a more marginal usefulness.

One proposal is that developed economies now have literacy needs which reflect an 'employment structure' that is increasingly polarised between jobs that are upskilling and those that are deskilling. In the United States, the labour market is seen as divided into two broad sectors. There is 'an econom-ically and socially advantaged sector' which places 'a high value on informa-tion technology' and its 'associated literacy skills', and 'a disadvantaged sector', where the routinisation and fragmentation of jobs makes literacy less and less relevant (Perie et al.1999). Yet one should be wary of assuming that all lower-level service sector jobs are being left with a low or declining literacy requirement. Some quite low categories of employment, such as shelf-stacking or care-work, might require a high literacy input. Shelf-stackers deal with product labelling and care-workers with medication, for example.

Literacy demands vary radically according to occupation. Yet there are also interesting variations between countries. Thus the literacy demands made upon managers in Poland are far lower than those made upon French-speaking managers in Switzerland (ibid.). This is a difference which cannot be disengaged from the large gap in wealth and productivity between these two countries. At the same time, the difference is not great between the literacy demands made upon a lower-status occupation. If the literacy demands on managers increases in line with economic output while those made on service personnel do not, then this gives an indication of a growing polarisation where company productivity is less likely to be affected by improved literacy among its blue-collar workers than among its managers. This conclusion is supported by Levine's (1986: 128) study of the US labour market. Levine found that lit-eracy problems constituted an insuperable barrier only to entry into jobs which had a supervisory component. He further cites the case of semi-skilled employees whose literacy problems seem to raise no barriers against their reaching productivity targets. Sub-literacy posed greater difficulties for job-seekers only when they had another attribute employers found unfavourable.

Despite these complications, the view put forward by scholars such as Bynner (2001) about the economic harm caused by poor literacy and numer-acy is uncompromising. When examining actual modern workplace situa-tions, Mikulecky and Kirkley (1998) cite 'vignettes' from modern industrial processes that question the assumption that automatisation reduces literacy needs. Their contention is that the rapidity of new technological processes can in fact multiply the cost of literacy-based errors.

In the developing world, the relationship between literacy levels and eco-nomic performance is also complicated. In 1968, it was calculated that a minimum threshold for economic growth was a 40 per cent literacy rate among a national population as a whole (Bowman and Anderson 1968). This rate would have to increase with economic growth if that growth was to be sustain-able. Yet this is not the same as saying that economic development will start to occur when a literacy rate of 40 per cent has been attained. Illiteracy rates of more than 60 per cent are now almost unknown. In all LDCs combined, the rate for adults was 31 per cent in the year 2000 (Todaro 2000), even though population increases have ensured that the total number of illiterates in the world rose in the last decades of the twentieth century. At the same time the decline in the number of illiterates as a proportion of population cannot always be identified as a factor that has encouraged economic growth in the areas where such growth has occurred. The lowest rates of economic growth by region have been seen in Africa, with some states such as Sierra Leone, Angola and Zimbabwe recording negative figures over the last decade. Yet Africa's 43 per cent illiteracy rate is lower than South Asia's 50 per cent, while Asia has been an area of quite high economic growth. Kerala, in India, on the other hand, has reduced country illiteracy rates but not developed country productivity.

Kerala's high literacy rate can be linked to two sets of unusual and conflicting circumstances, and these reveal the problem of generalising about literacy's socio-economic impact. The first feature is Kerala's long mercantile economic history (Gough 1968), perhaps testifying to how a rise in literacy rates is more a response to certain economic developments than a cause of them. The second set of circumstances adds a political rather than an economic dimension to Kerala's success. The state has a tradition of socialist government and replicates the socialist motivation for assuring widespread literacy.

Looking more widely, if we examine East Asia as opposed to Asia as a whole, we find an illiteracy rate of 16.9 per cent and a much higher economic growth rate than for Asia. Yet it is difficult to determine the extent to which East Asia's diminishing illiteracy rate is a product of higher economic growth or a contributor to it. In East Asian culture where Confucian traditions are deeply embedded, the quest for literacy cannot be separated from a wider emphasis upon the value of education and self-improvement. How far such an emphasis is connected to economic performance is unknown.

The optimistic post-war assumption that rising educational levels would trigger economic development has been increasingly subject to question. Quite early on, stern market economists such as Peter Bauer (1971) warned that economic development would not occur as a result of aid, whether in education or any other area. Development occurred when the right combination of social and market conditions were in place. In some parts of Africa the implantation of a literacy-based education in the medium of the colonial language may have drawn resources away from the need to establish stronger vocational training in lower-level job skills. When literacy is delivered in the colonial language, this can postpone its successful acquisition into the secondary level and beyond, creating a further drain on resources.

Literacy may have encouraged the development of bloated government bureaucracies in order to offer work to the literate products of schools and universities. These bureaucracies actually constrain economic activity by entangling business formation in a regulatory web that can be unravelled only by bribery. They also contribute to the inflation of wages beyond what is affordable because governments may prefer a secondary school or university graduate for a position that demands no more than primary qualifications.

'Under the pressure of the educated' wages are set, not at the level required for the job but according to the qualifications of the employee on entry (Todaro 2000: 337). According to Egbo (2000), colonial education may actually have contributed to a gender gap in Sub-Saharan Africa. Although patriarchal social structures were a feature of pre-colonial African society, her contention is that this patriarchal tendency was exaggerated by a school system that encouraged boys to acquire literacy while leaving girls at home.

The education system can itself become an economic drain on a country. The higher the educational level, the greater the cost of producing a graduate and the lower the likelihood of obtaining a satisfactory economic return. An investment in education may favour the individual who receives it, but this is not matched by the benefit obtained by the national economy (Todaro 2000). Yet the effect of these doubts about the wider benefits of formal education in LCDs has been to increase the interest in literacy projects during recent years. Uncertainty about the benefit of formal education has focused on the very high investment required by a tertiary student. Primary school pupils and adult literacy students cost less and offer the prospect of a more immediate economic return. A policy change by the aid agencies of the European Union and its member states means there is a new emphasis on poverty alleviation within localities or among particular communities and less focus on the larger development of a national economy. Poverty alleviation has placed an emphasis on literacy education because the poor of the LDCs tend to have low or non-existent levels of functional literacy.

There is also a growing interest in literacy as a component of a larger aid package. Literacy's impact should be perceived not at the macro-level as an effect on national development but as a micro-intervention in the lives of the poor and dispossessed. Literacy's function is the support of a project's other micro-objectives, whether these consist of improved community health, irrigation, lower rates of reproduction or a change in the terms of trade between a given community and the outside world. Literacy projects run in Uganda by the charity Actionaid, for example, combine literacy with practical instruction in reforestation, crop diversification and methods of improving crop storage (Eisemon et al. 1998).

Just as importantly, our concept of development has also changed. It is no longer determined by raw economic indicators such as per capita income (the average earnings of each member of a given country). We acknowledge that development should afford all people scope to realise their potential. Individual growth cannot be accomplished without providing for an individual's basic needs, but it also requires such core attributes as a respect for human rights and universal literacy. Thus the United Nations declared that 'an entitlement to literacy' is 'a basic human right' reflecting 'the central role of reading and writing in all societies' (UN Resolutions 45/199 and 50/143).

If we confine our concept of functionality to the micro-level, concentrating on what literacy allows an individual or a community to achieve, then it may also be easier to find literacy's economic effect. Functional illiteracy may come with a high functional price-tag for the individual even if its national impact is more muted. In developed nations, people with poor literacy may be consigned to the low-wage economy. Denny et al. (2000) produce good evidence for the positive effects of literacy upon earning power when literacy is taken in combination with cognitive ability and general education. However, the dominant positive effect seems to rest with what they term 'quantitative literacy', or an ability to understand and process numerical data. Thus key economic impacts come from a deficit in the larger area of basic skills and not just from poor literacy.

In developing countries, literacy does seem to offer clear economic benefits to the individuals who acquire it, even if this does not make a marked impact upon a given national economy. According to *human capital theory*, individuals invest in education because they will obtain a return in the form of higher earnings. Equally, households will cease to invest in education when the financial rewards of an additional year of schooling are less than its costs. A general eagerness to invest in education would indicate that the expected return is high. Support for this assertion comes from a study of the labour market of Ghana, which found a clear correlation between functional literacy and earnings (Blunch and Verner 1999). When the population is divided into five groups according to how much they earn, the lowest fifth have the lowest functional literacy rate at 13.55 per cent and the highest group have the best literacy rate at 54 per cent. The study's larger conclusion is that functional literacy is in fact a prerequisite for entry into a job market characterised by a labour surplus.

My larger conclusion is that literacy and economic development exist in a supply-and-demand relationship. Economic development stimulates a need for literacy and that development will be impeded without a literate population. It seems unlikely, however, that literacy will itself trigger economic development. We perhaps need to be more aware of the *symbiotic* relationship that exists between education and economy, or the relationship of mutual dependence. If one develops at the expense of the other, it may actually become detrimental to its future growth. At the individual level, the detrimental effects of poor functional literacy are clearer, in both the developing and the developed world. It is within the community and the individual life that we can make the clearest link between what literacy is and what it allows us to do.

How do we construct literacy according to what it allows us to do?

Another area of difficulty for functional literacy is even more central to the way the concept is constructed. Functionality refers to the literacy that allows the individual to manage their socio-economic existence, achieving what society requires of them and they require of it. Its usefulness for educational planning should relate to how it can identify literacy deficits, as for a manager who cannot process complicated graphs, or a machine operator who cannot read data printouts. This works when we want to ask if an individual has the literacy to do what they need or if their efficiency is impeded in some way. Yet when we specify functionality as the goal of a larger educational process, many problems emerge.

First, we do not know what a given individual is going to do in life when they are learning to become literate. Any attempt to declare that one group needs the functional literacy appropriate for doctors and another for tradespeople would undo the desire to foster social advance through education according to merit. This type of planning would have struck a chord of sympathy among those who clung to a fossilised social structure where those born to be labourers were destined to labour. Yet, it would be nonsensical in a modern knowledge economy which needs to find and foster ability wherever it might lie. This may be why the rhetoric of functional literacy will commonly link 'function' to an individual's achievement of 'their potential'. Yet when functionality is so linked it may collapse into a terminological vagueness that will no longer help us identify and remedy skills deficits. Functionality may be a useful concept for assessing the literacy of the workforce in relation to the tasks they have to perform. It may be relevant to workplace training but have less use for educational planning unless we treat literacy's function as the ability to cope with school curricula.

In the literature on testing and measurement, whether of literacy or any other ability, it is common to speak of *norm-referencing* and *criterion-referencing*. Norm-referencing means that we set our test levels according to what individuals commonly achieve. Thus, in British universities, BA degrees are divided into classes with a first being the best and a 'pass' the worst. These categories should be purely criterion-referenced. You get a first because you have satisfied the criteria that this category requires. Technically, 100 per cent of students could get this level in any given year, but in reality only a small percentage do. Recently, a university I know sent round a circular saying that not enough of its students were getting firsts; the percentage was lower than in other universities. This was an attempt at norm-referencing. It implied that each year a set percentage of students should get this grade. Getting a first was no longer about achieving the right standard; it was about being compared to other students and found to be better or worse than them. A problem for those who say they believe in maintaining standards is that criterion-referencing is in fact very difficult because one has to be able to identify absolutely what standards are and the criteria needed to meet them.

The functional literacy concept should be criterion-referenced against socio-economic needs. But a problem is that everybody's literacy needs are different. The literacy functions of a manager are different from those of the people who work for them. People's literacy needs are also liable to change. They may be promoted and find they have to produce written reports when before they did not. It is therefore difficult for educationists to talk about functional literacy targets when, logically, everybody will have different literacy functions and some of these may change over time.

It is impractical for a government to individualise literacy targets and perhaps this is why functional literacy was initially norm-referenced. In 1947, the Bureau of the Census held that a US citizen was 'functionally illiterate' if they had not completed five years' schooling. In the UK, an operational definition of functional literacy was a reading age of nine, certainly insufficient for many of the types of literacy required by trades-people today. This norm gave an adult literacy rate of around two million in the 1980s (Dalglish 1982: 8). UNESCO were perhaps more realistic about the demanding nature of the literacy required by some communities of practice when they raised the threshold to thirteen. What is interesting is that such measures of literacy are not functional at all. They do not relate literacy to socio-economic function but to how long an individual stays in school. There is also the suspect assumption that those in school learn what the school teaches.

A more sophisticated test for literacy uses the 'Fog' index'. This appeared in a variety of functional literacy studies such as Dalglish's (1982). The difficulty of a reading passage was held to depend upon such factors as average sentence length, average word length and the degree of familiarity of the subject matter. However, the Fog index was statistically calibrated against reading ages in the US. Thus a given calculation of average word and sentence length will be equivalent to a given reading age. Through this type of calibration, the Fog index has also been norm-referenced.

To norm-reference functional literacy may be to deny its essential nature. We are no longer talking about the literacy that a person needs, but the average reading age that a school-age population attains. An individual's functional literacy should be criterion-referenced to the tasks that they need to accomplish. Functional literacy may be a norm-referenced wolf in criterion-referenced clothing.

Some more recent literacy models have tried to specify criteria less according to norm or to the criterion of socio-economic function and more according to the type of literacy skill required. For example, the International Adult Literacy Survey, administered out of the US and Canada, put forward a familiar definition of literacy as 'using printed and written information to function in society' but broke down these skills of information processing into:

> *prose literacy* – the knowledge and skills needed to understand and to use information from texts, including editorials, news stories, poems and fiction;
> *document literacy* – the knowledge and skill required to locate and to use information contained in various formats, including job applications, payroll forms, transportation schedules, maps, tables and graphics; and
> *quantitative literacy* – the knowledge and skills required to apply arithmetic operations, either alone or sequentially, to numbers embedded in

printed materials, such as balancing a chequebook, figuring out a tip, completing an order form, or determining the amount of interest on a loan from an advertisement. (Perie et al. 1999: 6)

Such breakdowns provide a clearer method of skills specification.

Another, more complex model of what it really means to be functionally literate was put forward by the Adult Performance Level (APL) Study. It was based upon a study completed by the Office of Continuing Education at the University of Texas for the US Office of Education. The APL constructed 'a model of functional literacy on two dimensions', 'content and skills' (Lankshear and Lawler 1987: 63). The content areas relate to the knowledge or subject areas that an individual requires to assume a normal literacy function. These are divided among:

- consumer economics, or the capacity to make informed consumer choices and manage a household budget;
- occupational knowledge: literacy specific to the requirements of an individual's desired employment goals;
- community resources: understanding and being able to use the resources that the community makes available to an individual in order to support and enhance their life-style;
- health: knowledge that will ensure good health for the individual and their family;
- government and law: understanding one's civil rights and civic obligations, knowing the functions of different, key government agencies.

The APL also reaches beyond prose and document literacy to include numeracy and problem-solving, while focusing more generally on interpersonal and communication skills. The OECD created a prose literacy scale which included thirty-four tasks with difficulty values distributed across five levels. The values were determined by such factors as the number of categories of features the reader had to process and the obviousness of the link between a question and the text that it was about (Organisation for Economic Co-operation and Development 1997).

In general, whilst the criteria for functional literacy remain imprecise, there has been an attempt to move them away from the somewhat self-defeating types of norm-referencing with which the concept began.

The problem of treating literacy as a set of competencies: the need for a cultural literacy

Whether or not they can be actually determined and measured, there are also problems with treating literacy as a set of competencies or as a knowledge of different skills. The first is an *affective* problem. An affective pedagogy will try to engage people emotionally in what they do. A positive emotional engagement is more likely to foster motivation and achieve a stronger educational result. When literacy is reduced to a set of skills it may be separated from how it can foster an individual's emotional engagement with their culture and their community. It may become remote, automatist and demotivating.

There is a larger risk that people may acquire literacy to do something else but that they will not acquire a strong enough concept of what that 'something' is. We may understand more about this problem if we consider UK schools. The claim by the UK's National Literacy Strategy (NLS) that literacy 'unites' 'important' skills (DFEE 1998: 3) has resulted in the recognition of this importance by allotting it a large part of the timetable as a daily literacy hour. In the early phases of primary education, this may make perfect sense. The mastery of reading and writing skills is bound up with recognising, combining and producing the signs that make up the English writing system. Yet, as children move past the mastery of these literacy basics, the isolation of literacy as skills with their own timetable slot may enforce too strong a sense of the separateness of reading and writing from the practices to which they are central. As many teachers recognise, literacy is carried forward by reading story books, writing science reports, historical eyewitness accounts, identifying locations on maps, plotting and describing graphs, exchanging notes, text-messages or e-mails with classmates, writing poems or illustrating those that have already been written. A well-structured literacy hour may include such activities, and teachers are trained to make sure that it does. But when we give so much time to literacy we may squeeze out too many of the content parts of the curriculum. This may be because we fail to understand how literacy may be better acquired through an engagement in how it is practised. If we need to write history essays, then essay writing should be part of the history curriculum.

The treatment of literacy as an underlying skill takes too much time from the knowledge-giving portions of the curriculum. It may also distract children from an induction into the practices through which literacy is carried forward into adult life. When treated as a functional skill, literacy risks becoming a set of abstracted routines. It is a process of completing or interpreting short, photocopied texts whose applications are ring-fenced by the curriculum. The result is that the child does not receive a staged induction into such social practices as reading novels or writing poetry. Instead, they are taught reading and writing skills outside an evolving social context of use, and how well they fund such a context is hostage to the environment in which they live.

Street (2001: 293) relates the failure of many literacy campaigns to a failure to understand 'the cultural and conceptual nature of literacy'. Literacy fails to convince its students that it will empower them when it is extrapolated from their cultural existence and reformulated as possessing various functional skills. Functional literacy perceives the literacy student as being in a kind of educational 'holding pattern' where they await the level of literacy that will permit 'touch-down' on 'the runway' of socio-economic self-realisation.

Some of the risks implicit in an economic and skills-based view of literacy have also affected commentators in the United States. One perception was that it might make students illiterate in their larger cultural environment. According to this view, literacy should involve a measure of cultural understanding that would include knowing why some days were holidays and what being a citizen in a democratic society should really mean. There was therefore a revival of the nineteenth-century view that literacy could even promote social cohesion and propagate a better understanding of the common values, beliefs and traditions with which a society holds itself together. This common value system is traditionally defined as a culture. To be literate in that system is therefore to be culturally literate. The key proponent of *cultural literacy* was E. D. Hirsch (1987), who wielded considerable political influence during the 1980s and produced a list of what he thought every culturally literate American needed to know. This meant understanding the historical significance of public holidays such as Thanksgiving. It also meant being able to interpret the significance of cultural icons such as the American Eagle or the Stars and Stripes.

Because of a tradition of absorbing culturally distinct groups of immigrants, the US public school system has traditionally been less apologetic about inducting children into a set of largely secular cultural values than some of its European counterparts. The more established and less fractured identities of the European nation states may mean that they think a culture may be better at transmitting itself as part of a hidden curriculum, though citizenship classes are now coming onto the curriculum in the UK and Australia, for example. Not only may a cultural literacy concept fail to export well, but it also makes the false assumption that a culture consists of a single shared value system, assuming that the individual must fit these mores while society need do little to accommodate the individual. Lankshear and Lawler (1987: 66) are clear about the perils of a model of literacy that orients the student towards the passive consumption of a civic role but which does not teach them to appraise or criticise the wider social system by which such roles are allotted. Their view of the skills and knowledge model of functional literacy put forward by schemes such as that of the APL study in Texas is that they in fact propose a model of dysfunctionality (1987: 64) because of the way they ignore the 'writing competences' that are capable of 'initiating change', and 'personal' or 'social transformation' (Levine 1982: 262).

One culture exists inside another or beside another. Thus Native Americans operate cultures that may be distinct from those of African-Americans or American Jews. Yet all of these are allowed to coexist by the broader set of values that constitute the value system of the United States. Among these groups, there are also subsets with quite different systems of values. Within any given culture, value systems may be changed by the type of education received and the institutional affiliations of an individual. It could be, for example, that one could take two academics or two business people working for the same multinational but coming from different ethnic minorities or countries with distinct cultures and find that they have a stronger cultural affinity with each other than with many other members of their own minority. Different minorities can also perceive cultural iconography differently. The American feast of Thanksgiving may have a very different meaning for Native Americans than it does for the descendants of America's first settlers.

In both its functional and cultural forms, literacy has been defined according to a purpose. That purpose may be greater individual fulfilment, but the real consequence can be a heightened self-awareness that leaves the individual frustrated with the social role they have to occupy. Such concepts of literacy are like an induction into the rites of the Aztec priesthood, where initiates became literate in the purpose of human sacrifice but did not question whether the sunrise would really depend upon such recurrent ritual slaughters.

For many critics the assumption of individual passivity that lies behind the quite different concepts of functional and cultural literacy puts them into conflict with a belief that education should foster a critical understanding of our own circumstances. According to this argument, literacy acquisition should not assume the passivity of the individual when faced with their circumstances. It should not even be about helping the individual become aware of the nature of those circumstances. It should challenge the circumstances themselves and thus act as a medium for social change. The concept of a critical literacy is then born.

Conclusions

In this first chapter, I have introduced the concept of functional literacy and described it as categorising literacy according to a set of socio-economic competences. In order to understand this idea better, I introduced some of the basic econometric concepts of education as added value and the student or pupil as product. I explained this with the other concept of diminishing marginal productivity, then looked at how functional literacy had been applied in the area of development economics and educational planning in developed countries.

Functional literacy was perceived as a useful concept because it took us away from an idea of literacy as a set of very basic competencies in such areas as letter recognition and assignation, on the one hand, and as some effete social virtue associated with a middle- and upper-class recreational interest, on the other. Functionality raised the core questions of what society needs us to know and what we need to know in order to function in society. It also forced us to look at connections between failures in literacy acquisition and social dysfunctionality or criminality. As an econometric view of literacy, the topic of functionality instigated a discussion of the real links between literacy and economic success. Here, I warned against any straightforward equivalence, suggesting that literacy rates and economic growth rates exist in a complex and mutually supportive relationship. Literacy could not be isolated as a single factor able to promote economic growth, but it could be seen as an important weapon in the armoury of those who wish to tackle individual or community poverty. I also found functionality problematic on several counts. Three points to carry forward are:

1. Although it looked as if it could relate literacy to identifiable sets of skills, it was sometimes difficult to identify these skills and to decide how we should specify the level of competence that we needed to obtain.
2. It treated literacy too mechanistically, as skills with which we might have no real emotional identification. It risked separating literacy from our wider cultural existence whilst driving a wedge between our idea of what we do with literacy and how we learn it.
3. It treated the society in which we exist as an order that was not open to challenge, preparing us for the efficient but uncritical consumption of the texts that this social order produced.

The last point, in particular, takes us on to the next chapter and the concept of a *critical literacy.*

Exercises

1. Using the descriptions of prose, document and quantitative literacy, try to work out literacy profiles for an occupation with which you have some familiarity. Discuss whether this profile provides a full and meaningful description of the literacy needs of that occupation.
2. Discuss how we should or should not sustain a concept of functional literacy by using the economic idea of diminishing marginal productivity.
3. Take an institution or organisation that you know. Imagine that you have been asked to make a training intervention that will improve its effectiveness; discuss how literacy training would impact upon that organisation.
4. Imagine you had to write a report about the link between criminality and functional illiteracy. Would you perceive a connection and what actions would you advise?
   Does this correlation point to a causal relationship between illiteracy and criminality?
   Is there some other literacy effect on behaviour or behaviour effect on literacy?

Decide how you would design a larger study to provide clearer answers to one or more of these questions.

5. Try to find out more about the relationship between levels of literacy and economic performance; then discuss whether literacy is a condition or a precondition of national development.

2 Critical Literacy

Introduction

The critical literacy movement is partly explicable as a reaction against a core problem with the concept of functionality. This is that a functional pedagogy is about helping children and adults to participate effectively in society. It is not about challenging the social inequalities that may themselves be responsible for the uneven distribution of literacy that puts the adult student in the literacy class.

Critical literacy theory was fashioned by three different yet related movements in philosophy, linguistics and literacy education. These three movements are:

1. Post-modernism
2. Critical discourse analysis (CDA)
3. Participatory pedagogy

Each of these movements has been informed by the other. Post-modernism embraces a large and complicated body of thought about the way that we explore and represent reality. Critical discourse analysis (CDA) is an approach to understanding how a society and culture use language to transmit their way of thinking about the world. CDA's modes of analysis are developed from a broader attempt to understand how the structure of language reflects the need to communicate a given socially appropriate meaning. This approach to language is known as systemic functional linguistics (SFL). The critical or CDA interpretation of SFL is, however, very much post-modernist in kind. The third movement, participatory pedagogy, is an approach to literacy teaching that is sometimes named after its foremost exponent, Paulo Freire. It combines a practical approach to adult literacy teaching with a wider attempt to make its students aware of the social system that has denied them literacy in the first place.

In this chapter we will try to understand critical literacy through these three core concepts. I will look first at post-modernism as the most general and pervasive current of thought. Second, I will explain some of the tenets of critical discourse analysis as a post-modernist account of how language shapes meaning. Third, I will discuss participatory pedagogy, treating this as an unconscious application of post-modernism to pedagogy. Next, I will look at how these three sets of ideas can help us construct a clear idea of critical literacy itself. Finally, I will show how criticality is also problematic as a complete approach to literacy.

Two tenets of post-modernism

Post-modernism is an intellectual movement that influenced the study of art, architecture, sociology, philosophy and literature during the latter half of the twentieth century. Although post-modernist thought is also bound up with some other movements, such as post-structuralism and deconstructionism, I will not attempt to distinguish and explore these different intellectual currents here. My main interest will be to understand some of the core ideas that have shaped the critical literacy movement. This interest will treat the post-modernist movement as having two central tenets:

1. small is beautiful: we are all members of a minority;
2. who we are shapes how we see: we have 'no final vocabulary'.

I will now consider what these two statements mean and how they can change the way we perceive literacy, illiteracy and the process of moving from one state to the other.

Post-modernism and minority movements

Post-modernism begins as a reaction to *modernism* and may be best understood by an exploration of that earlier movement. Modernism and the post-modernist reaction affected many currents of thought in philosophy and the arts, but they are, perhaps, most easily understood through architecture.

As pioneered by Henri LeCorbusier and Frank Lloyd Wright, modernism tried to do away with the ornate and make a building into an expression of its function. A structure such as London's Tower Bridge epitomises a style where form disguises function. The steel structures that hold up the bridge's spans and the hydraulics that raise them are concealed within granite walls that resemble the towers of a medieval castle. Modernism, by contrast, gave buildings the singular presence that is typified by modern city skylines across the world. These skyscrapers are what they are, and changing one into another, offices into apartments for example, can be a very costly undertaking. The modernist building begins as one unified form which expresses the function to which it is dedicated. Thus one might conceive of an apartment block as a giant display shelf into which apartments are slotted like shoeboxes. Space is mastered by a single plan or idea. As Lloyd Wright put it, buildings were to be 'one great thing instead of a quarrelling collection of so many little things' (Gropius 1965).

Architectural modernism is also global in nature. The city skylines of New York, Hong Kong, Shanghai, London and Tokyo have all started to resemble each other. The global nature of modernism in architecture makes a larger ideological statement that is best summarised by the sociologist Marshall McLuan. McLuan used an architectural metaphor when he famously characterised the world as 'a global village'. The metaphor refers to how modern media such as television link us together in a single state of collective intimacy where once isolated societies are informed of each others' activities (McLuan 1964). In a global village people lose their sense of cultural difference because they have been wired into the one community consuming the same types of entertainment expressing the same world-view. McLuan characterised the media rather as if it were an enormous global wall or modernist dwelling into which the world's minority movements and individual cultures had to slot themselves like shoeboxes.

Very differently, the nineteenth-century co-author of the *Communist Manifesto*, Karl Marx, had also treated all human activity as a product of the same historical design. The all-encompassing nature of his analysis now seems to place the world in a singular modernist space. A core Marxist principle was the class conflict that revealed itself in all societies everywhere. For Marx, the religious and cultural differences of nations were finally interesting only for how they expressed the same economic principle of class warfare and exploitation.

We cannot, of course, call a nineteenth-century thinker such as Marx a modernist. Nevertheless, his analysis of class conflict has a familiar modernist sweep. It supposes that we are all subject to the same historical processes. It implies that minority cultures and interests must either find common cause with the larger currents of class conflict that sweep through the world, or risk being drowned out. Unsurprisingly, Marxism was another movement that post-modernism sought to modify.

The disdain for the minority interest expressed by both Marxist and global capitalist ideology can be seen in the modernist quest for a universal architectural solution and a consequent re-engineering of our social space as a classless and functional environment. We see the result in the 1960s and 1970s high-rise housing estates of Europe, the former Soviet Bloc and the United States. Like other global ideologies, this architecture assumed that the lives of all people everywhere should be controlled by the same functional designs. Cultural and community differences, the architectures of local materials and local crafts and practices, were all swept into Lloyd Wright's grand singular 'thing'. Yet almost from the outset, minorities started to protest against this culture of uniformity by vandalising the spaces they were forced to occupy.

One can interpret such vandalism as the beginning of an unconscious post-modernist rebellion.

Approaching our topic more closely, we can see the graffiti writer as launching a literacy rebellion against modernism's singular functional canvas. They want to differentiate one wall from another by marking it with a badge of their identity. When that eagerness for self-expression reaches beyond the paint spray and becomes a voice in favour of community action then we can talk of communities exerting control over their lives and setting out on a road to *self-empowerment*. The capacity of the community to empower itself and its members is central to the post-modernist design. In the actions of the graffiti writer, we might also see the affective need for self-expression that was criticised as lacking in the functional literacy concept.

Individuals are empowered by taking control of their interests through a focus on minority rights and community interests. The result is a fracturing of that larger Marxist sense of a conflict between classes into one of minorities and localities that are struggling for their rights. Post-modernism witnesses a shift towards women's rights, gay rights, children's rights, ethnic minority rights, language rights, animal rights and the rights of the locality or region. It reacts against the global spread of a single model of culture. The concept of empowerment suggests that individuals can start to overcome their sense of being helpless when faced with the forces of global capitalism. Macdonald's Restaurant chain epitomises the modernist monocultural model. It sells the same food sourced from the same places in the same kinds of building across the world. Equally, a counter-tendency can be seen in the reaction of the French farmers who vandalised one of the company's premises because they believed it was squeezing their own produce out of the local market. The post-modernist model would have those same farmers empowering themselves by setting up their own restaurants and sales outlets in order to promote their regional economy.

For Freire, the illiterates of the world are a disempowered minority and to become literate should be to engage in a process of empowerment. The literacy class itself, is now a forum for minority action. We should no longer treat illiteracy as a singular, minority condition that puts its members outside the social mainstream. The path to literacy should not spawn some great mass movement, as in UNESCO's rhetoric of an illiteracy virus that we must 'eradicate'. To invert Lloyd Wright's dictum, we should engage not in 'one great thing', the global campaign against illiteracy, but celebrate the fracture of that campaign into a 'quarrelling collection' of community actions or literacy classes that are all the disparate products of their own unique circumstances.

Who we are shapes how we see: we have no final vocabulary

Post-modernism is a reaction against the single, controlling texts of the modernist ethos. The post-modernist mistrust of any singular, overarching idea takes root in a complicated view of meaning and language. This view does not just affect how we see the actions through which communities acquire literacy. It also affects the literacy that communities acquire. The belief that our lives are not governed by a singular set of principles extends into the way we view meaning and science. Most fundamentally, our literacy texts can no longer be treated as operating with a discourse of fixed and universal meanings. We can understand this better if we turn back to a more modernist, or structuralist, analysis of language that should largely be associated with the linguist Ferdinand de Saussure.

Saussure (1974) treated language as a sign-system, where a sign or *signifier* represents a meaning or a *signified*. Thus far he held to a conventional distinction between a word, or sign, and the object in the world that it represents. However, the relationship between a signifier and signified is not a mere naming process where a word such as 'ch-air' names that object in the world. Saussure's contribution was to argue that the signified is not a particular object in the world but a concept. If we take a word such as 'tree', we can make it refer to a type of object we have never seen before. We can even travel from a cold to a warm country, see the very different palms or conifers they have there and know that these are trees without ever having seen such objects before. The sign 't-r-ee' must represent a concept, otherwise we would not be able to use it to name all the quite different examples of trees that we encounter in the world.

A second observation of Saussure's refers to the construction of the sign itself. A more traditional analysis would hold that the sign 't-r-ee' is made distinct from another sign by the different nature of what it represents. Our ability to see that the tree outside my window is different from a shrub beneath it is what gives the sign a distinct identity. Saussure saw that linguistic signs themselves are arbitrary agglomerations of sound that are made meaningful only because they are part of a system of other agglomerations of sound from which they are distinct.

The post-modernist philosopher Jacques Derrida (e.g. 1997) took Saussure's analysis one stage further. Saussure assumes that although a word represents a concept and not a thing in the world, that concept is deduced from our observation of things. From the trees that we see, we derive our concept of a tree. Derrida found this to be impossible. We cannot know what a tree is unless we already possess a sense of what that concept should be. Derrida inverted the traditional analysis of a world of phenomena to which we give names. He argued that we need the concepts in order for that world to exist in the form in which we perceive it and that we can obtain that network of concepts only from language. For Derrida, the mental image or concept that we have of a tree is given an identity by how it is different from other concepts such as that of 'bush' or 'animal' or 'building'. Therefore, effectively, the suggestion is that we do not begin with a world of things that we name. Rather, we begin with a set of categories and their names, and then use these to bring conceptual order to the world. The meanings we thought to be anchored in the world and referred to by language are in fact constructed out of language.

According to Derrida, language is not a system where signs differentiate themselves from each other so that they can represent different concepts. Language operates as a set of signified concepts. As said, language also allows us to share these concepts and it is this exchange which enables society to exist. Our sharing of concepts gives society a coherent form. A witness can say in court, 'the car went through a red light and hit the cyclist'. The judicial system operates because, although we may all see the same event differently, we can all agree a concept for 'cyclist' and 'the car'. Yet, according to Derrida, conceptual differentiation, the difference between 'cars' and 'bicycles', is a product of the concepts established in language by society. Since the concepts are to some extent common to a society, we can say that society is constructing reality through the conceptual differences that operate in its discourse or use of language.

At first sight this might sound completely improbable. There is a suggestion that 'car' and 'bicycle' do not have any clear difference, which means we have to construct that difference in language. In fact, wrong or right, the postmodernist argument is more interesting than that. We might imagine somebody who comes from a society where the wheel does not exist observing cars and bicycles for the first time. They might perceive cars simply as larger bicycles and give both the generic name 'vehicles'. They then introduce a concept 'vehicle' into their language without the bicycle–car distinction. Their society is therefore constructing the world of transport in a manner that is different from that of other societies.

Interestingly, the French word for car is 'voiture'. This used to mean carriage. Therefore an existing conceptual difference, as between a 'carriage/voiture' for people and a cart/charrette is used in order to mark out a new one. The conceptual area covered by the carriage extends to encompass a new machine that performs the same function, a car. The new vehicle concept does not come ready-made into the world. It is a product of an existing conceptual differentiation.

We might now argue that language becomes a mechanism through which society constructs its reality. When 'voiture' extends its meaning from carriage to car, this is an example of the phenomenon of metaphorical extension discussed in the first chapter. Metaphors create new meanings in language. Thus the term 'voiture' or 'carriage' is extended from a horse-drawn conveyance for people to mean the new 'horseless carriage', or car. This process can be used to support Derrida's larger point. Language is not reaching into the world and giving names to what already exists there. Language is extending and differentiating its own concepts to create a network of meanings with which we can construct our reality. Since these meanings are derived from our collective life in society, we can call this process *social construction*.

A way to illustrate the social construction of meanings is to think of a chunk of matter that we now call iron ore. We should then imagine a Stone Age person looking at the same rock. This piece would have an entirely different construction for them. It might be 'matter that wasn't much good for making axe heads', for example. Less exaggeratedly, an Iron Age person might see it as containing the material for weapons and utensils, but a modern person would see it as a source of steel. Changes in society do not change the lump of matter we hold in our hands, but they do change our construction of it.

The social scientist Michel Foucault has made a huge contribution to the post-modernist endeavour by looking at how meanings have been constructed differently over time. For example, in *Discipline and Punish* (1977), he describes how punishment was once an assault by one of society's appointed representative, the executioner or torturer, upon the body of the criminal. In the nineteenth century punishment began to focus more on the mind and took on the meaning of remoulding the criminal into an acceptable being.

Critical literacy deals with the methods that society uses to construct itself through written language. This construction involves literacy's larger use of both visual and linguistic systems of meaning representation. For example, as I write this, my eye falls on a headline in the paper on the floor beside me:

US divided on Saddam successor. (*Sunday Times*, 17 November 2002)

An uncritical reading of this headline would simply be that it is informing us that the article below it will be about a policy argument in the US administration. The argument concerns who should replace the then President of Iraq, Saddam Hussein. The issue of Saddam Hussein's presidency has since been resolved, but at the time of the headline, it was still an open question. My concern now is with the assumptions made by the headline at the time of writing.

First, 'US divided' is an interesting use of a rhetorical device known as *metonymy*. A *metonym* is traditionally a figure of speech where one part of an item, such as the wheels of a car, stands for the whole item, as when we say 'a nice set of wheels' and mean 'a nice car'. Another type of metonym is based on the spatial or semantic association between two concepts, as when we say 'Washington rift with Berlin' and are referring not to the cities but to the governments that they house. Metonyms are often constructed by our cultural sense of what is important in an idea. Thus, Washington is not an important city because it has some fine eighteenth-century architecture and is situated in the east of the US but because it houses the US government. It therefore represents that government and this is its most salient cultural function. We say 'wheels' to represent a car but not 'a nice set of seats', because arguably 'wheels' are more central to our construction of a car than its seats.

A post-modernist might also see metonymy as an example of how different concepts construct each other, building a network of meanings that we impose upon the world according to the cultural significance that we attach to something. Wheels represent a car, and Washington signifies the US government, not because of how these concepts really are but because our culture attaches huge importance to one function, as opposed to another.

The accidental metonym in our headline is that the US is its government. It is probably safe to say that at the time of writing, the people of America were not all arguing with each about the leader to replace Saddam Hussein. If they were arguing about anything political, it was about whether their country should go to war and replace this leader in the first place. The headline constructs a nation's government as if it were that nation. This representation may construct the government as having an authority that it does not properly possess. 'We, the government, are America and America is us', the text implies.

Another point is the larger assumption of the headline. It does not state that 'US will be divided if Saddam needs a successor'. The assumption signals to the paper's British readership that the war to replace Saddam is inevitable, whatever its rights and wrongs. This message is reinforced by a picture of Saddam in the middle of the article with a caption: 'Saddam: who comes next?' The events that will bring about a succession problem are already happening; therefore, they are no longer subject to question. We should simply decide what comes after, go to war and do our government's bidding.

Looking at the larger page we can start to construct another type of meaning that can be read as 'guilt by association'. At the time of writing, there was some debate about how far Saddam Hussein was involved in global terrorism and the 11 September 2001 attack on the US. The page is constructed in a way that suppresses that debate. The page has its own title or section heading called 'War on Terror'. To the left of the Saddam Hussein headline is a pictorial diagram which shows how the US will use a new microwave bomb, and an article which explains what the weapon will do. Saddam Hussein and the weapons that will be used against him are thus part of the US war against terrorism. By implication, we have moved on from a debate about whether Saddam Hussein was really involved in acts or terrorism against the United States.

My interest here is not to start a debate about the rights and wrongs of a given strategy. It is about how critical literacy theory can find that a five-word headline contains a very extensive *subtext* or set of unstated implications and meanings. This subtext is conveyed by the choice of language and the juxtaposition of one set of signs with another. In the use of a common metonymy 'US' for 'US government', we are not suggesting that the writer has made a conscious attempt to identify the will of a government with that of its people. What we see is how the language that society puts at the writer's disposal reflects a deeper set of power relations. For the critical literacy theorist the point is that if we are becoming literate only to consume these signs, then we are denying ourselves access to the larger set of meanings that literacy can make available to us. We do not have to ask how far the headline writer's manipulation of their readers is conscious or unconscious. The headline is a product of a process of social construction. It is brought into existence by a mind that is organising the world according to its socially constructed categories rather than itself being organised by the same. The solution is that real literacy involves having the awareness that will permit the reader partly to deconstruct the texts that they consume. I will now look at how the type of enquiry known as *critical discourse analysis* can advance our capacity to do that.

Critical discourse analysis

Critical discourse analysis (CDA) is an enquiry into how the forms and patterns adopted by language reflect the types of meaning that a language's users construct. Such an enquiry makes the post-modernist assumption that a language is in some sense a reflection of its larger social purpose. The social construction of language is evident in the words we select and the syntactic patterns that they adopt. We can understand this if we look briefly at our use of the passive.

A traditional grammatical analysis would hold that these two sentences are using different grammatical and syntactic patterns to represent the same meanings and the same events:

1. An unknown author wrote this tract in 1852.
2. The tract was written by an unknown author in 1852.

Some generative linguists (though not all) might see sentence 2 as a transformation of 1. In order to create the distinct method of expression we *transform* the first sentence by *movement*. Thus a noun-phrase (NP), 'the tract', is moved to a subject position that a generative grammarian would define as empty. This operation gives us the concept of a *transformational grammar*. But from the post-modernist perspective discussed in the previous section, we cannot talk about events in the world as if they were separate from the structures of the linguistic system by which they are expressed. Thus sentence 1, 'an author wrote this tract' provides the author with a pre-eminent role. An object or person that causes an action to occur can be seen as the *agent* of the action. In sentence 2, 'the tract was written . . .', the author or the agent is 'moved' to a prepositional phrase. We feel the tract has brought itself into being and the author is reduced to the unwitting agent of its production. When we look at form and meaning in this way, we have already begun a form of CDA.

CDA draws upon two perspectives. The first is the social-constructionist view that has just been outlined. CDA views discourse, or our use of language, as constructing the reality with which a given society will deal. The second perspective is that of systemic functional linguistics (SFL).

Systemic functional linguistics

Unlike the generative position just referred to, SFL assumes that the forms and patterns that a language adopts reflect the meanings it is trying to convey. Every text exists in a context. The context is the interface between the utterance and the social situation in which it occurs. To understand context is to understand the medium through which society constructs meaning as language.

In Halliday's (1985) analysis, a language itself should be perceived as the meanings that the members of a given society wish to represent so that they can communicate them to each other. Because a society will also furnish the context in which a given communication occurs and from which its meanings are derived, a language and its context are inextricable (Thompson 1996). A social context and a text affect each other. A social context is structured by a text, and structures language in its turn (Lemke 1995).

For example, writing a letter to someone I know by name but have never met might require me to use 'Dear + title + surname'. This is a response to context. When I use 'Dear + title + surname' this sets up a formal expectation. We might therefore anticipate that the salutation will be followed by a formal statement of the letter writer's purpose such as: 'Further to your letter of 19 January 2002, I am writing to inform you that . . .'. We would not expect a sentence that resembles one we speak such as: 'Nice to get yours, just to let you know that I'll . . .'. The writer responds to this context by selecting a traditional written mode of address. This address then becomes a part of the context in which the rest of the letter will unfold. What I use language to convey, how I want to convey it and to whom are attributes of the context that both shapes and is shaped by language.

In a development of Halliday (1985), Fairclough (1989: 146) bases his critical discourse model on a six-level model of text interpretation. I will illustrate this by using the short text below:

> Crumbly pastry encloses jammy fruit in a wodge of almond paste. If you want to really plump your tarts out, use Merchant Gourmet Mi-cuit semidried plums (call 0800 731 3549 for stockists). (author's data, Holme 2003a)

At level 1 we begin by decoding the primary signs in which the discourse is encoded. These signs could be the graphemes, or the letters and characters that constitute writing. Thus, in the passage above, we decode 't-a-r-t-s' as 'tarts', for example. If the text is delivered through speech, it might be the *phonemes*, or the smallest units of sound by which one word can be distinguished from another – The sound 'k' that makes 'cat' a different word from 'mat', for example.

Level 2 deals with the *semantics* and the *pragmatics* that give us the basic utterance meaning. Semantics refers to the basic meanings of the words used when they are combined into a grammatical sentence. Thus the first sentence, 'Crumbly pastry encloses jammy fruit in a wodge of almond paste', refers to the quality of the fruit and jam and to how they are encased in pastry of a certain kind. Pragmatics is about how we interpret what language means by using the context in which it occurs. For example, in this text, one reading might lead us to believe that the pastry uses 'almond paste' to 'enclose' the 'fruit', rather as I use my hand to enclose a small object. The pragmatics of the utterance tells us that this cannot be. A more relevant interpretation would be that this desert consists of two layers, pastry and almond paste, with a fruit centre (Holme 2003a).

Level 3 refers to how we use the cohesion of the larger text to make sense of it. For example, 'tarts' in the second sentence refers to the construction described in greater detail in the first. This reference carries the meaning of the first sentence forward into the second sentence. It allows us to manipulate that larger meaning without repeating it. But it also adds important information about what has just been described. It tells us that we are not talking about a 'roulade' or cylinder of pastry enclosing a centre, but a bottom layer of pastry that has been folded up to form sides to make a 'tart'.

Level 4 employs what we call discourse schemas. A *schema* refers to a pattern in which information is stored. Many of our ways of using language are schematised. To take a very simple example, a story puts forward an expectation that it will have an 'end' where the complications of the narrative are in someway resolved, either tragically or happily. As we interpret a narrative, we wait for that 'resolution' and are dissatisfied if the author does not provide it. We expect the resolution because we have a schema for what a good story should contain.

The first sentence above provides an expectation that this text could precede a recipe or come after it. We are either being tempted into trying the recipe by a description of its 'jammy' product, or we are reading about the outcome and are tempted again. The second sentence gives the impression that the latter is the case. We are invited to make the product perfect by buying one type of ingredient rather than another. As a means of closure, the reader is invited to place an order and start assembling the recipe's ingredients.

Levels 5 and 6 comprise the larger context. Level 5 is intertextual and refers to how the reader uses their knowledge of other texts to interpret this one. The reader may have a wider experience of reading recipes and this helps them to understand that this text is a description of what they will produce. A context consists of the variables, *field*, *mode* and *tenor*. Field focuses on institutional practices. We can think of these institutional practices as the environment in which the text operates and what it is about. This text appears in a Sunday newspaper magazine so that its field component belongs to magazines and their representation of the topic of cookery with the implicit advertising that may arise from this. Tenor identifies social relations. In the example of the letters we saw how formal and informal social relations change the nature of the language used. In newspapers, a lengthy broadsheet with quite high literacy demands makes very different assumptions about its readership from a tabloid with a front page that is mostly occupied by a headline. It is not uncommon for an event to receive front-page treatment in both tabloids and broadsheets. In this, the field is largely common. But because of the quite different writer–reader relationships in these two types of paper, the result will be two very different texts.

In the case of the text above, our understanding of tenor can also show how a very basic kind of discourse analysis can lead us into the territory of textual deconstruction, or critical discourse analysis. For example, the interpersonal and field characteristics of 'wodge' and 'jammy' are strong. In British English, this type of idiomatic diction belongs to certain social classes. It connotes the illicit treat afforded by the sweets that we ought not to like, perhaps because they are unhealthy or had to be stolen after-hours from the pantry in girls' boarding schools. The writer makes a classist and, perhaps, a gendered assumption about their readership. They are housewives of a wholesome and 'jolly' kind whose concept of a forbidden pleasure is sticking their fingers in the jam pot then licking them. Additionally, there is a field assumption of a newspaper magazine that reserves its serious content for the main reader in a broadsheet presentation, while spinning off recipes for the rest in its aptly named 'Supplement' (Holme 2003a). Some thought about mode will tell us that the text is written and writing may pressure language in certain ways. It will also emphasise that the text does not exist in isolation. One text creates its meaning by referring to others of a similar or contrasting kind. This text refers to brands, labels and telephone numbers, and borrows from the meanings of these accordingly.

By exemplifying the levels of textual interpretation we can start to understand how we might see these as the mechanisms through which a given social context constructs language. The levels through which we interpret or reproduce a larger meaning are the mechanisms that society has constructed within us to do the same. Any ability to use the heightened awareness that emerges from these analytical strata can also help us to deconstruct the manipulative purpose of a given text. Kress (1985) suggests as one example the type of public notice that one finds in parks or open urban spaces everywhere: 'Ball games are forbidden by order'. A core interpersonal characteristic of such texts is how they hide their authorship. According to Kress, they are like 'ghost ships', a metaphor that evokes the phenomenon of the *Mary Celeste*, the ship that was found in perfect condition but adrift and without its crew. Such notices heave into view, devoid of any creator and hence of anybody with whom one can discuss or otherwise engage. Writing is the 'mode' prerequisite of such an effect, since it can detach language from both the voice and the person. The mode is also responding to an ideational component, or to a field that is laden with a bureaucratic and legalistic agenda. By effacing themselves behind the passive tense 'are forbidden', the authors abandon their text and let it loose upon the world as something that is right because it is self-promulgating. The decree is simply part of a regulatory framework we must accept or deface, presenting itself with the bland factuality of the wall or post it hangs upon.

Critical discourse theory proposes different levels of textual interpretation. Each level concentrates within it the various ways in which society constructs textual meaning or conditions our response to the same. We can benefit from such understanding by moderating or reconfiguring our own responses. The concept of a critical literacy resides in this scrutiny of our own responses to text, by, for example, restoring the author to their utterance as a being whose views can be challenged.

A literate population suggests the possibility of the mass consumption of a given message and thus the manipulation of mass opinion. In his *Uses of Literacy*, a well-known book of the late 1950s, Richard Hoggart (1958) proposed how the spread of literacy had not created a more astute, analytical and aware working-class population but had instead subverted their cultural values. Mass literacy had turned what was once a commonsensical and intuitive response to the world into a celebration of ordinariness and a refusal to look beyond a shallow, consumerist gloss. The expression 'I'm as good as you', becomes 'you're no better than me', and typifies a refusal to accept that some people are more able than others (Street 1996). Everything is thus scaled down so that it can fit a small-minded vision. CDA would see this as a consequence of how literacy is socially constructed, where society is held in the thrall of consumerist egalitarianism.

In what could almost be read as a development of Hoggart's (1958) analysis, Fairclough (1995) identified a trend that he called the 'technologisation of discourse'. Accordingly, we are increasingly made aware of correct ways to produce the language we need to accomplish certain goals. Sales personnel are told how to structure presentations, teachers are taught as if there is an optimum way to arrange lessons, police are given interviewing procedures for suspects or witnesses, while business people believe there is a correct way and a wrong way to write a report. Such people undergo communications skills training, partly to learn about the kind of statement they should make at a given point in the discourse. Such attempts to organise discourse are not new. In sixteenth- and sevententh-century Europe, for example, writing poetry was thought to be part of the normal accomplishment of a courtier. Manuals were produced in order to help them do it. While in the nineteenth century a growing obsession with etiquette resulted in a literature that advised people about what they should say and when. Yet what is different now, warranting the coinage of Fairclough's term, is the pervasiveness of the media and hence the extension of how it can script our lives according to its models of language use. Thus even personal encounters, such as declarations of love, arguments with teenage children or the offer of condolences, are set out for us in the soap operas we consume. Intimate conversations are a re-enactment of episodes already run, risking that our emotions also are borrowed, like the language through which they are expressed.

While CDA makes us aware of how literacy can become a means to ensnare all spontaneity in a discourse of constructed feelings, it can also have a more practical role in the critical literacy process of empowerment through mastery of the relevant discourses. For example, students of academic writing may not be fully aware of how the way they cite a given authority may construct the view that they have of it. Such terms belong to what is called *metatext*. Metatext is the use of text to comment upon itself, or to explain what it is saying. When I preface my next paragraph with a sentence which explains what I am going to do, as in 'Now I will consider what critical literacy really means', I am being 'metatextual'. Metatext provides an implicit or explicit opportunity for the writer to give their own view on what they are saying. If we look at the following alternatives:

Smith stated that, argued that, understood that, claimed that, saw that, implied that.

'Stated' implies that a straightforward repetition of Smith's views will follow, yet these views are being attributed to their author only and not to a wider spectrum of opinion. 'Understood' acknowledges Smith's insights but attributes to others a failure of comprehension. 'Argued' suggests some uncertainty about Smith's opinions. Arguments await rebuttal. 'Claim' is generally weak. Claims seek a securer foundation. 'Implied' may not precede Smith's opinion at all. It implies that this has been read into the statement by the writer. At best it is an elaboration of Smith's views, at worst a false attribution. If teachers encourage students to deconstruct such metatext, they may impart a fuller understanding of how the student should manipulate it in their own work.

Metaphor and critical literacy

Another feature of discourse that CDA can help the critical literacy teacher explore is metaphor. We have already shown how metaphor was of considerable interest for such post-modernist thinkers as Derrida because, in their analysis, it demonstrated how one concept was spun off another by language, creating a system that arranged the world rather than simply representing it. The social scientist D. Schön (1963, 1993) stated how the solution to a given social, scientific or technical problem would lie in the way that the problem was framed. Schön (1993) discusses metaphors as 'generative' of a narrative that frames our approach to an issue. Thus we may think that if we face a planning problem such as urban renewal we will proceed in a rational manner, weighing up the different ways to move forward, then selecting the one which is affordable and likely to provide the greatest benefit to all parties. In fact, we frame the choices we make in the metaphors through which we grasp the issue and the narratives they generate. Accordingly, a slum may invoke a story of 'blight and renewal', constructing an approach which could lead to its demolition and a failure to recognise the community that the slum may in fact house.

Lakoff and Johnson (e.g. 1980, 1999) reject the post-modernist thesis, asserting that metaphors base their categories on what exists in the world instead of spinning them out of language's conceptual system and making the world conform to them. None the less, they also reveal how the way we think about abstract ideas depends upon the metaphors through which we grasp them. Lakoff and Johnson (1980) identified how the metaphors that grasp abstract ideas are linked together by common themes. A notion such as 'time' is part of the universe we inhabit, yet 'time' is not something we can grasp for how it is. We therefore have to *conceptualise* it through something else, creating the *conceptual metaphor* 'time is space'. We therefore use metaphor to conceptualise abstract thought and these conceptualisations affect our way of seeing the world.

Lakoff and Johnson (1999) suggest a thought experiment in which we try to think about time as time. We quickly realise that we cannot. We have to think of time as one of the metaphors through which it is expressed, as a clock or a line through space, for example. Very differently, 'love' and 'life' are both conceptualised as journeys. So we say that we 'have reached the end of the road' when we are near death or near the end of a relationship, or: 'we've been a long way together' and 'this can't go on forever'. The same holds for other abstract meanings, many of which are understood through a sense of the self as embodied or physical. For example, we conceptualise direction and location through associated body parts, talking about the *back* garden and the road *ahead.*

We also conceive of many activities through metaphor and may thus steer the nature of the activity itself. We think of business as war when we use phrases such as 'company HQ, hostile take-over', 'boardroom battle', 'dawn raid' or 'corporate in-fighting'. Arguably, such conceptualisations actually frame our approach to business. For example, it is fashionable for companies to prize warlike qualities among their personnel, looking for 'aggressive' salespeople with a 'win–win' philosophy. Some could even argue that such rhetoric closes down intellectual options, denying to managers the conceptual space in which they could ask whether 'aggressive' sales tactics are really effective.

Lakoff (1992) looked at how metaphors controlled the language that was used to lead the West into the first Gulf War and therefore gave the war a supposed inevitability. A predominant theme was the demonisation of the Iraqi leader, Saddam Hussein. Metaphor put the leader outside the frame of rational discourse and nullified the possibility of any reasonable pretext for the Iraqi invasion of Kuwait. Therefore, the Iraqi leadership was constructed as something with which one could only properly engage through warfare.

Whether metaphor creates or discovers concepts, it remains a key property of language and one with which the critical discourse analyst cannot but engage. Consider the passage below, taken from a car magazine lying on my desk. The underlined phrases are those which could be interpreted as metaphorical, and at first sight the passage is so suffused with metaphorical constructions of one kind or another that it is difficult to find any literal language:

> Despite inner-city gridlock, punitive petrol prices and the looming spectre of congestion charging, our love affair with the car shows no signs of waning. But at least we're boxing a bit clever now.
>   More exalted sectors of the market may be feeling the pinch, but supermini sales have never been more buoyant. Examine the three candidates we've gathered here for our latest bargain basement shoot-out and its easy to see why.

Obvious examples are the use of 'punitive' to describe petrol charges. Again, the phrase comes from a view of taxation as punishment for high earnings or high consumption instead of as a consensus about the wealth that a society should pool in order to foster its collective interest. The tax is accepted here as part of the status quo, but its punitive nature exonerates the motorist from responsibility for the gridlock that the tax must partly ameliorate.

Idioms are metaphors that have become an accepted part of how we use language yet still strike a chord as unusual or strange (e.g. Gibbs 1994). 'We're boxing a bit clever' is typical of this process. We know that car buying is nothing like boxing and we find it strange that we should think of it as such. Yet we also understand it as a conflict, because we conceptualise business transactions in that way and because of the pressures we feel when we engage in this activity. We are constructed as in conflict with a government that makes motoring expensive, so we fight back 'cleverly' and buy smaller cars. It does not matter that this is exactly what the government wants to see happen. We are constructed as canny consumers winning our right to drive forward with impunity. 'Buoyant' is also interesting. We conceptualise movement as liquid. Cash is liquid because it can be moved about easily. We flood the market with cash and the sales float on this pent-up demand. The market is 'buoyant', which is positive because its opposite is sinking or drowning.

Finally, despite our somewhat negative construction, the issue here is not one of how we regard the car and taxation. The interest is in how the writer makes use of metaphors that can construct the issues in a particular way, even when their objective is simply to debate which car is best. For the student of critical literacy and critical discourse, we need to understand those types of manipulation so that we become more than mere consumers of the printed word.

Towards a participatory pedagogy

So far, we have looked at two movements that can change the way we see literacy and language. Post-modernism was described as providing the larger world-view in which an approach to language such as CDA can operate. I have also begun to show how we can use the assertion that reality is socially constructed in our approach to literacy pedagogy. We can refuse to accept literacy as the unthinking consumption of written text and treat the consequent attainment of a critical literacy as an act of group or community empowerment. To know how to use these insights to inform our approach to literacy teaching we should look more closely at the development of a pedagogy that makes unconscious use of them. This will involve us in a discussion of the work of the Brazilian educator and educational theorist Paulo Freire.

In a more recent retrospective, or 'reliving', of his major work, Freire (1992: 13) remarks on how his earlier approach was post-modern without his knowing it. To become literate in the fullest sense, adult learners had to strip back the superficial meanings of words and discover the socio-economic forces that had left them illiterate in the first place. Freire (1974) cites Aldous Huxley (1937) when he calls this 'the art of disassociating ideas' 'as an antidote to the domesticating power of propaganda'. In keeping with a postmodern ethos, 'liberation' is achieved not by the struggle of one class against another but by a pedagogy of liberation that would help literacy students separate themselves from 'the masses' by carving out the fuller, critical identity of a 'person' (Freire 1974).

Freire's conception of literacy and of how it should be taught has its roots in the Socratean tradition of Ancient Greece (Gee 1990). In a famous passage in the *Phaedra* (1986: 275–6), Plato has his master Socrates declare that writing is like painting. Writing challenges the reader with the illusion that it is presenting something lifelike which they can question and talk back to, as if 'they had some thought in their heads', but it disappoints by always saying the same thing each time. Speech can be changed to fit a context, but writing is always 'trundled out everywhere in the same way', then 'abused', by a poor interpretation or an unwilling listener. Language needs its author, or 'father', 'to defend it' (Gee 1990: 32–3) but all too often, writing has divested itself of its parentage.

For Plato, true knowledge is obtained through dialogue. A dialogue allows the student to ask their teacher what they mean so that the teacher must find a different wording to put their message across. Plato is saying that writing nullifies the possibility of this Socratean method. Interestingly, Freire retains this ancient mistrust of the unquestioned word even though his objective is literacy. Freire's method is based on questioning language even as students learn how it should be alphabetically encoded and decoded. He advocates a process of questions that come from the student, of replies suggested by the class and framed by the assistance of the teacher where this is needed. In this process, Freire is making a wider challenge to what he terms a naïve *objectivism* and the *banking concept* of education, which he sees as that objectivism's product.

Objectivism treats the world as existing apart from us, the creatures who perceive it. In what is almost an early post-modernist formulation, Freire's view is that we should be neither subjectivist nor objectivist since both make a transformational pedagogy impossible (Freire 1972: 27). Naïve objectivism treats the world as the text that Plato thought resistant to dialogue. When the world is such a text, it is out there and apart from us. It follows its own course and cannot respond to our desire to question it. A naïve subjectivism, on the other hand, wraps us up in ourselves so that each of us fabricates our own reality, leaving the collective reality that we inhabit unchanged by our actions. In what is perhaps Freire's best-known phrase, he asserts that our objective should be to 'read the world'. This reading can emerge only from the interaction between the objective world and our critical response to it.

The 'banking' concept of education treats the student as passive or as a cerebral vault in which the teacher simply deposits knowledge against the possibility of the student's future need. The student–teacher relationship implied by 'the banking concept' reflects the wider socio-economic and philosophical framework in which the teacher as banker must operate. A banking pedagogy is fatalistic, having a 'tamed' or domesticated view of the future (Freire 1992: 101). This can be seen quite plainly in a functional model of literacy. A functional literacy derives its construction of what people will use literacy for from what people do with literacy now. Functionality commits students to a naïve objectivism that 'banks' the future as a version of the present.

For Freire, the vehicle of change is *praxis,* by which he means an instrument or set of practices that can transform our circumstances. Pedagogy should be that praxis, extending beyond the development of literacy and towards the attainment of a wider state of awareness as to the nature of society. Attaining that awareness is called *conscientizacao* (*consciencisation*, in a literal translation of the Portuguese term). Traditional banking concepts of education cast the teacher as the oppressor and the student as the oppressed. In a society where there are both oppressors and oppressed, each group is 'dehumanised' by their role. The liberation of the literate oppressors may actually be a harder task to accomplish since they do not suffer the same daily round of humiliation as the oppressed illiterate. A related risk is that the teacher's awareness of the oppressed circumstances of their students may result in a benign paternalism that sets the teacher apart from the students in order to dispense the knowledge that will lift them out of illiteracy. Teachers must share the class with their students as fellow interlocutors. Freire's emphasis upon dialogue is not just a sentimental return to Socratean method. It is a revolutionary gesture against how he perceives the power structure of society.

In sum, we can find six basic principles that underpin Freire's approach (Lankshear and Mclaren 1993):

1. Students must try to understand the world through their own experiences and circumstances.
2. Because the world is shaped by human consciousness we have the capacity to transform it with our learning.
3. Students must understand the connection between how they lead their own lives and how they see the world in which they live.
4. Connecting their circumstances to how they read the world will give students the capacity to transform that world.
5. 'New makings' of the world arise from their critical understanding of how that world expresses itself as the printed word.
6. Understanding how dominant discourses, or the uses of language that are called literate, are the means through which their learners can be oppressed or marginalised.

These principles take us far beyond the practice of the literacy class and the question of what it means to become literate. Yet what is perhaps most interesting about Freirean ideology is that it produces an approach to literacy teaching that is grounded in practice. With some adaptation and development, Freire's methods have been implemented throughout the developed and developing world. In the next section, I discuss their key principles as part of a wider examination of what critical literacy teaching means in practice.

Critical literacy in practice

Freire first triggers dialogue with pictorial situations, then through the examination of a word. In one case, the class looks at a picture of a man, a woman, a child and a well. The objective is to help the students understand the difference between the world of nature and the world of culture. By asking simple questions such as 'who made the well and why?' the teacher sets up a sense of the duality of a world that is natural and a world that is transformed by the combined knowledge and work that constitutes a human culture. The cultural transformation of the world supposes a human dominance over it. This becomes a metaphor through which the teacher examines and rejects the dominance of one person over another (Freire 1974).

Just as the teacher extends a picture into an exploration of how we represent the world and treat each other, so they also open up the significances of a given word even as they expose the systems through which it is written and read. Freire's well-known example is the 'favela', a slum. The slum is considered through a photograph that triggers a discussion of the problems of slum living and the dearth of facilities, such as education and clean water. The word itself is projected first as a whole and next as a combination of syllables: fave-la. A given syllable is extended into what is termed a phonemic family, or a set of syllables beginning with the same phoneme, 'fa, fe, fi, fo, fu'. After other sets of syllables are added, the class starts to combine them into words and the words are discussed. *Terreno* (land), for example, develops a discussion about economic domination, irrigation, natural resources and 'the defence of the natural patrimony' (Freire 1974). Pictures are used to establish an analytical dialogue while acting as a bridge between the physical reality with which we have to deal and the highly abstract medium that is written language. The move towards written language begins with an analysis of the word as both a phonetic entity and as one imbued with socio-cultural significance.

The dialogic principle enfolded in the Freirean exploration of the words has become a more general educational objective. Nystrand (1997) derives from it a more general need to reflect upon how the discourse of classroom interactions may either transform learning into a creative and dialogic dynamic or relegate it to a repetitive regurgitation of facts. Critical literacy can itself become a way of reflecting upon these classroom processes, their texts and their discourse.

Luke (1994) categorises critical literacy as the acquisition of four types of competence: coding, semantic, pragmatic and critical. *Coding competence* means learning to be a code-breaker, or acquiring the graphic systems in which literacy is encoded. *Semantic competence* involves learning your role as a text participant or a co-creator of the text's meanings and not simply their willing consumer. *Pragmatic competence* includes understanding what the text was for and what one has to do with it. It suggests the empowerment of the reader or writer as somebody who can understand or reproduce the texts required by particular social purpose, be this to inform, amuse or advance some business or academic enterprise. Finally and perhaps most centrally, *critical competence* is about understanding the text's manipulative purpose and perhaps being able to engage in the larger act of deconstruction that a text implies.

Critical literacy uses CDA to obtain a 'productive power' (Street 2001: 297) where the student can learn to exploit the expressive potential of society's discourse structures instead of being simply manipulated by them. For example, the Australian disadvantaged schools programme focused on *genre* (Martin 1999). A genre is a category of text, such as a fairy story, newspaper editorial or a science report. Arguably, a given genre has distinct linguistic features, and understanding how these realise meanings can give us an insight into how society organises our language in a way that suits its social purpose. Yet, this post-modernist position has always been moderated by Halliday's (1993) understanding of how a given textual arrangement or register may reflect a genuine disciplinary need. The use of difficult linguistic constructions reflects the difficulty of the ideas that the text expresses. In the Australian disadvantaged schools programme, an objective was to help students identify the features of a given genre so that they could learn to 'produce' more 'powerful' texts.

Christie (1999) has a similar interest when she adopts the analysis of the social scientist Basil Bernstein (1990, 1996) in order to consider how educational discourse can either empower or disempower its students. Bernstein had a concept he called a *pedagogic device*. The pedagogic device is a means of regulating our perception of the world and hence our actions within it. The device is 'a condition' that both sustains and transforms 'culture' (Christie 1999: 181). In her study of the discourse of secondary school literature classes, Christie found that one educational objective was to help students develop their own perspective upon texts. But the discourse through which this perspective was expressed never had its structures studied or explained, while the processes through which students were supposed to arrive at a given opinion were not consciously exposed. The implication was that the structures through which we controlled a given genre were not properly taught. The result was that students tended to absorb views which were handed down by the curriculum. None the less, as Bernstein makes clear, although the pedagogic device is the means through which the prevailing power structure exercises control over the students' development, it can also furnish us with a discourse through which we can challenge and oppose the educational processes to which we are subject. Christie's exposure of the generic processes that generate critical opinion is exactly the kind of pedagogic device that can help students to control texts which might otherwise control them.

Although activities with genre suggest a concern for developing literacy, critical and genre approaches can be brought back to children of quite a young age. One straightforward technique that will be familiar to many primary school teachers is to cut a story off before the end and to ask the children to discuss and supply their own conclusions. This constitutes critical literacy because it allows children to take control of a narrative and consider endings that may better express their lives and circumstances, challenging sexist or classist stereotypes for example.

With some explanatory examples, genre teaching can base itself upon questions whose answers identify the central features of the genre that is being employed:

> What is the topic?
> Who is the intended audience?
> Why has it been written?
> What is the attitude of the writer towards the topic?
> How else could it have been written about? (Hood et al. 1996: 90–2)

Fraser (1998: 54) attests to how the most interesting discussion can be about whose interests the text serves, as this is derived from why it has been written. This has the merit of 'revealing more clearly the writer's position, uncovering the purpose behind the choice of subject matter and the interests of the people at the centre of it' (Brown 1999: 10).

A writer's attitude to the topic can be determined through a wider consideration of how the text does not emerge 'from some timeless, placeless zone', carrying the same message down the ages. The way the text is read will change according to the social context of the reader (Mellor and Patterson 2001: 120).

Critical approaches can therefore mean making students aware of the situated nature of text. Again, teachers can do this with students of different ages. Mellor and Patterson (2001: 21–2) describe how they tell nine-year-olds the beginning of an Australian version of the fairy story 'Hansel and Gretel'. The parents are so poor they cannot feed their children and decide to leave them in the 'bush'. The class then discuss the motivation of the parents and are asked to agree or disagree with a range of statements saying that they are very mean, very nice, sensible or left without choice. Such statements can open out a Freirean dialogue about the societies that leave children neglected or abandoned in a time of trouble.

Working with adults, but with a procedure that could also be adapted for children, Holme (2003a) asked classes to treat popular stories as allegories. For example, a class were told that the story of Little Red Riding Hood was an allegory of the conflict between the United States and Iraq. The class were asked to assign representations to different characters, discussing whether President Bush was the wolf or Little Red Riding Hood. The process of trying to fit political personages and their nations to a well-known story can awaken the critical faculty of students who have no strong political interest or knowledge, forcing them to adopt positions when they might not normally do so. The critical understanding of learners can also be engaged through the deconstruction of metaphor in text. As we discussed in the section on critical discourse analysis, we now understand that metaphors influence how we view a given idea because they are often the means through which we are able to grasp that idea in the first place. In the now established fact or opinion exercise students try to identify what is fact or opinion in a given text. This is also a useful critical literacy technique since it helps students expose how opinion is expressed and how also it often borrows the discourse of fact in order to give itself greater credibility. An understanding of metaphor can further this process because it shows how metaphors can provide a topic with a certain construction that makes our opinion of it appear as an attribute of how it actually is.

Such techniques reveal how critical literacy teaching is finally about 'engagement', 'control' and 'empowerment'. 'Engagement' is to move beyond an automatised response to the meanings implicit in text and consider how they are actually constructed. 'Control' is to understand that the reader is an interpreter who can co-create the text's meaning with the author. 'Empowerment' enables them to take charge of the mechanisms of textual construction, either resisting its manipulations or assuming the mantle of its authority.

Difficulties with critical literacy

We have seen how critical literacy theory can challenge the idea that to be literate is simply to attain a level of reading and writing performance that permits a given socio-economic function. The critical literacy challenge bases itself upon a post-modernist and critical discourse view of how language implements the social construction of meaning. For Derrida, 'there is nothing outside the text' (1997: 41). By this he means that language as an expression of meaning, and 'the world' as a collection of phenomena to which language is traditionally thought to refer, are one and the same thing. We therefore live in a reality that our language has constructed for us and can achieve a measure of understanding only if we can deconstruct these linguistic operations. Achieving a satisfactory literacy 'function' is then the same as operating in the role that society has constructed for us.

If 'there is nothing outside the text', how do we know anything?

An obvious or commonsensical feature of language is the fact that it is *referential*. By this one means that the word 'dog' means a species of four-legged animal because we have identified that animal as existing in the world, then used the combination of phonemes 'd-o-g' to *refer to* that category of creature. Yet Derrida flies in the face of this commonsensical assumption when he claims that Saussure failed to understand how his view of linguistic relativism had in fact shown language to be *self-referential*. In other words, Derrida does not suggest that 'd-o-g' achieves a different capacity to refer to the world because it is different from the sounds of 'c-a-t', on the one hand, and 'r-a-t', on the other. He suggests this difference is what allows the language to create out of itself the meanings and the categories that are used to organise the world.

Such a radical view encounters many serious problems. First among these is the question of how this self-referential system of meanings evolved in the first place. The second issue concerns why we do not live in a world of extreme cultural and linguistic relativism. If linguistic meanings had evolved out of a language, then the differences between languages should be so great that translation would be impossible. In Derrida's conception, misunderstandings would not be intermittent but absolute. Language, as it is, could not have evolved (Southwell 1987); it would be a chaos of misunderstandings. Even if a given language's own rules of use were rigid, they would have no correspondence with another language's rules of use.

More pertinently, a post-modernist view of language denies it any scope for definitive self-analysis. If our language were largely self-referential, we would find it difficult to sustain that claim in an authoritative manner. The argument for that claim would be fluid and could never be more than a matter of opinion as there would be no conception of a world with its implicit modes of logical operation which we could use to validate or invalidate the argument. Philosophical discourse, including the discourse through which post-modernism makes its claim would have to attribute its success to some vague concept of relative power or weakness in order to make a claim. Theories would supplant each other not because of any issue of validity but of power, as this is perpetrated by their discourse. This would also have consequences for how we view our own society, making meaningful social criticism and deconstruction impossible. In this sense, a critical literacy that attempted the deconstruction of socially engineered meanings would merely be adding another layer of socially engineered meanings.

Problems with the concept of criticality

A related, and perhaps more productive, problem for the critical literacy theory rests in the concept of criticality itself and in how we move from the deconstruction of social meanings towards the assumption that such meanings may foster injustice and may be challenged. We have seen how in the classroom critical literacy approaches can be a useful analytical tool for helping learners understand and finally control 'the discourse of power', yet more questionable is the assumption that such a discourse is always propagated at the behest of a social purpose that is framed as conspiratorial or malign. Language, and above all literate language, may use prestigious types of text or genres in order to impose a particular world-view. Yet such genres may originally be a response to a genuine contextual need, or to the unique circumstances to which writers want to refer or the purpose they wish to see accomplished. In other words, they are a response to how language refers to the world and not to how it constructs that world out of language.

According to critical literacy theory, a culture is a shared value system through which a society 'constructs' the outlook of its people with forms of language. Literacy is then one of the many cultural practices that implements that act of social construction. We have described how post-modernism is to some extent a reaction against the perception of how we dwell in a single modernist space that structures our lives, thoughts and feelings. This post-modernist reaction leads us to a multicultural or sub-cultural ethos where we try to create the social spaces that are responsive to our own minority belief-systems. By the same token we fashion the cultural practices and the forms of literacy that orchestrate this response to our minority needs.

Yet in another way, the critical literacy view seems to return us to a larger, all-encompassing space that is constructed by literacy's one, overarching practice. Culture is then treated as monolithic and literacy is one of the practices through which it propagates its value system. Critical literacy's 'deterministic view of culture' treats it as 'a one-dimensional stable, homogeneous and consensual entity, with easily identifiable markers' and with 'members' who 'share equally in the knowledge of and ability to use its norms'. Such a monolithic view 'renders invisible the various lived experiences of individuals within groups' (Hall 2002: 2). It denies us an insight into the different ways in which they practise literacy.

Street (1996: 75–6) cites Lienhardt (1964: 27) and his criticism of Sir James Frazer's 'if I were a horse' approach to anthropology. Frazer's approach was simply to follow the example of the fictional detective Sherlock Holmes and imagine himself in the skin of his suspect. Such an act may work for a detective who shares the socio-cultural context of his suspect, but it fails as soon as these contexts start to differ. We cannot know how or why people will respond to different sets of meanings unless we occupy the context from which those meanings are being constructed. We also need to understand the cultural assumptions that we carry into a strange context and which will colour our judgement of it. We should not reconstruct a context in a manner that justifies our ideological position. A problem with the Freirean method was that of finding ways to foster genuine dialogue, a dialogue that was free from the facilitator's ideological control. The problem arises from the lack of a shared context for teacher and student. Such a lack forces the teacher to try to put themselves in the skin of the student, act out their responses for them, then to become disillusioned when they do not respond as predicted. The teacher's attempts at deconstruction may in fact become a form of contextual manipulation where students are brought to believe in what the teacher believes. A deconstructionist pedagogy is not this process of learning how to share in the teacher's belief system. Deconstruction is instead a celebration of the difference between one institutional or minority culture and another, and an expression of the different forms of understanding that emerge from the interactions between different minority groups.

Emerging from the misperception of culture as monolithic and heterogeneous is what Street (1996: 139–41) calls 'the dominant literacies' view. Genre-based critical literacy approaches are considered empowering because they help their students to use the types of text that permit one social group to hold sway over another. Yet 'empowerment' seems now to mean helping critical literacy students to acquire a dominant literacy so that they too can dominate. If these genres are primarily the expression of a power structure, an induction into them presupposes an acceptance of the monolithic culture that uses these texts as its all-pervasive mechanism of control. 'Empowerment' is now acquiescence. Such acquiescence amounts to the eventual invalidation of the minority practices and beliefs to which literacy can also give expression. These practices and their expressive genres are left aside because they are regressive and not part of a dominant and empowering literacy ethos.

Deconstruction implies a dialogue between the forces that shape the text and the forces that shape the reader. Yet in its critical literacy form, the dialogue becomes an act of cultural resistance. It is the reader's refusal to succumb to the enforced social construction implicit in an uncritical reading of text. In this negative view of culture, there is a risk that we will forget how culture is not an oppressive conspiracy but an interactive dynamic, or a meeting place between the plethora of beliefs and value systems, institutional subcultures, communities of practice, languages and patterns of language use. If literacy is a vehicle for cultural expression, then we need a concept of literacy that is able to express the larger dynamic of institutions, cultures, languages, genres and registers which our concept of culture implies. This more varied and responsive vision of literacy will be the subject of the next chapter.

Conclusions

In this chapter I have tried to understand critical literacy as a perception of literacy that evolves from other readings of the world. To do this, I first examined post-modernism as the larger intellectual movement inside which the critical literacy concept was formed. In post-modernism I found three strands of thought that have influenced critical literacy theory. The strands and their application to critical literacy are as follows:

1. The fluidity of meaning and the view that categories are socially constructed. This provides literacy practitioners with Freire's sense of the word as an entity that we should not graphically decode or encode without first exploring its multiplicity of meanings. Literacy can suppose decoding meaning to promote that meaning's uncritical consumption. Critical literacy entails an act of deconstruction.
2. The fragmentation of global ideas and the quest for universally applicable modes of analysis into a celebration of minority movements. This furnishes us with a sense of literacy pedagogy as a quest for minority empowerment.
3. An understanding of text as encoding the power relations implicit in the organisation of culture and society. The need for literacy pedagogy to expose those power relations, treating text not as a product of a given author but as a method of encoding the social and cultural forces to which that author is subject.

I next looked at how critical literacy borrowed from two other approaches in order to implement its post-modern agenda. First, I explained the use of a form of linguistic analysis, termed CDA. This was perceived as an instrument that was able to advance the deconstructionist agenda. I argued that this should not be perceived negatively, as an exploration of malign social forces, but positively as a method of exposing the generic structures and language forms which students must master if they are to function successfully in society. I further looked briefly at some modern theories of metaphor as a method of understanding how a text may achieve a given perspective on a given topic. Second, I looked at participatory pedagogy as this was developed by Paulo Freire. I perceived Freireanism as an ideological movement grounded in a very practical approach to pedagogy. In describing Freire's dialogic method, I treated this as the foundation of a larger search for a critical reading and for the act of group empowerment that such a reading implies.

When I looked at critical literacy itself, I described some of the key tenets of critical pedagogy, giving some thought to its interest in genre and the exposure of the discourse structures through which society's power relations are allegedly expressed. Finally, I considered the problems with the critical literacy approach. The first of these was that deconstruction is self-defeating because it denies us the intellectual authority to deconstruct. I also expressed concerns about the critical literacy assumption that culture was the singular and malign focus of social power relations, relations against which we must seek protection in critical understanding.

Exercises

1. Find a newspaper article. Do not worry about finding a correct technical vocabulary but present a critical analysis of it that considers the following:
   * the field, mode and tenor of the article and social context and its assumptions that these analyse;
   * the way in which the article's visual arrangement reinforces its meanings;
   * the use of grammatical structure to reinforce an attitude or prejudice, disguising opinion as fact, for example;
   * the use of co-ordination to reinforce an attitude or prejudice. You should think here about the words through which co-ordination is achieved – for example, do cause-and-effect co-ordinators ('so, and so, thus, therefore, etc.') express a secure cause-and-effect relationship?
   * the use of metaphor or metaphorical themes to reinforce a certain view or outlook.
2. Consider why you would view or not view each of the following classroom procedures as a way to implement the critical literacy approach:
   * children are asked to take the point of view of a minor character in a story and retell it from that perspective;
   * the teacher writes a set of letters on the board and the class make as many words as they can from them. The teacher then asks a child to read a word. After each reading they ask the class to make a very short story about that word;
   * a class are asked to alter a text so that it supports the opposite conclusion to the one put forward;
   * a class are asked to imagine the unknown author of a text and to construct a picture of their life and character;
   * a class are asked to look at a text, then to read it in turn, sentence by sentence. After each sentence, the reader is asked to say aloud what the purpose of that sentence is and how it contributes to the unfolding structure and purpose of the text.

3. Either take the text that you analysed above, or find another, and describe how you would present it to a critical literacy class. Try to unfold a procedure for the class step by step with numbered sentences.
4. Take the procedure that you described above and describe how it does or does not serve the critical literacy approach as a combination of Freirean, critical discourse and post-modernist perspectives.

3 From Literacy to Literacies

Introduction

Both the functional and critical models of literacy presuppose a dominant discourse which must be mastered at the expense of any others that exist. They suggest that we treat our ability to deal with this discourse as if it were an 'individual possession' (Gee 1990: 42). In the functional case they ask 'how much' the individual needs to possess (ibid.). Critical literacy, on the other hand, opens a debate about the quality of 'the possession'. However, 'reading' and 'writing', as the core components of literacy, suggest that one 'reads' and 'writes' about something (ibid.: 43). This is not simply a question of having a topic or subject. It is a matter of doing something with that topic, of treating it in a particular way then transmitting the facts of that treatment to someone else, perhaps to provoke some kind of action. Literacy by its nature is about what we do with certain types of text. It is about the purpose and variety of these texts and the activities to which they give rise.

In Chapter 2 we considered how a culture should not be interpreted as one set of values that mould people according to a consistent set of values. A culture devolves into communities that can be identified by their common activities and skills and by the way in which these bind their members together with their common preoccupations. Some of these communities may seem strange to the uninitiated. Philatelists, for example, have developed the activity of stamp collecting into a set of recognised practices that involve soaking stamps off letters, arranging them in an album according to certain agreed categories and using hinged, adhesive paper to substitute for the stamps' own gum. The transmission of an activity among group members and its repetition in order to sustain community objectives will groove it as a social practice. Thus, if people simply stick stamps onto the album page, risking damage to the stamp, they will place themselves on the margins of the community of philatelists because they do not sustain one of the practices that give that group its coherence.

Some common activities that bind communities involve literacy. Philatelists form a community of practice that has quite specialised literacy skills. For example, philatelists read stamp catalogues, exchange e-mails or study the markings on the stamps themselves. These activities can then be called *literacy practices* (e.g. Barton 1994, Gee 1990, Scribner and Cole 1981, Street 1984). In this chapter, I am going to explore what we mean by these practices. I will consider how they affect our discussion of literacy, changing the way it is both perceived and taught. I will look at how such practices carry literacy through time, reconfiguring the culture of which they are a part.

Social practice: literacy practice

Literacy practices are the recurrent literacy activities of a community. They become practices because they unfold according to a repeated pattern. For example, the practice of reading chess books does not mean reading the same text but the same type of text for the same purpose. Sometimes the structure of the text reflects and controls the structure of the practice. Chess books begin with an introduction that sets out the facet of the game which they examine. This introduction may be followed by a list of the abbreviations used. The chapters will then unfold through an interplay between an explanational text, strings of notations signifying chess moves and positional diagrams.

In the chess book example, there is a close relationship between a text genre, the instructional book and the practice that unfolds around it. One could argue that we would find something similar where the practice involves writing rather than reading. If two people play chess by e-mail, for example, sending moves to each other, then the very brief text expressing that move will also evolve its own generic pattern. The literacy practice, however, does not end with the consumption or production of the texts that lie at its heart. Chess players and cooks both consume instructional genres with the objective of acting upon those instructions. In the case of reading chess books, their associated literacy practices extend into solitary game-playing and the moving of pieces across a board in order to study the positions in practice. Once the knowledge from the book has been partly memorised, it will become part of a repertoire of play, affecting the pattern of the player's future games. When a recipe is the central genre, its reading may have a dish as its product. The implementation of such instructional texts also involves a very different type of reading from that associated with some other texts, a novel for example. It therefore provides a good example of how a literacy practice must be part of a larger social practice that binds reading and writing into their larger structure.

Some literacy practices involve an elaborate interplay between a spoken and written use of language. A formal institutional meeting in companies and other institutions will be steered by an agenda. The practice of agenda writing is therefore an attempt to steer the order in which an oral discussion will unfold. Legal systems and the practices of drafting or interpreting laws are an attempt to constrain the activities in which the members of a given society will engage. The interpretation and enforcement of law result in a host of other literacy practices, involving police reports, the search for legal precedents and the construction of a courtroom record.

We can now see how social practices give coherence to the communities that make up a society and its culture, giving coherence to their plethora of subcultures and institutions. Where society aspires to universal literacy, it is unusual for community practices not to involve literacy at some level. Even communities that are defined by practical crafts and trades will transmit skills through instructional materials and may, like the medieval guilds, bind themselves together with articles that enforce secrecy and endow the guardianship of those trade secrets with a quasi-mystical purpose.

The example of a legal and judicial framework also shows how different practices combine into a larger *literacy*. Thus the practices of drafting laws, writing court reports, consulting the law of precedent or writing letters and contracts that appeal to the possibility of legal enforcement will all combine into what we can call a *legal literacy*. In the same way, we can see how practices, such as research article writing, experiment note-taking and the exchange of official correspondence may combine as a *scientific literacy*. We should therefore no longer speak about literacy, but about *literacies*. These literacies bind different types of practice as a common social purpose (e.g. Barton 1994, Gee 1990, Street 1984).

In a literate society, a given individual is likely to engage in many different literacies and the practices to which they give rise. For example, one teenager I have observed engages in the recreational literacies of reading novels, using an internet chat-room, exchanging e-mails and exchanging text messages with their distinct graphic code. She also has to engage in different school-based literacies involving an induction to such communities of practice as science or literary criticism. She has failed, however, to absorb the practices of what one might call 'domestic literacy', rarely compiling task lists and never engaging in the practice of leaving written messages.

Although literacies and their practices will change with society, their very nature means that they confer a measure of stability upon the activities that surround them. This stability is partly passed down through the nature of the text genre and the text register from which they proceed or to which they give rise. Yet we can also identify how the practice gives rise to a *literacy event,* or to the moment when it is actually implemented (Barton 1994). This event is shaped by the practice. In the case of the telephone message, if somebody notes down a message from a caller and passes it on to the person they wanted to contact, then they have set in train two literacy events: the writing down of the message and its being read by a recipient. However, other unplanned events are also possible. For example, somebody other than the intended recipient may read the message. This invokes a different type of practice, one that could be called 'literate eavesdropping'. The unintended recipient may actu-

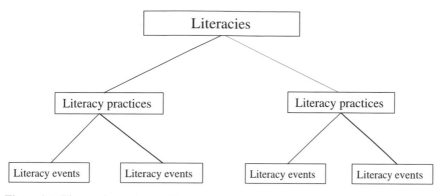

Figure 3.1 The configuration of literacies

ally want to divert the message or throw it away. Although such an example shows how the manner in which events unfold may be determined by the nature of social practice by which they are instigated, they can also develop their own form, responding to the unusual nature of a given circumstance. This typifies the inherent instability of 'the event'. We can now see a three-level model, as illustrated in figure 3.1.

Our social fabric is bound together by practices involving the use of literacy. These practices can be grouped as larger literacies or as configurations of similar practices. They are also analysed by the repeated events that they configure.

The practice as a context of use

In Chapter 1 we considered how one of the problems with the concept of functionality was how it led to curriculum planning where literacy was time-tabled as separate from the practices that it sustains. This meant that it developed literacy in a vacuum as a conglomeration of well-learnt but irrelevant knowledge. One example was how this could also result in a loss of the learning opportunities provided by school-based history or science literacies. Literacy did not develop as the means to expand a framework of knowledge. It prepared for the moment of knowledge expansion that may actually never occur. Such a state of affairs can be detrimental to both the larger process of knowledge acquisition and to the larger development of literacy that knowledge acquisition will set in train.

A practice concept of literacies returns the acquisition of a literacy to its context of use. It supposes that once children have mastered the basics of reading and writing, a literacy is learnt as a key to the mode of enquiry from which it has evolved. Other possibilities for learning also arise. Gee (1990) describes how an individual will have to cope with many different ways of using language, or with many different discourses. However, they will have a primary discourse, which is the one in which they are socialised from birth, and secondary ones, which will be acquired at a later point. In the case of middle-class American children, their primary discourse will be more closely modelled on accepted literate uses of language, or on what I have called 'the grapholect'. In the case of many less privileged children, school-based literacy forms a secondary discourse which imposes a greater learning burden. Because the school introduces children to a discourse that is 'dominant' because of its association with the power structure, it may fail to confer a proper value upon the linguistic practices of many of its children. This can apply as much to literate discourses as to spoken ones.

In what may first appear to be a reversal of this process, where language is seen as shaping the practice and not the reverse, Bernstein (1971) formulated the concept of *elaborate* and *restricted codes*. These codes fashioned the way we use language, determining our ability to find the appropriate linguistic form for a given meaning or to express the context that would give those meanings a more pertinent application. The codes transmitted the requirements of the social structures in which we existed, regulating our use of language. Restricted codes were perceived as 'public' because the user could assume community knowledge of their topic. A discourse that dealt with known or familiar topics deprived a speaker of the need to elaborate upon their meanings or to describe the remote context in which they may have been set. An elaborate code evolved out of an interest in constructing private or novel attitudes to a topic, hence supposing that language must work harder because it was not simply regurgitating sets of agreed, public attitudes.

Bernstein was often criticised for his association of the larger expressive potential of the elaborate code with literate middle-class speech and the restricted code with a working-class dialect. The working-class dialect was less influenced by a formal encouragement to construct a private response to a given set of circumstances, or by an interest in the formation of individual opinion. These criticisms were made by linguists such as Labov (1972), who may have been influenced by basic linguistic perceptions of the nature of language.

According to much mainstream linguistic theory, we can control a language and produce original sentences once we have acquired that language. An acquired language or grammar is a complete language or grammar, whatever its dialect, and the suggestion that our knowledge of language can be codified as restricted or elaborate, as if partly learnt, would be alien. Yet Bernstein was not making a qualitative judgement about literate versus non-literate language. His supposition was not that different class practices foster a different discourse, hence creating a disjunction between the impoverished language of the home and the richer discourse of the school. His suggestion was finally that different codes transmit different forms of linguistic behaviour and that these have different degrees of compatibility with those expected by school.

In a more recent practice view, our interest is no longer in the suggestion of a discrepancy between home and school behaviours, but simply in understanding the nature of the practices to which these different locations and their cultures give rise. Amy Shuman's (1986) study of urban adolescents reveals how their primary discourse may be quite different from a dominant, literate model. Yet this does not preclude them from primary literate practices. Black children, for example, may develop literacies within their primary discourse by writing rap songs and passing notes or messages. A 'practice' concept of literacies confers validity on these forms, holding them out not as activities that must somehow be brought into a formal curriculum but as ones that should be valued as part of the larger social world of the child. The practices should be developed and contrasted even as their owners are inducted into the dominant practices of the power structure and hence led towards a mastery of their discourse. Our interest now is less in a concept of all-controlling codes and more in a fractured picture of different practices, each of which can have a different way of using language.

There have been many other studies that examine how literacy practices evolve in different communities. Benson et al. (1994), for example, recount the induction of three students into academic literacy practices. One interesting observation expresses how individual socialisation can distort the dominant form of practice. A student from a working-class background recounted how her parents were ambitious for her, insisting that she do her homework, but did not make her go to the quiet of her room to write. Her habit of doing homework in the kitchen with its attendant activity and noise from the television meant that she constructed writing as a practice that had background disturbance and subsequently she had trouble adapting to the assumptions of silence and solitude demanded by an academic context.

The New London Group (2000) analyse the challenge of a literacy environment that is fragmenting into a plethora of practices stimulated by the spread of new media, the internet, multiculturalism and by the way in which globalisation is breaking down nationally distinct societies. The invasive ubiquity of modern media is appropriating 'the discourses of private life' and destroying 'the autonomy of private and community lifeworlds' (The New London Group 2000: 16). The new literacy challenge is to establish a 'space' in which 'different lifeworlds' can develop their full potential. The solution is to develop the modern concept of 'design' as this is used in the sense of designing office space to permit more effective working practices or a curriculum to permit a more powerful pedagogy. Situated 'practice' concepts of literacy pedagogy, where students absorb forms through a process of socialisation, are finally insufficient. Design must pertain to understanding the structures of discourse and shaping a critical pedagogy that responds to these insights. The view seems, finally, that we should combine the understanding of discourse structures obtained by critical literacy approaches with the realisation that these are rooted in the context of a practice, and acquired out of a socialisation into the same.

Martin-Jones and Bhatt (1998) showed how the literacies of Gujarati speakers in Britain spawned a complex and variable nexus of practices. Saxena (1994) recounts the complex web of literacies and literacy practices that have been evolved by the Punjabi-speaking minority in Southall, London. A feature of Punjabi that adds a particular dimension of complexity is how the process of becoming a minority language in London adjusts and even elaborates upon the already complicated set of practices that evolved in the Punjab, then were adapted by migration to Hindi-speaking Delhi. Punjabi can be written in any of three scripts, Gurmukhi, Devanagari or Arabic. The use of different scripts may reflect different practices and these will form a badge of identity. Arabic is identified with Islam, for example, and Gurmukhi with the Sikh religion. Different individuals operate different literacies with different degrees of success. A grandmother, for example, can only recognise the destination marked on the London bus she takes regularly because the shape of the word has become familiar. A child educated in an English school and only partly inducted into his parents' minority literacies will be an unknowing messenger when they take a Hindi script shopping list from home to a Punjabi-speaking shopkeeper.

Fundamental to the practice approach is the type of research perspective that evolves. When literacies are perceived as 'local' (Street 1996: 85), this is not simply in a straightforward geographic sense. Literacies are 'local' to their context of use and they cannot be understood outside this context. Context and literacy, as a form of linguistic practice are 'bound together, existing as two mutually constitutive components of systems of action' (Hall 2002: 128). As Street points out, this can have a quite fundamental effect on the conclusions that are drawn. A cultural construction of literacy as a singular autonomous way of reading and writing language denies the validity of whatever local practices may arise. Because literacy is itself a cultural value, the act of trying to propagate it in a different culture can prove sterile. Successful literacies evolve from the evolution of indigenous, local practices.

The variety and history of literacy practices

Literacy practices identify an almost limitless variety of activity. When we consider how they have evolved, we can see how they stimulate technological and organisational development while responding to it. A history of literacy would finally be a history of literacy practices and of how they relate one to another. There is no space to produce such a history here; all we can do is give some insight into the complexity and variety of this network of social activity as it has evolved over time.

Literacy practices evolved from other practices requiring sign use to denote ownership, value and transmit information through space and time. In the Tigris–Euphrates valley of what is now Iraq, literacy responded to the growing complexity of social organisation. A need for property marks and taxation records stimulated the development of increasingly elaborate systems for recording ownership and registering contributions to the larger community. The representation of a fiscal value and the assertion of ownership are two practices that stimulated the development of some of the earliest forms of literacy. After considerable evolution and multiplication these fiscal practices now underpin modern society, whether through the production of banknotes, the writing of cheques, the use of credit cards, signatures and PINs, or the elaborate accounting procedures by which these devices are underpinned.

The coin is an intermediary phase. When metallurgy was primitive, any fragment of metal had value. A royal assignation was stamped upon the metal disc in order to standardise its worth and to declare that this would not fluctuate according to the daily need for whatever metal it was made of (though this did not stop governments debasing their coinage). An increase in the availability of precious metals and the widening geographic spread of goods to be exchanged for them meant that by the sixteenth century the weight of coin might have restricted its use in making purchases or paying armies far from home. Additionally, there is an increasing need for secure storage. This invokes a parallel realisation that to be meaningful a sign does not have to be attached to what it means. What is needed is a form of words which guarantees their bearer that the equivalent in coin will be paid if it is required. Practices evolve that require the agreement of communities which are no longer identifiable by their occupancy of a given territory but by their agreement as to the value of certain arrangements of signs upon paper. We can therefore see the evolution of another literacy practice: the writing, reading and exchange of promissory notes. Literacy allows a fixed form of words to be carried across any distance that a human can travel. In sixteenth-century Europe some of the first great Italian banking dynasties such as the Fuggers could astonish contemporaries by making coin appear in distant locations without ever actually moving it. These promissory notes evolved into banknotes. In some countries, the origin of these notes in earlier promissory letters was, until recently, reflected in their promise 'to pay the bearer on demand the sum' that was their value.

Now another level of meaning representation has evolved. We no longer carry notes in significant quantities but cards or a cipher to indicate our right of access to notes. In the UK during the 1960s the coin and notes in circulation amounted to ten times the total value in 2000 as a proportion of overall economic activity. Effectively, we promise to pay a token signifying a consistent value that can be exchanged against goods or services. In actuality, we hand over our electronic code, our capacity to honour the promise is verified, and we receive the goods or services. Our socio-economic existence is made possible by widespread agreement as to how one sign signifies another. Literacy practices lead us into a realm of semiotic abstraction where we are dealing in networks of signs that rarely have to be exchanged for what they signify.

The code with which a credit card holder confers payment is effectively an electronic signature. The signature derives from another mode of authentication, the seal. In Ancient Sumeria, each significant person carried their own seal just as each now has their own distinct signature and their own PIN number. Such assignations confer our enduring agreement to a form of words.

A strongly attested attribute of literacy is its ability to confer a sense of permanence upon language. Promises also aspire to that sense of perpetuity. When the promise is spoken, those who reiterate its meaning may change its wording, resulting in greater debate about what exactly was said. Writing does not overcome the problem of interpretation because words mean different things to different people at different times, but it restricts the area of debate. Banking and finance group together a multitude of practices that exploit this capacity of literacy to assign enduring agreement to a form of words and to make an enduring social contract as to their meaning.

The use of literacy to hold and pass down enduring meanings allows the codification of society's regulatory structures as law. A legal system will in turn spawn a multitude of other literacy practices and their associated events. There are the more complicated promissory practices or drafting, signing, reading, interpreting and enforcing contracts. Other related practices are those of certification, whether of the person, as an artisan possessing a given body of skills or a graduate as having attained a certain level of education. We do not just vest proof of our identity in written documents but proof of our knowledge, good character and personal history. There are the very specialised activities associated with drafting laws and recording courtroom proceedings. In the British and US legal systems, courtroom proceedings establish a body of case law, which is in its turn read and interpreted.

The belief that writing's permanence can constitute an assertion of authority or truth lingers naively in phrases such as 'it must have happened because I read it in the papers'. Yet more subtly it associates itself with practices of handing down knowledge as a precise formulation of words or as a testament to something seen that is not subject to subsequent distortion. Once signed, the written confession can condemn the confessor even after the confession has been retracted. Legal literacies developed within a respect for a given written formulation or law, which then required interpretation. They also admitted the concept of evidence and a written assertion of the truth or testament. Such concerns cannot be dissociated from the development of science. Written proof promotes great opportunities for verification by others whilst contributing to a larger archive of knowledge. Science even encloses the universe in a network of regulatory principles that they call 'laws'. The ability to capture events as an enduring form of words permits the transmission of them as repeatable formulae. The concept of verification depends upon a record that can be verified. Science requires literacy, even if literacy does not always foster science.

Societies do not simply perpetuate themselves through regulatory frameworks but through core belief systems and shared myths. However, the writing of myth confers upon it a degree of permanence and can affirm it not simply as a society's evolving birth narrative but as the society's enduring contract with itself, or a revealed text that will determine its future existence. Legal and early scientific literacies sought authority in religious ones. Literacy practices operate elaborate intertextual webs where revealed texts buttress legal texts and legal texts confer authority on other enduring contractual practices.

The transmission of a form of words through time, whether of law or creed, suggests that meaning can also be delivered intact from the moment of its revelation, immune to the insights of its future readers. An interpretation invokes analogy because it explains one meaning through another. The risk is then that analogy will corrupt or even destroy the real message. A consequence is a metaphor of *reification*, where the text is treated as an object or thing, the container of a meaning which is there even when an interpreter or a reader is absent. Understanding is then incidental to the act of reading. Simply to read the text, even without proper understanding, is to release its meaning and put it to work in the world.

The metaphor of a reified text, or of the text as an enduring object, is no better encapsulated than in the monumental literacies of the Egyptians or the Central American Maya. The Egyptians carved their narrative into obelisks asserting how the event and its language will command public attention through time. Histories are fixed by a formulation of language, and literacy fixed language in stone. This carving out of a record predicates a larger consolidation of past activity as a single process or 'history' and our self-construction as that process's grateful product. In another act of reification, the word 'book' has come to connote not an object made of leaves of paper bound together but a text trapped inside that object. The text is reified by association. It is no longer created out of the act of perception, or readership. The text is the book. In our legal processes we therefore swear upon a book, confident that the truth of its entrapped message will attest to our own truthfulness.

Some linguistic practices attribute to language the capacity to act upon the world and make it other than what it is. When a prayer or other acknowledgement of the deity is repeated daily, people purge themselves of responsibility of wrong-doing. Likewise, sickness is driven out with incantation. The daily affirmation of what is good may set that goodness to work. In the late medieval and Renaissance period the Pope's representatives would sell documents called 'indulgences'. These were papers that guaranteed forgiveness of the holder's sin. The paper circumvented the extended process of confession and absolution. When entrapped by writing, absolution would exert a continuing effect. Once written down, the words repeat themselves endlessly, exerting their protective power. Much earlier, Socrates had described how the sick would place an inscription next to a herbal remedy that they wore in an amulet. Without the inscription, the power of the remedy would not be released (Drucker 1999). Similar practices endure. In twentieth-century Yemen, there was a suggestion that an inscribed cup could impart healing properties to the liquid it contained. The word of the prophet that was engraved upon the cup would combat the effects of all poisons and sorcery, or of a snake or dog bite (Breton-Gravereau and Thibault 1998). In some practices, writing thus fosters the illusion of a voice that is forever speaking. The Buddhist prayer-flags that rise above a Tibetan mountainside also promise this repeated release of meaning. The wind's whipping of the flag assures the release of the signs from the cloth and perpetuates the distribution of their sense.

Writing allows a use of language to endure in time and this fact has impacted upon our wider perception of time itself. Few literacy practices have been so central to other social and historical developments as those which are bound up with our division, measurement and control of time. For pre-literate societies, time is a property of the phenomena it affects. Time is made manifest through seasonal change or the movement of the moon and the planets. Few practices are as central to early literacies as calendar construction, and few exert a more profound effect, recreating time as a distinct and measurable entity. Calendars put time outside the phenomena and processes in which it resides, displaying it as an entity that can be understood and organised. Calendars also bring power into the hands of those who can read and write them, giving them the ability to apportion activities to future slots, determining who must do what and when.

Attali (1982) describes how monastic communities programmed their existence as complex series of routines. This practice of compiling and writing schedules would shape the life of a community. Within the day, the movement of the monks from 'matins' to 'vespers' marked out time, regulating the surrounding community like a great clock before clocks had yet come to exist.

In medieval Europe the ecclesiastical control of literacy permits the ecclesiastical reconstruction of the temporal space that ordinary people inhabit. Lives are steered by an ecclesiastical road-map with its 'Book of the Days', and its invasive demarcation of Saturnalian licence with Lenten denial. A more recent and very different consequence is the effort at self-empowerment in the construction of a life according to a personal agenda and the plethora of practices that are an individual's attempt to take control of future time.

Writing does not just carry text through time, but across space also. Letter-writing was another early literacy practice. The high cost of producing writing materials and the problems of carriage meant that for centuries this remained the practice of a few, devoted most commonly to the dissemination of proclamations and assertions of royal or imperial power. The phrase 'within the King's writ' testifies to the distance within which a given monarch could respond to a request for legal redress, thus defining the limits of their authority.

The rise of recreational letter-writing in eighteenth-century Europe began to make a common event of dialogues whose interlocutors where separated in space and time. Such letters were made possible by a plethora of inventions and newly evolved practices. For example, a key invention was a practical writing material. This required the invention of paper in first-century China, more than a thousand years before paper-making technologies began to spread throughout Europe during the thirteenth and fourteenth centuries. Letter writers also needed a system of distribution and payment. The response to this need was a further development in ancillary practices such as stamp production and interpretation. These finally came of age in 1874 when all countries of the world agreed to link themselves together with a system of flat-rate postage (Vincent 2000). Practices associated with correspondence both developed and evolved from the sense that reading was not a public activity where several people listened to the reading of one. Letters developed the practice of confidentiality and the address of a written text to one reader only, with an evolving need to restrict circulation and develop a new set of ways to control readership. When many early literacies had been associated with public stipulations and controls, letter writers evolved a private voice, one that anticipates a response from another voice that almost seems to be close by. Even a very early journal such as *The Pillow Book* from eleventh-century Japan still seems to impart confidences to its modern reader. Lady Sarashina, as the anonymous author is known, recounts the blossoming of a plum tree and how it reminds her of an absent friend: 'utterly dejected', she breaks off a branch and sends it with a poem, confiding in verse how 'she promised to return' (Sarashina 1972: 45).

Many early literacy practices were public in nature. Recreational literacies involved the use of written prompts to sustain an oral performance. The dominance of drama as a preferred mode of recreational literacy in Ancient Greece reflects that. Acting enabled the broadcast of a single written text without an unending process of reproduction and distribution. In medieval Europe, the high cost of literacy materials and the problems of portage, storage and manufacture precluded our modern concept of an individual engaged in the silent consumption of text. Reading was reading aloud or the oral improvisation upon a written text. One consequence may have been the elimination of word spaces in alphabetic script. Spoken language does not mark the spaces between words. Word separation is more a property of semantics and syntax than phonology. A script that was written to be read aloud did not require word spaces as one understood it through its vocalisation. One read as one spoke and the result was a *scriptura continua* which no longer marked the boundaries between words. In its time, this was not a regression, or a loss of the sense of the word chiselled out by the users of hieroglyphs and other early scripts. It could even be interpreted as a celebration of the capacity of writing to represent language as sound. Silent reading was unnecessary. The materials and technologies needed to supply large numbers of people with books for silent consumption were simply not there. Scripts were designed to support their oral performance. They were therefore written as they were spoken (Saenger 1997). It is suggested that word separation, which permitted the silent processing of meaning and silent reading, arose in Europe together.

Yet silent reading was not the only development needed to support intimate recreational literacies. Few developments can be accorded the importance as that of printing with a moveable typeface, though the success of this innovation was also dependent upon other innovations in metallurgy and paper production. Block printing began in China, though arguably the earlier use of a seal to leave an imprint on a material such as clay is simply a version of the same process (Gaur 1984). The Chinese use of this process was crucial to the dissemination of Buddhist texts and even to the rapid spread of Buddhism itself (ibid.). The Chinese development of a moveable typeface meant one could represent different combinations of words with the same set of signs. However, this was more effectively harnessed in Europe, because one had to deal only with combinations of 26 letters and not 50,000 characters. The technology was harnessed by the Gutenberg's screw press in the middle of the fifteenth century. Central to printing's many effects was how it gave the writer a readership of individuals able to construct a personal and interpretative relationship with text.

Like the innovation of block printing in China before it, the screw press arguably made possible another set of religious literacy practices, those associated with the spread of Protestantism, allowing the individual to read religious text without ecclesiastical mediation. Print literacy weakened the ecclesiastical organisation of time by providing more individuals with the mechanisms that would help them regulate their own lives. During the seventeenth, eighteenth and nineteenth centuries, printing stimulated the evolution of new narrative genres, or types of novel, which no longer transmitted meaning for future oral broadcast but were written for the reader's silent consumption, closeting them in an individual and unspoken interaction with another's text. It may also have been that the intimate way in which these narratives could be consumed was bound up in their adoption of a more private subject matter, one which was sometimes unfolded by mimicking an exchange of letters, as in such eighteenth-century works as Samuel Richardson's *Clarissa*. A result was the increasing spread of literacy practices away from the consumption and creation of histories and myths towards the exploration of the motivations that drive less elevated lives.

Whatever their nature, literacy practices depend upon the formal and informal systems of education through which their necessary skills are imparted. Printing itself stimulates a demand for a literate population. Yet printing also responds to the demand for materials that assist literacy education. The informal schools of the poor taught with whatever scraps of material they could find. At the same time the rise of mass literacy during the seventeenth, eighteenth and nineteenth centuries spurred the production of purpose-designed reading materials. One eighteenth-century English publisher produced as many as half a million cheap reading books, for example (Vincent 2000: 32). Yet few materials found their way to the deprived. The peasant children who attended the Irish hedge schools of the early nineteenth century would have been fortunate to have slates to write on, though the attendance of many children at such schools attests to how a general perception of literacy's importance had filtered down through all the social strata.

The state interest in controlling what was taught in its schools may have often been motivated by the interest in ensuring a curriculum that was favourable to its larger interests and in treating literacy itself as a vehicle for greater social cohesion. School literacy practices must therefore become much more than the development of a route to literacy. They become ends in themselves, reflecting the values of the state or the narrower institutional values that motivate their curriculum.

Even as popular wisdom predicts the decline of such recreational pursuits as the reading of novels or histories, literacy practices infiltrate almost every aspect of life in economically developed societies. They underscore social and economic organisation, affirming the terms of association and the terms' interpretation in the organisations' future actions. They script broadcast performances and fashion the interface between information technologies and their users. We can caption them as recreational, bureaucratic, political, religious or educational, but in their larger existence as social practices we can understand their fuller nature only within their context of use.

Conclusions

I began this chapter by arguing that we impoverish literacy if we treat it as a set of skills that we must acquire. We need rather to consider it as a set of practices into which we are inducted. This argument is both an educational and a socio-linguistic one. The socio-linguistic argument is based on our ability to achieve a consistent representation of the huge array of activity that comprises reading and writing. It also evolves from the unsatisfactory nature of the other types of representation. We do not really know what any given individual's functional requirements are. We certainly cannot generalise about them in a way that permits the construction of a satisfactory literacy curriculum. The same 'ownership' problem applies to the critical literacy concepts. We do not know what a satisfactory level of critical awareness would really be. But the greater problem is perhaps educational. The treatment of literacy as a set of decontextualised skills would deny to children their need for an induction into the practices of which it is actually composed. It is also divisive by promoting the practices of one group against those of another.

After describing the nature of literacy practices, I showed how this concept would be used to elucidate our literacy history and the evolution of its attendant technologies. However, simply to name social practices or to relate them briefly, one to another, is rather to distort the nature of what is at stake. The nature of a social practice is best uncovered by those who can engage in it. It emerges from the interactions and unfolding narratives of its participants. In short it requires a type of study that is *ethnographic.*

The fuller understanding of a literacy practice might need Layder's (1993) model of how culture and society combine as a context of use. Such an understanding would come from the identification of sociocultural structures and the frameworks within which different groups relate to each other. For example, the sense that the language of a dominant majority is fit for literacy while that of the minority is not would do much to determine how literacy practices emerge from a given language culture. It would mean finding out the institutional zone of use and the institutional culture that this imparts. Different institutions may drive a practice in different directions, evolving their own forms of letter-writing, for example. It would further require the discovery of how communicative activities are differentiated, as between the hand-to-hand exchange of a secret note by students in class and the drafting of a legal framework to be passed down through time. Finally, it needs some insight into how individuals vest their observation or realisation of a practice with the uniqueness of their personal history and its collected experiences. It is within this deeper sense of a context that we might start to tease out a full understanding of some among this plethora of practices.

A further and hitherto unaddressed issue concerns the language in which literacy is taught. Functional and critical models of literacy tend to vest literacy in national or majority languages, if only because these are perceived as best able to maximise the ways in which we can use literacy, and hence the empowerment of the individual who acquires it. Such models ignore key affective factors, forgetting how finally a successful literacy must be grounded in the social practices with which an individual can make a strong emotional identification. There are fewer greater barriers to the achievement of such an emotional identification than language. If the language is strange, poorly learnt or seen as the property of another cultural community, then the literacy vested in it may be viewed in the same light. A multiple-literacy view embeds our conception of literacy into the cultural and linguistic life of the locality, forcing greater thought about the languages that should be used and the affective identification than can be made with them. This topic will be raised in the next chapter.

Exercises

1. List the problems associated with the critical and functional views of literacy, then discuss how your list supports a view of literacy as a socially embedded activity.
2. Discuss how far we can identify a literacy with a community of practice.

3. Identify one or more of the following types of subject:
    a. a child of 8–11 years;
    b. a high school or university student;
    c. an employed adult.

Design a series of interview questions that will help you to find out about the types of literacy practices in which your subject may be engaged and the kinds of events to which they lead. You should try to develop a semi-structured interview with open-ended 'wh-' questions.

Ask a colleague to read it before you use it or even try it out with them. Discuss whether it should be modified. When you conduct the interview, take a tape-recorder and begin by asking the subject and/or their parent if they mind you using it. Do not stick rigidly to the questions you have written down but make sure you cover the areas the questions enquire about. Try to conduct the interview as an informal conversation. When your subject starts to talk about something relevant or unusual, do not hesitate to digress from the topic and explore what they are talking about with them. Listen to your tape later and, if you have time, transcribe it. Either use your listening or your transcription to identify the different themes that the subject talked about, if these cut across your questions. Finally, write a short case study of the literacy practices of your subject, discussing how this experience has informed your concept of literacy and the literacy practice.

4. Refer to the last section of this chapter dealing with the history and variety of literacy practices. Take any practice mentioned there or any other about which you have knowledge. Think what the practice involves and consider any others to which it may be related. List the technological innovations and skills on which it may be dependent. Try to identify any texts with which it is associated. Using any references that are appropriate, produce a written profile of the practice. Discuss how well or how poorly the profiling methods you have used respond to the concept of a practice as it is presented here.

4 Literacy and Language Choice

Introduction

The question of *language choice* for literacy arises in communities where more than one language is in current use. Such communities are common because national borders rarely coincide with linguistic borders. One can identify several overlapping sets of circumstances where a child's mother-tongue may not be the language through which they become literate.

In this chapter we will look first at why the choice of language for literacy is not always straightforward and consider why this dilemma may arise and the way in which literacy policies may respond. We will then consider why language choice arouses a quite passionate advocacy of one strategy or another, examining how literacy policies can be associated with language attrition or death. The theory of linguistic imperialism will also be described, so that we can consider how the languages that are associated with larger, more powerful nations may conspire against the right to choose literacy in a minority language. Finally, we will explore the questions one might ask if we had to construct a framework in which to place literacy and language policy.

Why there is a language choice

A language such as English, Spanish, French or Russian may have taken on the role as the medium through which education is delivered and administration conducted during a period of colonisation. The colonial language is then treated as a knowledge-bearing or high-status language. There are many nations where this is the case.

In the nations of Central and West Africa, which were once French or English colonies, the colonial language has been retained as a medium of national education and hence of literacy. In the successor-states of the former Soviet Union (USSR), Huskey (1995) and Kolstoe (1995) attest to a conflict between maintaining an education system in which the Russian language is deeply embedded and reviving local languages for literacy to express a rediscovered national identity (cited in Koenig 1999). In Tajikistan, Russian, as if by neglect, has maintained some of its status as a language for literacy education in a fractured and unstable political climate. Kyrgyzstan, however, at first instituted monolingual language policies and introduced the Latin script as a medium for Kyrgyz, rejecting the Russian Cyrillic. A 1990 language law denied Russian an official status and may have contributed to the migration of skilled Russian labour out of the republic (ibid.). Yet, the recent tendency has been more pragmatic, with the economic importance of Russian having been acknowledged and an official bilingualism adopted in 1996 (Koenig 1999: 78).

The linguistic effects of invasion, colonisation or occupation can endure through centuries. Peoples who are indigenous to a territory but have been made a minority by colonisation or conquest are best described as *national minorities* (Kymlicka 1995). One such can be found in the Andean countries of South America where many of their people are the descendants of the indigenous Inca and use Quechua as their vernacular. This state of affairs was given some recognition in Peru in 1973, when thirty articles of the by-laws for bilingual education were published. The articles recognise the existence of bilingual school districts and specify that their language of literacy instruction should be Spanish and the vernacular, Quechua (Hornberger 1988: 27).

The national minorities of Wales and Scotland in the British Isles show how the effects of invasion are more enduring. It is now far from the norm for the inhabitants of these nations to speak a Celtic language as their mother-tongue, yet the desire to preserve these languages and the sense of cultural identity they confer raise a language-choice question. In the case of Basque, the language is more ancient still and may pre-date the Stone Age spread of the proto-Indo-European from which all other European languages, apart from Finnish, are derived. However, the language has also been associated with regional nationalism. Before the fascist unification of Spain, Basque's ancient origins were seen as revealing how its native speakers possessed a unique ethnic purity (Le Page 1997). Fascist Hispanisation led to the language's suppression as a medium of literacy, with its revival being assured by more recent democratisation. The United States also shows linguistic residues of a nation built on conquest and settlement. Despite a quite brutal colonisation and an extended phase of language suppression, the size of the USA and the relatively recent process of settlement mean that more than twenty-five indigenous languages still survive. The most commonly spoken is Navaho, which has almost 150,000 speakers, and the smaller, Blackfoot, Cree and Arapho are close to extinction with only 1,000 each.

A less considered but important type of minority language which is found in many nations is one that is a product of disability or deafness. Sign languages such as American Sign Language (ASL) or British Sign Language (BSL) also boast communities of speakers and pose strong and quite specialised literacy needs. The fact that these languages are not spoken should not lead us to doubt their status as full and rich vehicles of communication with their own syntax and lexis.

The language-choice question also arises when a country feels that it requires a single national language to achieve unity and administrative coherence, but has several indigenous languages that could take this role. Assigning primacy to one indigenous language may risk the dominance of one group of speakers over others. A common solution has been to adopt a colonial language as a national language. Because the colonial language is then retained as a passport to government employment, it becomes the medium for literacy education. In India, for example, the southern states, which spoke several different languages, feared dominance by the Hindi-speaking north. The 1960s saw a series of language riots when the south thought they would be disadvantaged by a nationalist interest in promoting the national use of Hindi and downgrading the use of the colonial language, English. This difficulty has largely passed with Hindi becoming the preferred national language, and literacy being delivered in a variety of local languages. A common consequence has been a tri-literacy requirement, with each demanding a different script. English still holds high status, however, and is a common medium for higher education and thus a precondition for joining the economic and governing elite.

As this example shows, the high status of colonial languages may lead to their promotion as the preferred language of literacy and schooling. Added to this is the problem of how English as the language of the largest and most diverse empire has also developed into an international, knowledge-bearing medium in which much international business is conducted, not just between English native speakers and other nationals, but between other nationals for whom English is a second language.

A given community or nation can have a large number of languages with no clear reason to favour one over another as an agreed medium of education. Again, the result may be that a colonial language is used as the prime vehicle of knowledge transmission. Such a situation holds in Freetown, the capital of the West African state of Sierra Leone, or in other areas where the city has collected many disparate tribal groups from the countryside. Because these groups live side by side, one cannot even set up different schools to cater for different mother-tongues. When indigenous languages are not even localised according to urban catchment areas, *community languages* take root in order to allow communication between members of a community.

Ethnic minorities are a product of emigration as when, for example, Gujarati-speaking African-Asians migrated to the UK or the Vietnamese formed communities in Australia and the US. Ethnic minorities produce language-choice issues of their own. Many immigrant communities in North America, Australia and Western Europe are keen to promote mother-tongue literacy while their children are schooled in the languages of their adopted nations. For example, Chinese Saturday schools are a common feature of life for many children of Chinese emigrants in the US, UK and elsewhere. Among Muslim and Jewish children these types of literacy education have a religious motivation and involve the learning of classical Arabic and Hebrew respectively in order to read sacred texts. The US plays host to one of the world's largest and most diverse emigrant communities. The picture of the US as a monolingual nation that expects the world to speak its dominant language while harbouring little interest in the rest of the world should be treated as a myth (Wiley 1996). More than thirty million of the inhabitants of the US speak a language other than English (Wiley 1996) with most of these being ethnic minority rather than an indigenous languages.

Some countries may have evolved national languages whilst retaining a rich and diverse linguistic landscape. In East Africa, Swahili evolved from a mixture of African languages with Arabic. It was spread as a *lingua franca*, or trading language, evolved from two more languages, and was also found to be useful by East African colonists. It was the language used by British colonial regiments such as the East African Rifles and for this reason has recently been adopted in Uganda as a language of literacy despite having little indigenous history there. In such cases, the *lingua franca* may be adopted as a unifying national language.

Responding to the language-choice question

The above summary reveals that there are in fact few, if any, significant nations that are truly monolingual. Whether their linguistic diversity originates in a history of colonisation, conquest or immigration, most must confront the question of how to ensure the education of their minorities whilst maintaining national coherence and ensuring access to the mainstream economy for all. Methods of response to the language-choice question diverge considerably as conditioned by the following factors:

1. attitudes to language and the view that one language is better, more evolved or richer than another;
2. positive and negative views of bilingualism and biliteracy;
3. analyses of how the use of languages is predicated upon economic, political and military power relationships.

Attitudes to language

Nationalism may often result in an excessive and unfounded celebration of the qualities of a given national language. Few readers will be unfamiliar with statements about the expressive power of one or other of the world's larger languages. Such statements are often uttered by politicians or other commentators eager to strengthen a national identity by assuring people that they have the good fortune to know a language which is more expressive or more beautiful than others. Often this type of unfounded celebration refers to language's literature and the assumption that a national genius such as William Shakespeare did not simply use their available linguistic resources to powerful effect but somehow extended the expressive potential of their language. The self-congratulatory promotion of a given language entails the contrary depreciation of other languages. These have even been viewed as degraded or ill-formed, particularly when they are associated with defeated peoples who may lack advanced technologies. This type of opinion pervaded mission schools on many nineteenth and early twentieth-century native American reservations with native American children being punished if they used their mother-tongue. Whilst we should still be aware of a popular view that languages do not all possess an equal potential, this is not a serious opinion among linguists anywhere. Language inequality attests only to the unequal power relations between peoples. In language choice it arises only as the economic question of whether a given language has a sufficient number of speakers to make literacy a viable possibility or as the functional question of whether a given language has a large enough written archive to make literacy acquisition economically worthwhile.

The fact that languages may be viewed negatively by their own community of speakers can pose a more difficult problem, however. *Creoles* are types of language formed by the fusion of two or more other languages. According to one analysis, one language forms the *substrata language*, furnishing the syntax while the other contributes the larger part of the lexis (Bickerton 1975). By this theory, the fusion of two languages creates *a Pidgin* from which a more stable Creole is derived once it has been passed down through a generation. Perhaps because they are of relatively recent origin, Creoles may be popularly associated with the unstable and syntactically limited Pidgins from which they are derived, often connoting a substandard language. Further, their development in a culture of oracy may mean that they lack a high-status written form.

In the Indian Ocean island of Mauritius, Mauritian Creole has evolved largely from a fusion of French and some African languages. Like other Creoles it began as an attempt by slaves speaking different African languages to communicate with each other and their masters. Mauritian Creole is the nation's common mother-tongue, being used inside and outside the home by both the Asian and the French-African communities. Yet, it is not seen as a serious candidate for literacy education, which occurs in English even though that language is almost nobody's mother-tongue (Mahadeo 2003). Because Creoles are often slave languages, their origins as well as their geographic dislocation may exaggerate their low status. Yet we should remember how, after the Norman Conquest in 1066, French was for three centuries the language of England's elite, while Latin, with its grammatical and morphological complexity, remained the language of ecclesiastical literacy. Chaucer's use of English in the fourteenth century to rewrite the classical *Troilus and Cressyde*, or recount the *Canterbury Tales*, therefore, demanded something of a revolution in the common perception of an appropriate language for literacy. The revolution was accompanied by the dawning realisation that literacy skills were not simply the preserve of the clergy, court entertainers or a new class of administrators. More widespread literacy created demands for recreational literacy in a more widely understood language. Before becoming the object of increasing literacy activity, English bore some of the hallmarks of a Creole that had evolved from the superimposition of a French or Latin vocabulary onto Anglo-Saxon.

Melanesian Creole (Tok Pisin) is also used across the diverse and language-rich communities of Papua New Guinea but was often held to be a debased, 'native' form of English. The Creole's low status and the rise of English as the language of globalisation has meant that New Guinea's national education system uses English as the language of literacy. In Mauritius, New Guinea, and the Caribbean, Creoles have begun to evolve a written form. Tok Pisin can boast a newspaper, for example.

Yet although the case of English may show how a Creole can develop into a powerful language of literacy, a problem now is the perception that colonial languages afford global access to knowledge and employment, helping to maintain them as a medium of literacy education in cultures where they have no indigenous roots. A vicious circle also arises where a language is seen as having low status because it has failed to develop a strong literate culture and therefore consolidates that lack of status because literacy activity is concentrated in the colonial or international language by writers searching for a larger international audience.

Situations where there is a Creole and another higher-status, better codified language from which the Creole has evolved are examples of a *diglossia*. A diglossia arises when a community has one or more very distinct dialects and there is a superimposed variety that may be more highly codified and grammatically more complex (Ferguson 1959: 315). This highly codified variety is often the written form. Such a situation holds in the German-speaking cantons of Switzerland, where people switch between Swiss German and Standard German (Trudgill 1995). In much of the Arabic-speaking world there is a diglossia between standard Arabic and the many regional varieties of this widely spoken, international language. This can mean that although the language in which literacy is taught is nominally the same as the mother-tongue of the students, it may in fact differ markedly, entailing that literacy teaching is also a disguised form of language teaching.

There is no notable movement for Arabic literacy in dialects that correspond more closely to the mother-tongue, in part because of the perception of a unified Islamic culture and the belief that literacy will anyway require new modes of language understanding if it is to unlock the still more remote classical Arabic of the Muslim Quran. Yet, a more controversial case has arisen in the US around the question of African-American Vernacular English (AAVE) or African American Language (AAL). The names AAVE and AAL reflect a change in perception as to the status of this Creole from dialect to language. According to its proponents, AAL began as a Creole that evolved from a fusion of English and various West African languages in the plantations of the southern US. More contact between white and black communities and a greater use of English resulted in a process called *decreolisation* where AAL lost some of its distinctiveness and began to resemble standard English to a greater degree (Roy 1987). However, AAL still possesses quite distinct features that are consistent across the states and remarkably unaffected by regional variation (Labov 2001). This can be used as an argument in favour of treating it as a language rather than a dialect that is a product of its region. Despite this consistency, Labov's larger view is that AAL/AAVE's origins are no longer an issue, since most of its forms can be related back to English (2001).

Arguments for the recognition of AAL therefore raise familiar language-choice issues. The earlier interest was not in the development of a Creole or vernacular literacy as this would have been seen as disempowering, leading to the construction of a linguistic ghetto. In a famous legal challenge of 1979, the objective was to reduce functional illiteracy among African-Americans by requesting special educational help to overcome linguistic differences (Wiley 1996: 127). A consequence of recognising this diglossia of English and AAL, or any other for that matter, was therefore an argument for the equal status of the elaborate, codified dialect and the regional vernacular. An emphasis could then be placed on allowing language choice through the development of a vernacular literacy, or a written form of the local language or dialect. The 1970s also saw the development, but less than wholesale adoption, of such a bridging reading programme which introduced literacy in AAL then took the student towards standard English.

More recently the debate has been framed in the rhetoric of language rights and the assertion, often made by white linguists, that African-American children had the same right to literacy in their mother-tongue as any child anywhere (Wiley 1996: 127). Williams (1991), who rejects the dialect label for AAL, sees the education system as complicit in convincing the African-American minority of their low status because it does not build literacy on their dialect but instead tries to reform their language habits. A contrary view would be that failure to inculcate a minority in their nation's high-status language practices and modes of expression amounts to an act of social exclusion, which will leave them isolated in a linguistic ghetto. As Wiley (1996) points out, a white dialect such as Appalachian is probably as remote from standard written English as AAL and a core need is finally for literacy teachers to understand standard written English as a dialect whose genres and use of language may need to taught.

Bilingualism and biliteracy

As discussed, the use of two or more languages is more common than is often appreciated. In what could be interpreted as a deliberate commitment to multilingualism, the Tukano people of the north-west Amazon insist that men marry women who are speakers of another language and that the women must then move into a Tukano longhouse, bringing their language with them (Sorensen 1971). In Europe and America, attitudes towards multilingualism have not always been so tolerant. Opinions about the benefits of bilingualism have oscillated between theories that its effect was to create a *cognitive deficit* to those where it was associated with a *cognitive surplus*. In this case, a cognitive deficit or surplus refers to the extent to which bilingualism may detract from or benefit a subject's strengths in other areas, such as IQ. Hakuta (1986) has described how, prior to the 1960s, traditionally monolingual developed nations associated bilingualism with emigrant groups and hence with social and educational deprivation. This association spawned the view that bilingualism itself retarded educational progress, and not socio-economic circumstance. A consequence could be a greater insistence on the need for language support within education in order to help put children on the track of successful monolingual literacy education. In the 1960s and 1970s various studies gave a more positive construction to bilingualism with the suggestion that they revealed a cognitive surplus (Hakuta 1986, cited in Wiley 1996). Lambert (1974) produced a model that connected the cognitive effects of bilingualism to socio-economic circumstance. Thus, bilinguals who were well nurtured by an appropriate education and upbringing would show a cognitive surplus, and vice versa.

The need to nurture bilingual abilities has led to the view that the promotion of mother-tongue education among minority groups is a duty of the state, attesting to a commitment to a multilingual and multicultural society. Since the 1970s there has been a variety of schemes to bring mother-tongue literacy education into some UK primary and secondary schools. A 1984 survey by the Schools Council of Great Britain revealed that about one third of local education authorities (LEAs) had a policy to support mother-tongue teaching (Tansley 1986: 36). The now disbanded Inner London Education Authority advocated one of the more consistent policies, asserting that 'all minority children' had the right to know that their mother-tongues were valued by their schools (ibid.). As regards projects that introduced mother-tongue teaching into schools, a marked rise in the self-esteem of the children involved was often observed, but the success of initiatives was affected by such notable variables as teaching styles and the way in which they were sold to school staff (ibid.: 112–13).

More radical approaches involve bilingual education policies where schools operating against the background of a majority language promote a local vernacular or community language through *biliteracy* (literacy in two languages) policies. These can extend to the delivery of most of the curriculum in the vernacular. In the UK, Welsh language schools have enjoyed some success, while immersion programmes have scored some notable successes in Canada (French-English).

There is some debate about the meanings of immersion. Thus one might discuss whether, for example, alternative-language day programmes qualify, with Spanish one day and English the next, for example (Cummings 2001c: 155). Yet broadly we are talking about a sustained school-time exposure to a language, not just as an article of the curriculum to be conveyed but as a medium for the conveyance of literacy and knowledge. The alternative, and more avowedly bilingual/biliterate, Spanish-English programmes in North America have also enjoyed some of the success reported for the Canadian French-English programmes, but may also have occasioned greater opposition.

The Milwaukee 'magnet' schools in the US provide one interesting example. These schools were set up in the 1970s as 'an alternative' to the 'forced bussing' of children out of their residential districts to achieve a less segregated school population. The idea was that the schools would offer something unique in their curriculum which would attract pupils from outlying districts. One interest was the development of language skills through bilingual programmes. Their aim was to use two languages equally by grade 5. 'The results' were 'remarkable in view of the fact that' in one language, English, reading' was 'formally taught' for only one year and the school population represented a wide spectrum of social strata (Cummings 2001c: 158).

Yet many biliteracy immersion programmes are dogged by adverse comment about the failure of the education system fully to induct its pupils into the majority language and the potential threat to the primacy of that language. The Hispanisation of some communities in the United States has been greeted with considerable alarm in some sections of the English language press and has been treated as a threat to the sense of national cohesion that is supposed to arise from the sharing of a common tongue. A consequence has been 'the English-only movement', and it prominence in a state such as California, which is seeing one of the largest growth rates in its Hispanic population. May (2001: 223) regrets how this view is 'shared by both liberal and conservative commentators'. He cites Kathryn Bricker, former executive director of US English, and her warning that the US must reaffirm its common language or 'go down the road of division on language lines'. Yet there appears little evidence for the view that multilingualism is a factor in promoting a lack of social cohesion. Furthermore, in Florida, where the Cuban minority dominates some school districts, there is evidence that despite the high-profile role of Spanish as a community language, second-generation Hispanic children are increasingly ignoring the language in favour of English (Cummings 2001c).

Accompanying this evocation of multilingualism as a threat to social cohesion is the reiteration of a cognitive-deficit view that bilingualism undermines literacy standards. This research is largely based on the poor attainment of some minorities in English-medium schools, Hispanics in the US, for example. The view of early studies that bilingualism itself results in a cognitive and hence literacy deficit is also discredited (Cummings 2001a). Such results may have emerged from educational programmes that failed to optimise a child's performance in both languages with a strong biliteracy programme. A certain recipe for failure is the lack of proper language immersion and comprehensible teaching in both languages. If good teaching and sustained immersion are present, then the 'optimal development of a minority child's cognitive and academic potential' is best obtained by school programmes that 'promote an additive form of bilingualism involving literacy in both the L1 and L2' (Cummings 2001b: 91).

How the use of languages is predicated upon economic, political and military power relationships

Advocates of mother-tongue literacy or of biliteracy programmes also seek sustenance in the broader insistence upon *language rights* and in the more specific theory of *linguistic imperialism*. A concept of language rights apportions the right of the individual to their language in the same way as the their right to free speech or justice. Clearly, there are wide differences in how a given state or individual will interpret the concept of a language right. For example, while many would acknowledge that indigenous people or national minorities have a right to their language, and to literacy education in it, *assimilationists* might argue that ethnic minorities give up the right to their language when they choose to emigrate. Language rights affirm the need for instruction in a majority language so that they can share the same educational privileges as the host community. The opposite view would see their language rights as encompassing the delivery of education in their own language.

The theory of *linguistic imperialism* (Phillipson 1992) originates in neo-Marxist economic theory. The theory of neo-colonialism holds that imperialism formalised a process of economic exploitation of the less-developed nations by the developed. Europe colonised Africa and Asia so that its manufacturing industries could gain exclusive access to their resources. Decolonisation may have provided the newly independent nations with the freedom to establish a manufacturing base, but it did not necessarily provide the capital investment that this required or allow right of access to developed country markets. According to neo-colonial theory, the same inequitable relationship between the developed and developing worlds has been perpetuated throughout the post-colonial era but with a freedom from political responsibility on the part of the developing world. The developed world no longer exploits the less-developed nations through their own administrators but through a governing class drawn from the newly independent nation, but educated in the language and cultural traditions of the colonial power. Often that class is forged anew by the institutions and policies of the larger, dominant superpower as its interests supplant the colonial nation. This elite are afforded a privileged life-style by their conscious or unconscious furtherance of the interests of the Western powers. Often educated in the universities of the colonial nations, they make knowledge of the colonial language a condition of access to their class.

This exploitative relationship between the developed and less-developed countries (LDCs) is cemented by a parallel trade in culture, language and knowledge. In the immediate post-colonial period the retreating imperial powers established education systems that were modelled on their own. The colonial language was then perceived not simply as a means of access to local positions of power; it also afforded access to the knowledge produced by the ex-colonial powers. When the language was English, this scope of access was widened further by its *internationalisation*. This internationalisation meant the use of the language outside the British, Australasian and North American (BANA) countries, not simply in the ex-colonies, but as a means of communication between speakers of other languages, as between French and Japanese citizens, for example. Such a process fostered a growing inequality in the linguistic terms of trade.

The international status of a language exaggerates its status as a knowledge-bearing medium that is the prerequisite of a professional career. It downgrades still further the perception of local and minority languages. The BANA countries locate themselves at a global linguistic and cultural 'centre' from which they spread knowledge outwards to a world that is placed on a linguistic and intellectual 'periphery' (Phillipson 1992). Contributions to the global stock of knowledge must be expressed in the *international language*. They must therefore conform to organisational or generic principles that underlie the BANA construction of knowledge. The BANA nations further reinforce their place at the centre of knowledge-creation by producing a cadre of 'experts' who disseminate their supposed insights into effective methods of obtaining access to this language and its accompanying cultural models of literacy. Even if experts in the LDCs contribute to the language's dissemination of trade, they do so like the Indian farmers who once sent cloth back to British mills so that it could be spun into the clothes they had to purchase. In other words, their work is published in a language that is not their own by organisations that they do not control, then disseminated back to them in a process that reinforces the sense of a life lived on a disenfranchised periphery.

The alleged consequence for language choice is a reinforcement of the primacy of one international language and a growing perception that local languages are 'useless' for any extended educational purpose. If literacy affords access to knowledge, both within the school and beyond, then literacy is not useful if it is not in the language which maximises that access.

A more complicated and related issue is that of *language death* and its contrary, *language maintenance*. Phillipson (1992) implies a linkage between linguistic imperialism and language death. Languages that do not develop extensive literacies and which have poor status as a knowledge-bearing medium may suffer from neglect. Perceived as useless or confined to a small community of users, their speakers lose interest in them. The language then starts to die.

In actuality, it is difficult to associate language death with the promotion of a single international language. Even where the international language is used as a medium of education, there is no evidence that a community of speakers will reject their own language as a direct consequence. Language death has complicated and varying causes. These generally relate to the extinction or assimilation of their community of speakers. In the 1990s, this author had some involvement with the threatened Central African language of Bongili. One problem was the reputation of Bongili women for infertility. A consequence was that the women would look for husbands outside the tribal group and adopt their husband's language. The combined result was the dwindling of a community of speakers. French-medium education ensured that literacy was largely the preserve of that language, but this did not stop the development of healthy communities of other African languages such as Lingala or Kikongo. Whether it resulted in a fractured cultural landscape and an impoverished intellectual life that was overly focused on France is a more difficult and, finally, unknowable point.

What may also be true is that the prestige of a colonial or larger national language as a knowledge-bearing medium may compensate for the greater efforts that non-native speakers must make while devaluing the easier process of mother-tongue literacy. An effortful road to literacy will then become a value in itself, as Hornberger (1988) observed of the attitude to literacy in Spanish among some Quechua speakers.

In actuality, the process of making a distinction between the damage wrought by the propagation of literacy in a single international language and in a powerful local language will always be difficult to quantify and very much a process of perception. Phillipson makes some controversial assumptions about the linkage between language and culture and the role of an international, as opposed to neo-colonial, language. It is not certain that languages are so steeped in the cultures of their host communities that the learning of them amounts to an induction into their hidden cultural agenda. The relationship of language and culture is debated across a spectrum of opinion that runs from universalism, where all languages reflect common ways of seeing, to strong relativism, where how we look at the world is a product of a culture's way of seeing. This cannot be debated in any detail here. What must be remembered is our conclusion that cultures are not a monolithic value system (e.g. Hall 2002). They represent a fluid and interactive dynamic that is responding and adapting to other sets of values and ideas. In an age of international languages, the identification of a language and a culture is itself false. The concept of internationalisation may itself promote the adaptation of language to culture as the vehicle of locally embedded literacy practices.

Conclusions

The relationship between the language-choice issue and the question of language and minority rights ensures that few issues in literacy studies arouse so much controversy, However, there is one definitive conclusion. This is that a concerted initiative in *language planning* that promotes literacy in a threatened mother-tongue can drastically alter the prospects of a language that is threatened by its minority status. Much cited cases are those of Basque and Catalan in Spain, Welsh in the United Kingdom or the revival of Hebrew in Israel. Of varying but still often positive outcome are the many programmes that foster mother-tongue education among Native Americans. Successful cases like that of Welsh may be reinforced by legislation that imposes language requirements on certain government-controlled categories of employment. In Wales, this is one reason why Welsh-medium schools are popular with some parents who have moved from England. In the case of Basque in Spain, it is significant that the success of that language has been accompanied by political devolution and active promotion. On the French side, Basque was never proscribed but still suffers from neglect at the hands of a suffocating and largely nineteenth-century tendency to see education as an act of nation-building fostered by the literacy instruction in one language that has one carefully conserved grapholect.

The above programmes have all been promoted by the substantial resources of developed nations, and language planning may be more problematic when it can be less well resourced. In Peru the impact upon language maintenance of bilingual, Quechua–Spanish programmes has been more difficult to document. Hornberger (1988) reports how the bilingual literacy programmes were introduced not simply to raise the status of a language and promote its speakers' sense of self-worth. They were also a counter to the ineffective practice of teaching literacy through methods that assumed knowledge of a language that few children actually understood. Another consequence of Spanish language literacy was sometimes a quite rapid attrition when pupils returned to Quechua-speaking communities and found no culturally embedded practices to exercise their new skills. Mother-tongue programmes fostered the integration of literacy into prevailing language practices encouraging its perpetuation as part of a local culture. In this way also, the mere fact of mother-tongue literacy ensured the greater usage of that language, carrying it from educational practices into religious and other community activity. Such an increase in usage is itself a form of language maintenance (ibid.).

Yet language choice is not always between literacy in a colonial language or an indigenous one that is embedded in a community and remains quite widely spoken. As we have already indicated, a language's survival can be more threatened by a local language than a colonial or international one. Literacy in the more powerful local language enhances that threat because it will raise its status and ground its practices in those that are culturally more familiar. When languages fall to a few hundred speakers, or when the resources of a nation can barely provide the materials and curricula required by a single language, let alone those needed for a multilingual programme, then some pragmatic language-planning decisions are required. Yet in assessing such cases, it is also worth remembering that the cost of providing education in a second language can be prohibitive and, if not fully met, may lead to the still greater cost of jeopardising literacy acquisition and of maintaining an ineffective education system.

We can consider a nation with the linguistic resources of Papua New Guinea which has over 850 vernacular languages for a population of four to five million, so that on average a given language has no more than 5,000 speakers. A mountainous landscape has meant that adjoining communities have lived in complete isolation one from another, speaking languages that may not even share an attribute as fundamental as tonality. It would be difficult to establish literacies in all such languages. At the same time if literacy were promoted in schools in the national Creole, Tok Pisin, the easy familiarity of that language might make its effect on the maintenance of this rich linguistic tapestry more marked than that of English.

An additional demand upon scarce educational resources is the effort needed to create literacy materials in languages that have no literacy tradition. This reaches beyond the need for school primers and extends to a body of reading matter that will sustain literacy once it has been acquired and make that effort worthwhile. An early and fascinating instance of how literacy can take root in a language was the North American case of the Iroquois. In the eighteenth century this substantial Native-American nation developed its own literacy after contact with the first English colonies. This was not some imported system but more the borrowing of the idea of writing in a form that would serve their own cultural needs. The system's decline mirrored that of the nation itself as they fell victim to US Western expansion after backing the losing side in the War of Independence. West Africa has seen the development of several indigenous scripts during the nineteenth-century colonial period, such as Loma and Vai, as did other North American nations, such as the Cherokee and the Cree.

Carrington (1997: 84–92) sets out some useful preconditions for successful local-language literacy. The first of these is a shared language where literate and non-literate people use the same vernacular with no requirement for a new literate form to be introduced. A difficulty here lies with the concept of 'shared', particularly when such sharing may overlie a pattern of indigenous language use. A second precondition concerns the perception of literacy in the vernacular. If users share the negative perceptions, then it can be difficult to overcome these. Equally, when economic advancement attaches to a higher-status national or international language then vernacular literacy can be perceived as education for disadvantage. Another issue is legal status. If a language remains deprived of official legal status, then interest in it may be reduced. Some form of legal recognition or active promotion of the vernacular has often preceded successful vernacular literacy campaigns such as in Spain (Basque and Catalan) or Peru (Quechua).

A final element involves the creation of a successful environment for the spread of vernacular literacy. This involves the understanding of several features. First is how the success of literacy campaigns is often dependent on ideological and revolutionary motivation as in sixteenth-century, post-Reformation Scotland or twentieth-century China. Clearly, 'revolution' cannot be a workable precondition for vernacular literacy, but one can implement strategies that involve community mobilisation and the awareness-raising of society as to the wider benefits of such literacy. Second is the identification and action upon areas of common good, such as health promotion, where an accessible literacy can establish an uncontroversial role. Third is the search for 'pathways' through which a vernacular can filter its literacy practices into the domains that were previously the preserve of one mainstream language. Thus, if street, shop or restaurant signs are written in the vernacular, these can open a pathway to associated texts, moving from a vernacular restaurant sign to a restaurant menu, for example (Carrington 1997). A final aspect involves such technical considerations as a readily employable script, preferably one that already has common local use; the development of appropriate written language conventions; and the creation of a larger literacy infrastructure involving the production of material that is useful, culturally central or recreational.

Finally, language choice may not be a problem that is open to a general solution. Another approach could be a needs-analysis one, which although driven by the guiding principles of language rights and linguistic diversity, must focus upon the particularities of each situation. Questions that must be studied should concern:

1. the viability of the language, its number of speakers and its potential as a widespread vehicle of literacy;
2. the language's affective dimension, or the loyalty and strength of attachment it commands among its speakers;
3. the literacy resources that a language already possesses and availability of finance to assure further development;
4. the larger linguistic topography in which it exists and how easily this can accommodate a bilingual school system.

If a local language cannot be sacrificed to literacy in a prestigious international or national language, the gift of literacy in a powerful international language cannot be sacrificed to a linguistic interest of keeping a handful of dwindling community speakers in an exotic but poorly resourced literacy ghetto.

Exercises

1. List the ethnographic conditions under which language choice issues are likely to arise. Use the internet or your reference library to research countries that exemplify the problems you identify (for example, the US: ethnic minority languages, indigenous minority languages). Select the country about which you know least, and research a short presentation analysing its language-choice problem.
2. Imagine that you were about to be employed as a consultant who would advise on a country's language and literacy strategy. Draw up a list of questions which you would need to answer. Take two of the countries that you studied in question 1 and use the case of each to provide answers to your questions. Review whether there are important aspects of language choice that your questions have failed to raise. If necessary, adjust or expand the number of questions. Use the answers to the questions to write a short report about the language-choice problem in the country under study, making recommendations for an appropriate literacy policy.
3. Review the theory of linguistic imperialism and discuss its relevance to the language choice question.

Part II

Sign

5 Understanding Sign

Introduction

Part I took a wide-ranging look at what the term literacy means. The insight that literacy is not itself a frozen mental 'state' or a threshold of knowledge changes how we see the written texts that lie at the centre of literacy practices. How we process a text is bound up with the society and culture in which we exist, ensuring that the same text engenders different practices and meanings among different people.

The sociolinguist Del Hymes (1974: 196) saw language as 'socially constituted'. By this he meant that what we do in society and the knowledge we have of this will be responsible for the linguistic forms that we use. We should, therefore, not only see language as an expression of a social function, we should also understand that language is such a function. We should treat language as part of the larger system of communication that creates society and makes it what it is. Language is a form of social action, in other words. If we accept this description, we can treat a written text as bound into the larger social dynamic that is language. For example, a student completes research, revises their notes, writes an essay, takes it to a tutor who reads it and discusses it with them. Their essay text is not the product of the practice of essay writing and it is not the departure point for discursive reading. The text is central to a larger social practice, and, when vested with meaning by our reading of it, will become the practice's defining process. To understand literacy practices, therefore, we must also understand the texts that make them what they are.

We can see this clearly if we refer to Chapter 3 and our discussion of Saenger's (1997) suggestion that silent reading needed and hence fostered the reintroduction of a text with spaces between the words. By the same token, the continuous scripts of the early medieval period were skewed towards their oral performance. When word separation was reintroduced or new languages were written down, it became essential to think about what words were within a given language. Principles had to be discovered that would determine whether a morpheme was simply a morpheme or whether it was also a word. For example, we now assume that 'n-o-t' is both a *morpheme* and a word in 'he is not known', whereas 'u-n' in 'he is unknown' is only a morpheme and must be part of a word. Modern language users acquire such distinctions with literacy, but the principles on which they are based were not always easily established. Combinations of morphemes, the smallest units of meaning in a language, had to be distinguished from words. In this way, we can see how the shape of a text and the representations it contains must be interpreted as inseparable from its social function. The text's design is an attribute of whether it is for private or public reading, and of whether it is primarily functional in the sense of storing language, or decorative, in the sense of trying to extend language's meaning by giving it an aesthetic form.

Literacy practices employ an elaborate array of sign systems. According to Saussure (1974), one of these systems is language itself. Yet, for the purposes of this book, I will defer our discussion of the relationship between literacy and language to Part III, and will focus here upon literacy's conveyance of complex meaning through visual means. I will start by providing the student with a basic analytic vocabulary and will raise the question of how this basic understanding of sign systems can provide a greater insight into the nature of writing.

The nature of sign

Signs are any form of meaningful entity. They can be accidental, like the footprint that betrays the presence of a thief. They can be an intuitive response that is also a deliberate attempt to mean, as when we shake our head to show that we do not want to do something. They can involve careful and deliberate acts of meaning construction as when we scratch a musical note on a page.

Charles Peirce (1931–58) described 'a sign as something by which we know something more'. Because the human mind has an almost overpowering need to vest phenomena with meaning or to seek meaning from phenomena, it is sometimes difficult to look at an object and not see it as a sign. If we take the example of a stone lying by the roadside, we can see that this might simply be a stone or it might also be a sign according to the state of mind with which we examine it. The stone is only itself if we observe it as an object that has a separate identity to those it lies among. The stone becomes a sign if we are looking for building material. It might then signify an object that we can integrate into our wall.

For Saussure (1974), we should remember that a sign did not represent or refer to something out there in the world (see Chapter 3). A sign embodied the mental concept that we have of a thing. For Saussure, the sign consisted of the signifier and the signified. These were interdependent: 'language was comparable to a sheet of paper, thought is the front and sound is the back', one could not cut the one without cutting the other (Saussure 1974, cited in Genosko 1994: 24).

The sounds of language break down into phonemes. Phonemes are not meaningful in themselves and therefore do not qualify as signs. However, phonemes construct *morphemes*, the smallest units of meaning in a language. For Saussure, therefore, a letter is a type of metasign, or a sign that signifies the components of other signs (Harris 1996). How far writing is really a system of metasigns will be discussed in subsequent chapters. What is clear is that the phoneme signified by a given letter is not an actual sound that we hear but the concept of one, in exactly the way that the tree, signified by t-r-ee, is also a concept, and not an object out in the world.

Just as 'tree' signifies a concept and not the object in my garden so 'd' signifies a phonemic concept and not the sound I make when I say 'duck'. If that is the case, the concept must be fairly flexible and accommodate many different ways of saying 'd'. Accordingly, it may not have a specific signification so much as a potential to refer to a broad family of different sounds. We call these differing realisations of a given phoneme *allophones*. Let us take a more extreme example, the letter 'a'. In English, this might signify the sound with which we construct the animal 'c-a-t'. Yet we also use this sign in combination with two others, to represent the indefinite article. The two other signs we use here are the spaces that separate the 'a' from other letters, giving 'kick a cat' and not 'kickacat'. Any student who has had to learn English spelling will also know that 'a' does not always represent the same phoneme. More confusingly, in a word such as 'foal', it combines with another grapheme 'o' to represent a quite different vowel. We can see now how a visual sign can contain within it many possible meanings. Therefore, when thinking about how signs contain their meanings within them, we should remember Halliday's (1985) phrase, *meaning potential*. Signs contain within them a potential to mean many quite different things. What they come to mean will finally be a function of the context they operate in and the semiotic environment that expresses that context. The text furnishes that environment, providing the spaces, for example, that isolate the grapheme 'a' to make it signify the indefinite article.

For Peirce (1931–58) the sign had three parts. First there is the *sign* itself; next there is the sign *object*; and third, the *interpretant*. The sign object is what the sign represents. In the case of the stone, this would be building material. The object has a dual existence. It is an object that actually becomes part of a wall and it is the image of that object that we hold in our minds. The interpretant also has different forms. A key distinction is between the *immediate* and the *dynamic interpretant*. The *immediate interpretant* is 'the meaning potential' of the sign before it is interpreted. In a sense this is a text without a reader or a letter without a context. When we read the text, then our understanding is a dynamic interpretant.

Different kinds of sign

In his early but enduring account, Peirce (1931–58) identifies three types of sign: *the indexical, the iconic* and *the symbolic*. Indexical signs are meaningful either because they are caused by what they represent and are thus directly indicative of it, or because they lead us back to their meaning. According to Peirce there are two types of indexical signs, *tracks* and *symptoms*. When a phenomenon signifies itself with tracks, the sign is like the footprint that, while it may not point directly to the presence of a person, leads us to surmise their presence. A symptom, whether it is the temperature that means a fever, the red that signifies embarrassment or the bending tree that shows the wind, is triggered by the meaning it represents.

Iconic signs are meaningful because they are similar to what they represent. The colour blue can be an icon for sky because it shares the property of colour. When this happens, blue is an iconic sign for sky. Peirce suggests that there are three types of iconic signs: *images, diagrams* and *metaphors*.

Images make deliberate attempts to match or reproduce the features of the meaning that they signify. An obvious example is the photograph or portrait of a person. Early signs in writing, called pictographs, were also images because they looked like the concept that they represented.

Diagrams share relational properties with the object they represent. If we take a city map as an example, it is evident that there is almost no visual similarity between this type of diagram and the object it represents. However, if we walk 20 metres to 'Street A' then note that the map indicates 'Street B' is twice as far again, we can assume that it is 40 metres further. This is because the map will be drawn to scale and scale is a relational property between the diagrammatic icon and what it represents. There are more basic relational properties than scale, however. Another relational property is knowing that one town is between two others because it is marked as between them upon the map. Another example is a sales graph. This bears no iconic relationship to what is being sold. Its meaning lies in the relationship between the fluctuations of a line and the quantity sold at one time. Interestingly, diagrams are also an early form of visual text. The Churinga of the Australian aboriginals have lines carved into wood. The lines are half-map, half-narrative prompt, relating the mythical journies of man's ancestors to the landscape in which a tribe now lives (Gaur 1984).

We should be careful when discussing the iconic properties of *metaphor* about confusing these with the larger sense in which metaphor will be used in this book. A traditional analysis of metaphor, however, holds that it treats unlike things as similar. One much cited examples is Shakespeare's 'Juliet is the sun'. There is no sense in which 'the sun' and 'Juliet', a girl of fourteen, are similar. The girl and the sun have quite different domains of meaning. Yet within these domains there are properties that the poet wants us to match. The girl is beautiful and her beauty illuminates the lives of those around her. The sun warms the earth. Juliet warms Romeo with the prospect of love. The sun can scorch the world. Juliet may scorch those who become involved with her. In Peirce's understanding, the sun can stand as an icon for Juliet, so that when we say 'sun' we actually mean Juliet. The fact that the 'sun' has a potential to mean both a fiery object in space and a young girl is what makes it metaphorical.

The symbol is arbitrary and contains its meaning only because it has been vested with it by convention. Most of language exemplifies this. Words that are onomatopoeic, or which try to imitate the sound of what they signify, such as 'splash' or 'creak', are arguably iconic, though the extent to which these meanings are in fact conventionalised is very much a matter of debate. It is well known, for example, that different languages represent the same animal sound quite differently. Thus, although these would seem to be icons representing a given animal sound, they are actually quite conventionalised within the phonological system of the language. Pronouns such as 'this' or 'he' fulfil an indexical function in that they are meaningful by pointing to other meanings. Yet they do this by having a trace-meaning which allows them to point in the first place. However, the vast majority of linguistic signs are symbolic. In writing, the graphic symbols that writing now uses to represent meanings or sounds are also symbolic. We can understand them only if we are party to the *code* with which they were constructed.

Codes are the principles that differentiate one sign from another (Johansen and Larsen 2002). In a symbol, they organise the conventions through which they are understood. If we consider the Roman alphabet, we can see that its letters are differentiated through the contrast of different combinations of curved and straight lines. For example, if we take 'q' and 'd', in their printed form, we can see that both use a vertical straight line on the right and a semi-circle on its left. They are different because of where the semi-circle and straight lines are placed relative to each other. The semiotic code combines the straight line and the semi-circle in different ways to create different letter-signs.

Deacon (1998) found that the defining feature of humanity was the capacity to engage in symbolic representation. With one type of cry, a species of monkey will identify the direction of approach of an animal that may prey upon them. Yet the cry is triggered by the presence of the creature it signifies. It is indexical in the sense that the movement of trees may also signify the creature's presence. Some animals blend with their surroundings. This capacity is iconic sign-creation, because they become similar to their immediate environment. A symbol, by contrast, is not meaningful because it can be compared to something outside itself or because it may point to the same. A symbol is not informed by a meaning with which it finds properties in common. It is meaningful by convention or social agreement. For this reason, the symbol does not have to be vested with meaning by a context. If a chameleon changes to the colour of the leaf it sits on, this act of camouflage is made meaningful only by the presence of the leaf. Equally, the cry of the monkey is meaningful only when there is a predator there to indicate. But for Deacon a symbol is quite different. Wedded to the concept that it represents, the symbol allows us to carry that meaning from context to context, or even to use it to create another context. Thus, if we take Peirce's example of a tree bent by the wind as an indexical sign for wind, then further imagine that we represent the wind as a bent tree, then a bent line, we have engaged in a process of conventionalisation. Finally, if we agree that the bent line means the wind, whether or not the wind is present, then we have a symbol. This is how we can talk about 'snow' when we are suffering from heat exhaustion in the Sahara desert or construct imperceptible meanings, using a wide array of abstract lexis.

Signs and the development of pre-writing

We can plot the difference between these types of signs in the development of pre-writing systems. When we recognise that one person has features that make them different from another, the signs of that person's individuality are attached to them. They are indexically meaningful. If we make a portrait of them, this is iconically meaningful; it is an image. Seals were used by the Sumerians before they developed writing. The seal begins as a combination of iconic or indexical signs. It may have an image upon it, which means the person who is its bearer. It may be indexical by virtue of being carried round its bearer's neck on a string. When the cylindrical seal presses the identity of its bearer into clay, and the clay imprint is removed to another location, the seal mark has become an unequivocal symbol, one which confers the authority of the person on whatever transaction has occurred.

In Chapter 3, we discussed how many literacy practices surround and support our concepts of money and the transfer of value in society. For example, the insignia on a coin was an early guarantee of its value as currency. The face of a coin is an icon in that its head takes its meaning from the person it represents. Originally, it was also indexical. It was attached to the value of the piece of metal to which it attested. It took much longer for us to entrust our fiscal systems to our capacity to deal in symbols. When a similar insignia was stamped onto paper and had a value agreed by convention, we had moved away from an indexical and iconic realm towards a symbolic one. A process of conventionalisation occurred where the sign could recreate its meaning or value, even in its absence. The last indexical concession on the English bank note was a promise to pay the bearer the sum in silver or gold that the note was worth. Now this has gone and we accept it as the symbol of value that it is.

Symbol interpretation: categories and prototype theory

In the introduction to this book, I mentioned Plato's comment on Socrates' mistrust of writing. His concern was that 'writing (like a tape recording) is not language in vivo', but merely 'the trace that language leaves behind' (Harris 2000: 18). Aristotle, by contrast, asserted that one must see writing and speech as possessing different functions (ibid.: 21). Writing was not the lifeless 'shell' of speech (ibid.: 18) but rather symbols of sounds. In their turn, these sounds of the voice were symbols of 'affections of the soul' (ibid.: 22). A key point is that different people make different sounds or draw different graphic forms to represent them, but the concepts that we represent with these sounds can be shared and interpreted among us as if they were the same.

While restoring alphabetic writing to a fuller semiotic function, Aristotle also recognises an important point about its phonological meaning and about the meanings of its combined *phonemes*. This is that, while our representations of a given sound may vary, the meaning that we attach to it is finally unvarying. If it were not, communication would be impossible. We can understand this both from a phonological perspective and from a semantic one. Phonologically, we know that the speakers of different dialects will pronounce a given vowel or dialect differently. Equally, there are differences in the way speakers of the same dialect will say the same phoneme. Yet at some level we have a shared representation of that phoneme which allows us to interpret different realisations of it in the same way. In the semantic case, two people will have a different idea of what they mean by a common word such as 'house' or 'table'. Yet we communicate with our different semantic or phonological interpretations, knowing what we all mean by 'table'.

At first sight the meanings that we represent with signs differ so markedly from one individual to another that it is a wonder we can communicate at all.

The solution to how communication is possible lies in the idea of *category*. We encountered category when we intimated that this was how we should understand the concepts that Saussure found to be the meanings of signs. This means that when we write 'exit' we are referring to a category of locations, which could actually be very different from each other. An 'exit' from an aircraft is not the same as an 'exit' from a lecture theatre. More strangely an 'exit' from life may not actually lead anywhere at all. 'Exit', therefore, does not represent a meaning, but a category of different meanings. I could analyse this category as having a set of common *semantic features*. Thus we might say that 'exits' all share the feature of being a route out of a location. In traditional philosophy, these common features were held to be inviolable properties of the category. They were what made one category different from another (Lakoff 1987). Whether we were dealing with phonemes or other phenomena, if we could determine what the features of a category were, we could tell how the meaning had been constructed and what it could or could not refer to. A problem now arises, one which is perhaps the defining problem of formal semantics, this is that the meanings we use form a network of almost impossible complexity. One set of features begets another. For example, if we take the common feature of 'exits' suggested above, we must ask what a location is. Is the exit 'a point in space', for example, and if so, what is 'space' and where is that space when, for example, we 'exit' from life?

The same problem arises when we think about phonology. I have already discussed how, in English, Roman letters represent many quite different sounds. This does not simply vary within the community of English users and among dialects but even among individuals who share a dialect. For example, my children were brought up in the north-east of England, and in conformity with the local dialect they pronounce the 'a' in 'bath' in the same way as the 'a' in 'at', whereas I pronounce it in the same way as I say 'car'. This difference is relatively easy to distinguish, even though it makes clear how a letter does not represent a given phonetic value so much as a complex of the same. However, the speech of my daughter is not as different from mine as that of my son. Pronunciations vary quite subtly, not just between groups of speakers but between individuals. It is difficult to imagine a mind that could sift through these elaborate networks of phonological and semantic features as it searches for the correct interpretation of a given sound. Additionally, some categories do not seem to have common features at all. Lakoff's (1987) famous example, providing the title for his book, is an Australian aboriginal language category, 'women, fire and dangerous things'. How, he asks, can we possibly treat these phenomena as the same?

Part of the solution lies in the work of Eleanor Rosch on category theory. Rosch's (1975, 1978) revolutionary contention was that categories are not stable and consistent sets of features which phenomena do or do not possess. Thus, we did not recognise robins, eagles and ostriches as birds because they share such features as beaks, wings and feathers. Further, we do not set up a 'bird' category as meaning the sharing of the features 'beaks, wings and feathers'. Rosch found categories to be anchored in cognition by a prototypical example. When studying how Americans formed the category of 'a bird', Rosch showed that it was most often around the robin. The robin was central to their idea of what a bird is, with such species as the blue jay, canary and blackbird also being important. Thus we operate the category 'bird' by typifying it as one of its subordinate members. Some species such as the ostrich were clearly peripheral, with the penguin and the bat (a different species) ranked at the extreme edge of the class (Rosch 1975). Most importantly, when somebody says 'bird', we do not conjure a mental image of a creature with common 'bird' features, but one of the birds we find prototypical – 'a robin' in the common American case. A category, then, is not a defining set of features that preselects which items belong to it and which do not.

Lakoff's (1987) radial category model makes a more powerful assertion of Rosch's contention that there is no set of shared features which predetermine whether something is a category member. The members of a category which radiate out from the central prototype do not always share any of the features of the prototype. Lakoff (1987: 85) cites the case of Japanese young women giving their child to an older woman to raise. That older woman does not exist within the English language model of motherhood and cannot be predicted by our prototypical example of it. She does not have a core biological or legal relationship to the child. Yet within Japanese language and culture she would traditionally have been incorporated into the category 'mother' and evoked by its more central representation. Yet even if we grasp that we manipulate categories through prototypes and not through our knowledge of their features, this does not explain how we can hold together such diverse and unstructured sets of phenomena well enough to manipulate them with a single sign. For Lakoff (1987) and Gibbs (1994) the answer lies in another concept that we introduced in the last section, that of metonymy.

Symbol manipulation: the importance of metonymy

When we introduced metonymy in Chapter 2 we thought of it more in the traditional sense of a feature of rhetoric or of a figure of speech. Thus we said that a metonym is prototypically a relationship where the part of an object stands for another – 'wheels' for 'car', for example – or where the part of a semantic category such as 'an oak' evokes the subordinate category as a whole – 'trees', in this case. This last case of metonymy is very common. For example, we find it in this description:

> He walked past a line of trees; beeches and oaks; guards of the dark forest beyond.

The trees specified, 'beeches' and 'oaks', evoke the larger mass of trees that make up the forest 'beyond'. Metonymy allows us to evoke a given concept of a family or category despite the fact that there is no dominant set of features which every member will possess (Lakoff 1987). Such an evocation may depend on a metonymic facet of mind. Just as metonymy allows us to evoke a whole car through one of its parts, so it can let us evoke a whole category through one of its members. Metonymy may therefore play a part in how we grasp and manipulate categories. Metonymy is a figure of speech, but one which represents a ubiquitous cognitive process where we evoke and manipulate a larger network of concepts through one of their number (Gibbs 1994, Lakoff 1987).

Another question is why we make a metonym from one part of a category and not another. For example, why do we say 'All hands on deck!' instead of 'All feet on deck!'? This is because the activity for which sailors are required makes their hands salient. People are 'hands' because of the cultural perception of certain types of work. The domain of work sets up the metonym, making 'hands' culturally salient. We can see how the same effect operates in the area of language change. In many varieties of English we say 'glasses' to mean 'spectacles'. The word 'spectacles' is already starting to sound anachronistic. In time it may disappear from the language altogether. Let us think of 'spectacles' as a field of different meanings, frames (with ear and nose pieces), screws, springs and, pre-eminently, lenses or glasses. We can see with the glass alone. We would never have the implement if we had not learnt to grind lenses.

Everything follows from that. Because glasses are the most important feature of the object, they become its name. In the same way, the prototypical centre of a category is also culturally salient, becoming the means through which we manipulate it cognitively. If we build our idea of birds round 'the robin', then the robin can be the means through which we manipulate the bird category, meaning that we think of birds as robins.

We can observe something similar in the case of alphabetic script. When confronted by the sign 'a' we have to determine which category of meanings it represents. This is not the straightforward task it might first appear. At the outset we might see any number of different versions of the same letter: '*a*, a, a, a, a,' or '**a**', for example, with handwriting positing many more individual ways to render the same basic form. We then have to recognise and process these as a given category, 'a'. The metonymic process involves our use of a prototype to represent the larger visual category, and hence to provide a benchmark through which to process its meaning. We next have to recognise a phonological category, the sound or element represented by the letter. Again, a multitude of different versions is possible. Again, metonymy allows us to focus on a single representation, discarding those that are irrelevant to the broader issue of meaning. At the same time, we retain the larger network of significations for 'a', for when a different context requires another attribute or some larger sense. Metonymy, therefore, foregrounds the aspect of a category that a culture or context treats as most important.

Metonymy and indexical signs

There is one further point I should make about the relationship between metonymy, category and sign. There is a link between what Peirce understands as an indexical sign and metonymy (Al-Sharafah 2000). Prototypically, an indexical relationship is one of attachment or of cause and effect. Thus, when smoke is an indexical sign for fire, it is caused by that fire and sometimes visually attached to it. Metonymy is not a type of sign; it is a type of relationship between signs. Yet, indexical signs are often a type of metonym. We can observe this more closely by considering some principles of basic literacy systems.

In my example of coin, we argued that when the metal in the coin had residual value, the mark on it could be described as an indexical sign. This is true in the sense that the mark meant a real value only when it was attached to the metal in which the value lay. When we transferred the mark to paper, and we treated it as being of equivalent value to the coin, we had moved into a realm of symbol. It is our capacity for dealing in metonymy that makes this possible.

First, a society develops a consensus about the nature of value. It does this because it is useful to have a portable means of exchange. The sign once had value conferred upon it as an indexical sign. The insignia of the monarch was made valuable only by the weight of metal upon which it was imprinted. Traditionally, a pound or 'livre', for example, signified the exchange value of a certain weight of silver. Yet a coin is not important because it is a lump of metal of agreed weight. The significance of a coin lies in the fact that it has a value conferred upon it. In the coin construction, we can say that the value is salient. This value, or indexical sign, is the salient feature of the coin. It is so salient that it is finally detached from the larger category it represents, becoming a category in itself, the currency, sterling. Second, this 'value' is now a symbol, containing its meaning within it and defined by how it is differentiated from other 'values' such as dollars or, most recently, Euros.

We can also note how we cannot conceptualise abstract ideas such as 'value' without giving them physical form, as metal, for example. Metal was once valuable because it was difficult to extract from ore. Metal also had the advantage of portability and durability. Metal, therefore, underwrote value. The metal of the coin was used to conceptualise our idea of value. Yet as urban society and fiscal literacy developed, all we really needed was the value, and this became the salient attribute. It was no longer an indexical sign attached to its meaning in the form of a weight of metal. It was a symbol which represented a concept of value. This process of sign development underpins many other literacy texts, revealing how they take the form that they do.

Conclusions

In this Chapter I have stated that we should expand our exploration of literacy as social practices towards the texts that are those practices' focal point. By definition, literacy texts are written texts, using the visual sign systems that make them what they are. I have therefore introduced some of the terms and concepts that we can use to analyse these systems. I considered, first, what we meant by a 'sign'. Next, I looked at how there were different types of sign that could be meaningful in different ways. I introduced Peirce's three types of sign, the indexical, the iconic and the symbolic. I looked at them through Deacon's (1998) perspective and its argument that human cognition was made distinct by its capacity to deal in symbol. I suggested that although writing systems were largely constructed from symbols, iconic and indexical signs also played a role in the development of these.

Finally, I looked at the concept of category and considered how all signs represented a category of meanings. I argued that they were able to do this by using the cognitive process expressed by a rhetorical device, metonymy. This brief introduction to the issue of signs and how they construct and manipulate meaning will now be used in a more extended analysis of the visual construction of written text and the development of the semiotic systems that it employs.

Exercises

1. Describe Peirce's three different categories of sign, showing how they are distinct. Take any newspaper and see if you can identify one or more examples of each of these different types of sign. Give reasons for your conclusions.
2. Describe how you think it is possible for one letter sign to mean many different kinds of sound without creating impossible orthographic confusion.
3. A recent article about fishing described modern trawlers as 'hoovering up fish'. (The term derives from the name of the leading manufacturer of vacuum cleaners.) Write an account of the three phases of change in the word's meaning, from the make of vacuum cleaner to vacuum cleaner (metonymic), from vacuum cleaner to the action of cleaning (metaphoric), from cleaning to taking fish from the sea in large numbers. Discuss how an understanding of metonymy might elucidate these changes. Decide whether this process of change illustrates any common points with the development of our use of paper money. Say what, if anything, such a process tells you about how one type of sign, an icon, for example, can turn into another such as a symbol.
4. Try the following experiment. Write out a nonsense word of at least three syllables, using what you understand as the English spelling system. Pass the word to a classmate, but do not read it aloud. Ask them to write out the same pronunciation in another way without saying anything. Ask them to fold the paper over your version of the word but to leave the one they wrote visible. They should also copy their spelling and keep it on another paper before passing yours along. Ask each student to read out their version of the word. Assess how far their pronunciations diverge. Discuss what this exercise tells you about signs, the concepts that they represent and how they represent them.

6 Writing

Introduction

In this chapter, I shall explore the literacy text as a visual act of meaning creation and representation by looking at the writing systems on which this depends. I will consider how we should analyse writing as sign and raise the question of what the term 'writing' really means. In doing this, I will begin to consider the very complicated relationship of writing to language, asking whether we should agree with Saussure that writing is simply a way to represent spoken language. To ask that question, I will first consider the types of writing that now exist in the world and the terms that we use to analyse them. I will then refer back to Chapter 4 by thinking about the kind of sign systems that writing uses.

Writing systems

Broadly, there are really only three types of writing system currently in use. The terms we use for two of these, the *alphabet* and the *syllabary*, are relatively uncontroversial, though their use may overlap in some scripts. The third type of writing was once termed *ideographic* and more recently *logographic*. Both these last terms are probably inaccurate. The term that will be used here belongs to DeFrancis (1989): *morphosyllabic*.

The alphabet

The term 'alphabet' derives from the Greek letters 'alpha' and 'beta', the first two letters of the Greek alphabet. This is appropriate when two of the world's major alphabets, the Roman and the Cyrillic, are derived from the Ancient Greek or owe their existence to the principle that it encapsulated. This is the analysis of words as phonemes or as the smallest units of sound through which their meaning can be differentiated. Thus, the English words 'rat' and 'bat' are different only because of their initial phonemes, represented by the graphemes 'r' and 'b'.

Two points about alphabets should be remembered. The first is that there is no exact equivalence between one grapheme and one phoneme. The second is that a given alphabet will not always provide a distinct grapheme for every phoneme used by a language. We can see the problem of equivalence in the English use of 'kn' and 'n' and 'ow' and 'o' to spell two *homophones*, or words that sound the same but which mean something different, 'know' and 'no'. Though they may now serve the purpose of helping to differentiate meanings and thus create a less ambiguous script, such anomalies are often historical in origin. These words will once have been pronounced differently with the 'k' in 'kn' being pronounced, for example.

The second point concerns how a given phoneme does not always have an alphabetic sign to represent it. In many cases the transfer of the alphabet from one language or dialect to another has meant that some graphemes have become redundant and dropped out because the new language does not possess an equivalent phoneme for the one that the grapheme represented. In other cases, new graphemes have been created in order to represent phonemes that were not present in the language from which an alphabet has been imported. For example, the letter theta, 'Θ', in Greek was used to represent a sound equivalent to 'th' in the English 'thatch'. When the Greek alphabet evolved into the Roman, via Etruscan, the letter became redundant because Latin does not have an equivalent sound. After the decline of the Roman Empire, Latin was no longer spoken across Western Europe and a series of vernacular literacies evolved where the Roman alphabet was used to represent other European languages. In Britain, Roman script supplanted the Runic alphabet that had been used to represent Anglo-Saxon, it had to adapt again and represent the phoneme encoded by the Greek 'theta'. The grapheme was not reinvented in a Roman form, however. Instead, English uses a *digraph* for this phoneme. A digraph is a combination of two letters to represent one phoneme, as in the now familiar, 'th'. A combination of three letters, or a trigraph, is sometimes used to represent a single phoneme as in the French 'eau' as in 'beau' or 'l'eau'. Such letter combinations can also exist because the single phoneme they represent may once have been pronounced as two or more phonemes, as in the example of k and n. In old English, the letter, æ was used to represent the long 'a'. This form dropped out and was replaced by the use digraphs such as 'ai', 'ay' or 'vowel-consonant-e,' as in 'ite' and 'ate'.

Another option for dealing with phonemes for which the alphabet does not have a sign is to add a *diacritic* to one of the imported graphemes. Diacritics are marks which change the phonetic value of a grapheme. We can see this in the use of accents to adapt the Roman alphabet to many European and some non-European languages. The acute accent in French signals that the encoded vowel is longer, changing 'e' as in 'le' or 'the' to 'é' as in 'était' or the consonant 'n' in Spanish as in 'non' to 'ñ' as in 'señor'.

The above examples reveal that the task of adapting an alphabet to a different language is not always straightforward. Furthermore, the solutions adopted were neither uncontested nor stable. The English use of 'e' to lengthen a vowel before the preceding consonant, as in 'ate', did not become a standard innovation until the spread of printing made it important to have consistent systems controlled by agreed codes. Yet alphabetic systems are highly adaptable because they exploit how all languages construct large numbers of words from quite limited sets of phonemes. When one moves from the phoneme to the syllable then the number of possible units in a language will vary hugely. English, for example, has over 8,000 possible syllables (DeFrancis 1989: 55). If we were to represent syllables and not phonemes with our script, we would need to learn and process 8,000 distinct syllabic signs, making the writing system cumbersome and inefficient. Alphabetic systems have spread rapidly because they encode the common, numerically limited units of language. Their deficiency may lie in how these units are not ones into which we can segment language without a quite sophisticated and conscious act of analysis.

The syllabary

A *syllabary* uses one symbol to represent an entire syllable. For example, Japanese can use one of two syllabaries, or Kana, to represent almost fifty syllables. Japanese is in fact written using a combination of scripts that employ both syllabic and other principles. However, in themselves, the Kana can encode the entire Japanese language and form one of the clearer examples of the syllabary. There are in fact two Kana: Hiragana, a 'rounded, flowing script' derived from the cursive form of Chinese characters, and Katakana, 'a squarer, flowing type' (Hosking and Meredith-Owens 1966: 47). The Hiragana syllabary is shown in figure 6.1.

The area of the syllabary's greatest use is in the languages of the Indian subcontinent. This partly relates to how almost all Indian scripts originate from Brahmi, which although it bears some of the hallmarks of an alphabet, in fact represents consonants and the vowel 'a' with a single character, thus taking on some of the attributes of a syllabary. This vowel is by far the most ubiquitous in North Indian languages, although there are, of course, other vowels, which are represented with different independent signs. Other derivations of Brahmi, such as Tamil or the Hindi script, Devanagari, demonstrate the attributes of a syllabary more clearly because they have evolved single signs to represent an entire syllable.

あ	か	さ	た	な	は	ま	や	ら	わ
a	ka	sa	ta	na	ha	ma	ya	ra	wa

い	き	し	ち	に	ひ	み		り	
i	ki	shi	chi	ni	hi	mi		ri	

う	く	す	つ	ぬ	ふ	む	ゆ	る	
u	ku	su	tsu	nu	fu	mu	yu	ru	

え	け	せ	て	ね	へ	め		れ	
e	ke	se	te	ne	he	me		re	

お	こ	そ	と	の	ほ	も	よ	ろ	を	ん
o	ko	so	to	no	ho	mo	yo	ro	wo	n

Figure 6.1 The Hiragana syllabary

Distinguishing syllabaries from alphabets

The case of Brahmi shows that it is not always easy to divide scripts into the three distinct categories mentioned above as largely syllabic scripts sometimes represent individual vowels. The Semitic writing systems from which Brahmi is probably derived evolved early as *consonantal scripts*. This was made possible by the phonological properties of the languages they evolved to represent. A feature of Semitic languages is that their word roots are *consonantal* and *triliteral*, in that three consonants are used to shape a basic meaning. We can see this in a transcription of the form 'to write'. Figure 6.2 shows the widely cited example of how a stem-word provides the consonantal structure of a wider field of meaning. Thus, 'write' (*katab*) furnishes the string of three consonants, k-t-b, which are re-used in other words that portray the person who engages in the activity, the writer, the place where writing is carried out, the office, and its product, the book.

The nature of the Arabic and other Semitic scripts has led scholars to differentiate it from other alphabetic forms, calling it consonantal (DeFrancis 1989). Others have dubbed it a syllabary by treating a given sign as encoding both the consonantal sound phoneme as well as that of a following or preceding vowel (Gelb 1963). In fact, we may not be able to decode Semitic scripts or resolve ambiguities by decoding consonants alone with quite the ease that this analysis seems to assume (Hosking and Meredith-Owens 1966). Arabic in fact has six vowel signs, three short and three long, though the short are very

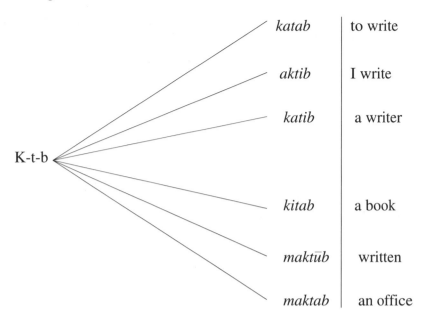

Figure 6.2 The triliteral root in Arabic (DeFrancis 1989: 172)

rarely used. Because these vowels are written above or below the line, they can be interpreted as diacritics that alter the sound value encoded in a given letter. This is why some scholars interpret the script as a syllabary. For example, the letter, 'ba', equivalent to the roman 'b', is written as:

ب

and the vowel sign for the long 'a', or 'ar' is written over it to give:

بَ

or ba. Yet the existence of signs to mark vowels suggests the interpretation of the script as a syllabary is incorrect, even though these signs are positioned rather as diacritics might be, forming a graphic unit with the consonant they mark. Arabic also marks the absence of a vowel, showing that a consonant does not have one following it with a sign called a *sukûn*.

The Korean writing system, Hangûl, also blurs the boundaries between the syllabary and the alphabet but in a quite different and unique way. Hangûl was developed in Korea in the fifteenth century, partly in response to concerns that the adaptation of the Chinese script to the Korean language had created a writing system that was too complicated to become a vehicle for widespread literacy. Hangûl is known as the world's only featural writing system in that it has a unique capacity to reproduce the 'distinguishing features of its host language' (Fischer 2001: 190). Unlike the Semitic scripts, with which Hangul's developers may have had some contact, the script gives equal graphic status to both vowels and consonants. In this sense, it is a full alphabet. Thus one has a grapheme that is equivalent to 'd' for example, or 'ㄷ'. There is also a grapheme to represent the vowel 'a', 'ㅓ'. Yet if we want to make a syllable that is equivalent to 'da', we would combine the two elements to make a block, thus creating the elements of a syllabary, as in 'ㄷㅓ'

Another intriguing aspect of Hangûl lies in how its graphemes are supposedly based upon a representation of the mouth positions required to produce the phonemes that they encode. This would give the graphemes an unusual element of iconicity, at least during their development. The graphic combination of signs that represent phonemes into ones that represent syllables has meant that Hangûl has been called a syllabic alphabet. The underlying principle, however, is indubitably alphabetic.

We should not forget that although the Roman alphabet is based upon an inviolable principle of phoneme representation, the representations that sometimes evolve become syllabic in nature. If we take '-ough' in the English 'en-ough', for example, this is perhaps most easily processed as one sign representing a syllable that can be combined with other phonemes into other syllabic units as in 'tough' or 'rough'. This may be for two reasons, one of which is historical, the other psycholinguistic.

The historical principle is very clear in English. Here, the importation of different words from different languages has been accompanied by the importation of different orthographic principles. This results in many representations of the same phoneme. For example, 'gh', 'f', 'ff' and 'ph' can all represent the phoneme 'f' when in a final position as in 'tough', 'half', 'staff' and 'graph'. These different encodings may represent historical changes in pronunciation, or the fact that the word originates in another language where a different alphabetic principle operated. 'Ph' represents the English transcription of the Greek letter 'Ø' (phi), for example. Yet there may be another psycholinguistic principle at work here. Phoneme segmentation is difficult and needs to be learnt. Syllables are the normal unit through which we perceive speech (Liberman et al. 1974, Morris 1992: 56). 'Illiterate members of a literate alphabetic culture have been found to have no phoneme awareness' (Morais et al. 1979). Older literate Chinese taught only in a character script cannot 'segment phonemes', unlike their younger peers, who have gleaned this knowledge from learning in the Chinese version of the Roman alphabet (Read et al. 1986, cited in Henderson 1992: 22). The clear conclusion is that phoneme discrimination is either taught consciously as a facet of phonic instruction or is acquired through the process of learning to manipulate alphabetic signs. The natural salience of the syllable, on the other hand, means that it would be surprising if we did not process recurring alphabetic patterns such as 'ough' as if they were single graphemes that represented syllables. A pedagogical point is that these can be taught to children as syllabic signs, though with some caution, since a given string can have two values, with 'ough' also representing a vowel, as in 'furlough'.

The Chinese writing system: a morphosyllabic script?

Syllabaries and alphabets may overlap in some sense, either in the assemblage of their graphic components or in the way in which they are processed. However, their salient principle encodes quite different phonological units, making them distinct and relatively easy to define. Finding the principles that encode the distinctiveness of Chinese *morphosyllabic* script is more complicated, however.

A common myth about the Chinese writing system is that it is *ideographic*. An ideographic script would be one that encodes a meaning rather than the phonetic value of a word. Thus we would have to imagine that a sign for 'house' encoded the house 'concept' rather than the phonetic values that build the word: 'h-ou-se'. In seventeenth- and eighteenth-century Europe, the ideographic interpretation of Chinese suggested a universal writing system that could transmit meanings without recourse to language. In 1714, the philosopher Gottfried Liebniz was so influenced by this idea of an ideographic script that he became interested in developing a universal writing (DeFrancis 1989). The concept of a universal system suggests that one can break down any language into the same set of constituent meanings, then encode those meanings as ideographs which would be known to everybody, whatever language they spoke. This posits a naïve view of the nature of language and its relationship to meaning. It forgets that language does not just encode a series of meanings as a series of different signs. Languages use syntax to combine the same signs in different ways to create different meanings, giving two different combinations of the same words two quite different meanings, as in 'the lion ate the boy' and 'the boy ate the lion'. Languages also use *grammar* and *inflection* to change the relationship between words, meaning that 'the man's monster' means something different from 'the man monster'. As every language learner knows, different languages use syntax and grammar differently. Therefore, the way a Korean person encoded language into a universal writing system would be quite different from the way an English- or Chinese-speaking person did it. Effectively, a universal writing system would need its own grammar, one on which all its users would have to agree, then learn. Finally, it would become another language, a sign language in fact.

Attempts to design successful languages generally meet with failure. They fail because the features of language are not fully understood, and more conclusively because a language is a response to community needs and not to the communicative concerns of one or two inventive individuals. Attempts to create universal writing failed for the same reason.

The Chinese writing system does not codify meanings but a language. If it did not, its signs and their graphic arrangement would constitute a language. The fact that each word in Chinese is represented by a different character has produced the term *logographic,* suggesting a script that does not represent phonemes or syllables but words. However, we should not forget that Chinese is a *monosyllabic* language. A character may therefore stand not for a word but for the syllable of which it is composed. This would mean that Chinese was not logographic but syllabic. The view that Chinese is a syllabary would be reinforced by the observation that as many as 25 per cent of Chinese characters encode phonetic information. These can sometimes be used as phonetic elements to build other characters or to distinguish one type of phonetic representation from another (DeFrancis 1989).

Chinese encodes phonetic information through a device called a *rebus.* As we will discover when we look more closely at the history of writing, the rebus principle has been central to the development of all the writing systems in use today. Basically, rebus means taking a sign that was developed to encode meaning, then using the phonetic value of that meaning to encode an equivalent sound which can stand for another meaning. Children and adults often use rebus to create visual puns. For example, because 'eye' and 'I' or 'eight' and 'ate' have the same phonetic value we can represent the phrase 'I ate' through signs as shown in figure 6.3.

Figure 6.3 'I ate': an illustration of the rebus principle

DeFrancis (1998) illustrates this principle with the Chinese sign for 'mǎ', meaning horse. Historically, the sign for 'horse' evolves from a *pictograph.* In origin, pictographic signs are iconic, in that their meaning evolves from a similarity to what they represent. We can see this clearly in figure 6.4, which shows the evolution of the Chinese character for 'mǎ':

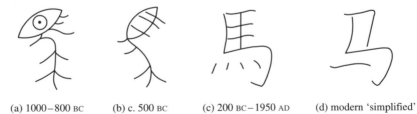

(a) 1000–800 BC   (b) c. 500 BC   (c) 200 BC–1950 AD   (d) modern 'simplified'

Figure 6.4 The evolution of the Chinese character for horse 'mǎ' (Halliday 1979)

The Chinese syllable, 'mǎ', which gives the word 'horse', can also mean 'mother', though the vowel will have a different tonal value in each. In writing, the use of a rebus allows the sign for 'horse' to mean 'mother'. For the originators of a script this would be extremely useful, as a concept such as 'mother' might be quite difficult to represent pictographically. When the character for 'horse' represents 'mother', it is no longer pictographic in any sense. It is representing the sound of the word 'mother' and has therefore evolved from a pictograph into a *phonograph,* or a character that represents a sound.

The phonograph, however, creates a problem of ambiguity. If the same sign is being used for both 'mother' and 'horse', then we depend on context in order to find which meaning is intended. If a large number of signs generated their meaning with a rebus, then the script would become highly ambiguous. To disambiguate the script, another type of sign called a *determinative* is used. *Determinatives* are signs that represent a semantic element in scripts. They are used to indicate the area of meaning in which another sign is designed to operate. In the case of 'ma', a character nü, meaning female, shown on the left, is added to the phonograph meaning 'ma' shown on the right (DeFrancis 1989: 98), as follows:

mă (meaning horse)   → 馬

nŭ (meaning female)   → 女

mā (meaning mother) → 媽

We can now see how the Chinese writing system embodies three principles, the pictographic, phonographic and ideographic or determinative. Another principle that can be identified is called *compound indicative.* The principle involves the addition of one character to another in order to create a meaning with which both are associated, but which neither fully represents. The principle is most frequently illustrated by the addition of the character for 'sun' to that of 'moon' in order to create the meaning 'bright' (ibid.: 98).

The sun   → 日

The moon → 月

Brightness → 明

This example charts the process discussed in Chapter 5 by which an indexical sign is evolved through a metonymic principle, in the way that the smoke points to the fire so the smoke means fire. The moon and the sun are seen through their light, and that brightness is their most salient attribute, so the moon and the sun together mean brightness. They are compounded because, individually, the sun and moon have several other areas of meaning with which they could be associated. Another metonym for the sun would be 'heat' or 'warmth'. The right amount of sunshine ripens fruit but the wrong amount scorches crops. The moon might be associated with tides. Yet when the sun and moon are taken together their repertoire of potential metonyms or indicative meanings may start to reduce. The moon scorches nothing, the sun and the tides are not associated. In short, the sun and moon create a context for each other which makes salient their shared attribute, brightness. This is also the sign's indicative meaning.

Chinese writing, then, is not ideographic. It is not itself a sign language but originates as a spoken language. It does not just encode the meanings of speech but speech itself through phonographs that originate in a rebus. But Chinese writing does not encode a current dialect in any direct sense. Even the most popular Chinese language, Mandarin, does not achieve anything approaching a direct representation in Chinese script and the exact nature of the language that is encoded remains mysterious. Although a character may represent a syllable that is also a word, it gives no clue as to the pronunciation of that syllable (Don Starr, personal communication). In this sense, it can be written by the speaker of one Chinese dialect, Mandarin, for example, then read back in another, such as Cantonese, though strictly these dialects retain a few character differences. Yet the fate of Chinese characters when they were taken to represent languages from completely different groups such as Japanese or Korean shows how far Chinese is from being an ideographic script that can transcribe meanings regardless of the language in which they are expressed. Chinese has a quite different syntax, grammar and phonology from Korean and Japanese. Chinese writing could not simply be extrapolated from the language it first encoded in order to represent the meanings of another.

Where Chinese is monosyllabic and uninflected, Japanese is polysyllabic and *agglutinative.* Languages that are agglutinative form compound words from other shorter words or morphemes. We see an example of agglutination in an English word such as hopeless, which is built out of a *stem word* 'hope' and a suffix 'less' meaning 'without'. Japanese also has many fewer syllables than Chinese, only about one hundred in all as opposed to more than a thousand in Chinese (DeFrancis 1989). These fundamental linguistic differences were crucial to the development of Japanese as a different script.

When the Japanese began to develop literacy by borrowing Chinese writing in the fifth century they also borrowed much of the Chinese language as well. However, the smaller number of Japanese syllables meant that several different syllables in Chinese would be pronounced the same way when read in Japanese. Also interesting was how they read classical Chinese texts as if they were Japanese. Like English, Chinese has an SVO (subject, verb, object) word order. Japanese is SOV (subject, object, verb), however, so Japanese scribes read early character scripts by 'mentally changing' the word order as they did so (DeFrancis 1989: 132). More difficult was the problem of representing the grammar of Japanese which uses inflections. Inflections are a result of agglutination. They change the grammatical relationship of one word to others in the sentence. Modern English has only a few inflections. One is the Saxon genitive "'s'. If we were to imagine a situation where we would not represent "'s' in the phrase 'the children's book', we can see that we have a problem even in a slightly inflected language. In Japanese, the problem was on a larger scale. They needed a more consistent phonological principle in their language. To achieve this they borrowed the rebus principle from Chinese, where some Kanji (the Japanese name for Chinese characters) were used as phonographs to represent the sounds of syllables. A polysyllabic word in Japanese was therefore written with two Chinese characters, one to represent the root meaning the other to represent the necessary phonetic information. These phonographs, which were generally written smaller than the main characters, were called Kana. There were two forms, Hiragana, derived from the 'cursive', hand-written form of Chinese characters, and Katakana, derived from the conventional printed form. The development of the syllabaries was not immediate, and even after the standardisation of the script in the nineteenth century, there remain many superfluous signs, or more graphic symbols than there are syllables in modern Japanese (DeFrancis 1989). Also, although Japanese can be written as a syllabary, it is more often written as a combination of Kanji and Kana.

When we look in greater detail at the history of writing systems, we will see how the process of adapting Chinese script to the Japanese language is revealing for how it expresses a larger process of adapting writing systems to languages for which they were not designed. It is a process which often results in the development of more efficient, phonographic representations. Chinese script did not carry across to Japan and Korea as a ready-made communication system. It underwent substantial adaptation in order to fit these very different languages. Writing cannot simply make a language fit its system. It is, in some measure, a semiotic system that must adapt to principles of a given language.

Writing and non-writing: semasiographic systems

In the above analysis of the Chinese writing system, we can start to see how we might apply Peirce's taxonomy of signs either to different elements in contemporary scripts or to the phases through which they have evolved. Early writing evidences pictographic or iconic phases where the characters draw their meaning from their resemblance to what they represent. There are also indexical signs such as the Chinese compound indicative (brightness), which make a metonymic representation of a field of meaning. Some determinatives are also indexical, at least in their early phases of development. However, most evolved systems are highly conventionalised and symbolic in nature. One might thus be tempted to see the evolution of writing systems as a development away from iconic and indexical signs towards the symbolic. The most obvious example of an iconic sign is the naturalistic drawing or painting, and Stone Age cave paintings have been seen as the precursors of writing (e.g. Fischer 2001, Gaur 1984, 2000). The pictographic signs might then evolve into a somewhat cumbersome but more conventionalised system of meaning representation before they turned into a phonograph through the use of rebus. The last phase would see phonographic systems evolving into ones that were purely phonemic or alphabetic. The alphabet would then be seen as sitting on the evolutionary pinnacle because of its ability to analyse the shared core units from which all lexical signs or lexemes are generated. Contemporary scripts, such as the morphosyllabic Chinese, would stand as cumbersome anachronisms.

Earlier accounts give some credence to this Darwinian view. Gelb's (1963) perception was that all writing emerges from what he termed a *semasiographic* phase before evolving towards a full phonetic representation of language. A semasiographic writing system is one that represents meaning and not language. DeFrancis (1989) argues persuasively that most such 'systems' proffer their users an incomplete vehicle for communication, one which fails to match the larger resources of language. For DeFrancis a full communication system posits the evolution of the sign system towards a position where it can fully represent language. However, some of DeFrancis's detractors point to the significant information-bearing role played by semasiographic systems in Meso-American or Andean civilisations. These never developed a *glottic,* or sound-encoding writing system (see, for example, Hill Boone and Mignolo 1994) but could construct archives and records sufficient to maintain the civilisations of which they were a part. One information-encoding system for which the Inca are well known is the quipu. This is a set of strings that could be knotted, with knots forming a record of transactions or tallies.

At first sight, a distinction between a semasiographic, or meaning-representing system and a language-encoding one might seem simplistic or flawed since the precise relationship of language to meaning is complex and subject to intense debate. The relationship involves such questions as how far cognition is dependent upon our capacity for language. Yet the distinction between a script that represents meaning and one that represents language is relatively straightforward and is illustrated in figure 6.5.

We can see two texts on the left figure 6.5. The first is an iconic sign warning people not to drink and drive. The second is the Chinese character for the word 'mù' meaning 'eye' in English. Because the first text does not represent a specific item of language but a meaning, we are free to represent its meaning with different combinations of words. Arguably, we can also represent it in a different language. The second text makes the contrast clear. This symbolises a syllable that in Chinese also corresponds to a word. That word will then be decoded into a meaning. Thus example sets up the distinction clearly between the linguistic sign systems that represent a language, such as Chinese, and the semasiographic ones that represent meaning. Two types of semasiographic

Semiotic Perspectives on Literacy

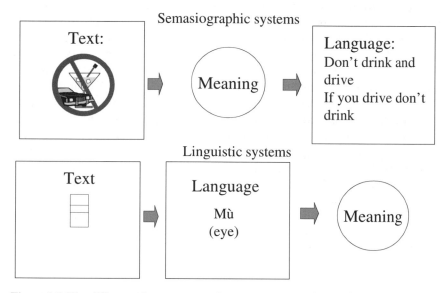

Figure 6.5 The difference between texts that represent meaning and texts that represent language

scripts have also been identified. These have been categorised as iconic and conventional (Gelb 1963).

The meaning of an *iconic semasiographic script* and a *conventional* one should be clear from our previous analysis of sign systems. In Peirce's taxonomy, we may remember that iconic signs are those that draw meaning from a resemblance to what they represent. We can say that they are coded analogically. The same holds for semasiographic systems that are iconic. Our use of conventional systems, on the other hand, is completely dependent on our knowledge of their conventions. A typical conventional semasiographic system is our current version of Arabic numerals: '0,1, 2, 3, 4, 5, 6, 7, 8, 9'. A musical score is another example. A well-practised musician may feel that a score may directly steer their fingers to the appropriate note without their actually thinking what that note is. They touch the score's meaning, unaided by language. I have observed another interesting example in pre-literate children.

Company logos are typical of semasiographic writing systems, where a given sign does not spell out a word but signifies a company and may also summarise what it tries to stand for. A well-known and quite typical method of logo-formation involves taking the first consonant of a name, or the name-word itself and creating a decorative sign from it. A ubiquitous example is the

'M' from Macdonald's fast-food restaurants. This is often hoisted on a column above the restaurants themselves. Children can decode these signs long before they have approached alphabetic literacy, decoding it not as an 'M' for Macdonald's but as the sign for a restaurant where they want to stop because free toys are distributed with the meals. They read the logo as a conventional semograph, or as an element of a semasiographic script. In this vein, Kress (1997) has observed how pre-literate children will decipher signs through such aspects as orientation (the direction it is pointing) and size. Determining that 'E' has three bars, for example, and 'L' only one, is difficult, perhaps because that core distinction is without apparent reason and is based only on a cultural convention that has evolved through time. Macdonald's logo might have been interpreted through brightness, colour, location and perhaps some general attribute of shape. But a key issue is the indexical nature of the sign. For the pre-literate child, it is meaningful as long as its column will hoist it above the restaurant itself. Implicit in this observation is that children will latch on earlier to iconic and indexical modes of sign interpretation, finding no difficulty, for example, in recognising that a 'doll' is a sign meaning baby whilst not being a real baby.

Conventional and iconic semasiographic systems: the role of metonymy in visual meaning representation

The shift between glottic and semasiographic systems should be seen as spread along a continuum. An example of an iconic sign is given in the warning against drink-driving given above. Yet this sign also illustrates how conventional and iconic modes operate together, while showing much about the role of metaphor and metonymy in sign construction.

First, the line drawn across the drinking glass to indicate its prohibition is partly derived from our knowledge of Western semiotic convention. If we arrived from another culture and another time, it is difficult to know whether we would derive the meaning simply through metaphorical processing or by intuiting that to draw a line through something means to prohibit it. Our understanding of the sign derives from two conventions of visual literacy. The first is that drawing a line through a picture or a word, or 'crossing it out', indicates that the word should not be read. In origin, this is iconic. The line through the letters makes them less legible, thus indicating illegibility. In the modern world, this crossing-out convention is used by road signs to prohibit an activity such as overtaking. We can thus see a metaphorical transfer and a further conventionalisation of one code by another.

Even number systems, though now highly conventionalised, are often iconic in origin. We can see this in the case of Roman numerals. The iconicity of 'I', 'II', 'III' is evident and the meaning of these signs is consequently transparent (Harris 1996). Less evident is that of 'IV' or 'V'. To look more deeply at this we should recall our discussion of critical literacy in Chapter 2 and the observation that one of the core insights of the new discipline of cognitive linguistics is how all abstract concepts are developed from bodily experience. The same is true of number. We understand it from the fingers we can hold up before us (Heine 1997). The strength of a finger metaphor for numbers underlies more than the use of vertical strokes in the Roman number system. The 'V' that stands for five may be an iconic derivative from the shape made by the raised fingers and thumb of the hand. When they write 'VI' they may be suggesting 'a full hand raised with one additional finger.

Even if they are iconic in origin, numbers do represent a clear case of how signs can become entirely conventional in nature. Harris (1996) reminds us that this process is further exaggerated when numbers are dissociated from quantification and are used as the elements of codes that may signify locations (as in ZIP codes), identity (as in student or prisoner numbers) or signature (as in PINs). In this instance, a given formulation or code simply becomes a sign for something because we choose to make it so. It thus represents a conscious deployment of our ability to deal in symbols.

The example of Roman numerals reveals how a *diachronic* perspective, or perspective that examines the development of signs over time, will uncover a core iconicity even in apparently conventional patterns.

Many of the texts and writing systems of ancient civilisations show clear evidence of an interaction between iconic and conventional modes of sign construction and between semasiographic and glottic forms of writing. In the script of Nahuatl, the language spoken by the Aztecs of pre-Columbian South America, the central units of the system are called *glyphs*. These are distinguished by their spatial isolation and by the fact that they are not always recognisable as people or other forms. The glyphs are clusters of phonographs that represent different linguistic features: syllables, entire words or their roots (Thouvenot 2002). However a second element is the figure or portrait, and there is considerable disagreement as to whether this form should be treated as iconic and representative of a person or constituted out of phonographic elements like the glyphs. The use of lines or links is another typical Aztec device. The links also permit a multidirectional process of sense construction, one which challenges the alphabetic assumption that meaning arises when the eye tracks signs along a line. The larger possibility is that the combination of iconic, indexical and conventional symbolic principles permits different choices of words to convey a secure and unvarying sense (Thouvenot 1997).

Interestingly, on the other side of the world and at an earlier moment in time, Morpurgo Davis (1984) notes how the ancient Hittite script also combined international or extralinguistic semographs with a glottic system closely tied to the sounds of that language. Her argument supports the overlap between conventionalised and iconic modes of sign construction as well as between the larger spectrum of semasiographic forms of sign construction and those of glottic scripts. This overlap persists throughout writing history and continues during the present time.

Few practices reveal the overlap between semasiographic and glottic scripts as powerfully as the medieval and pre-medieval practice of manuscript illumination. This practice reveals how the unquestioned supremacy of an alphabetic script in Western Europe may have left scribes with the sense that the transposition of language into a visual medium opened up the semiotic potential of that medium. This exploration of the semiotic potential of writing as a visual sign system can be either as a development of the letter forms we inherit or as a regression to the pictographic and semasiographic system from which they have evolved.

We can see the development of letter forms in the illuminated lettering of pre-medieval and medieval European manuscripts or in the calligraphy of Arabic and Persian texts. In the last case, cultural interdictions against the visual image may mitigate against the distortion of letter forms into the decorative animal images engraved by Christian scribes. But this did not rule out all forms of iconicity. For example, one practice formalised the use of margin notes to comment upon a central text. In one document the commentary was arranged as an elaborate frame that held the main text at its centre as if in an act of deferential ornamentation. The contrastive metaphors of a frame, or a periphery, and centre point, are used to create the sense of textual embroidery upon a 'core' meaning. Such a use attests to an underlying iconicity despite the larger refusal to represent the world of things visually.

The graphic or diagrammatic representation of information is also increasingly used, making new demands on popular literacy. The ease with which computers can help writers to create and insert graphs and diagrams means that these methods of representing information are increasingly popular, offering as they do a condensed and effective method of conveying some forms of quite complicated information. Figure 6.6 shows clearly how a text and bar graph interact using iconic and conventional forms of semiosis in order to convey a quite complex meaning in an effective and straightforward manner.

Figure 6.6 shows a breakdown of expenditure in a conventional stack graph with an accompanying textual explanation. The convention of bars indicates quantity against a scale according to their height, and can be called a convention which, as in others we have examined, derives from an iconic form of representation. The metaphors 'up is more' and 'down is less' (Lakoff and Johnson 1980), pervade our conception of quantity. In this case they translate directly into a graphic metaphor, which has been conventionalised as the symbols shown above.

Underneath, the text that refers to the graph provides only a brief explanation as to its meaning. We obtain our larger understanding of how the cost of education increases with the age of the pupils from the stepped bars of the graph. The text and graph interact through a reference to the figure number,

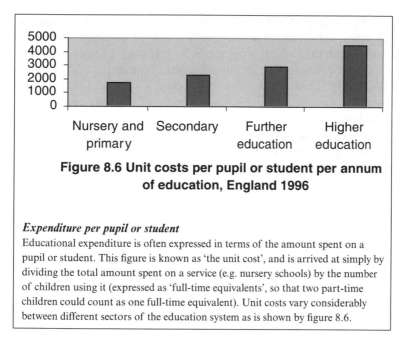

Figure 8.6 Unit costs per pupil or student per annum of education, England 1996

Expenditure per pupil or student

Educational expenditure is often expressed in terms of the amount spent on a pupil or student. This figure is known as 'the unit cost', and is arrived at simply by dividing the total amount spent on a service (e.g. nursery schools) by the number of children using it (expressed as 'full-time equivalents', so that two part-time children could count as one full-time equivalent). Unit costs vary considerably between different sectors of the education system as is shown by figure 8.6.

Figure 6.6 Graphic extensions of alphabetic text

figure 6.6, which shows how the use of numbers as notation is made meaningful by the metonymic principle of proximity (we know that figure 8.6 means this diagram because the numbers are placed under it).

In modern text, the overlap between semiasographic and glottic modes is seen most clearly in the practice of text-messaging where the mobile phone's small numeric key-pad and the high cost of transmission have forced some creative modern solutions to the representation of meaning. The sociolinguistic factors of intimacy, peer group communication, and youthful creativity have also promoted a greater willingness to shrug off convention and engage in innovative literacy practices that consolidate the group's sense of itself by using codes that are peculiar to it. The resultant texts employ creative processes that will be familiar to any student of ancient writing. For example, they employ iconic or pictographic modes of communication with the use of 'emotions' or icons such as smileys to show states of mind. In an extreme form this can mean the suppression of all glottic text, as in a recent advertisement for handsets that take and transmit photographs. The ad showed a young woman walking home to her room with a new boyfriend, saying goodnight, then texting him a picture of a mug of coffee. The picture reveals the overlap between iconic and indexical forms of semiosis. The immediate meaning is iconic in that the picture signifies the coffee mug that it represents. However, it is indexical because it marks out the act of drinking coffee and not the coffee itself. This is a clear instance of how our capacity to deal with metonymy then metaphor allows a straightforward icon to mean more than that which it resembles by invoking a larger semantic field. First, a metonym extends the semantic field to make a coffee-mug mean coffee-drinking. Then a metaphor maps onto a new field where nocturnal coffee-drinking evokes a larger semantic frame of intimate conversation and sexual liaison.

Text messages also make a constant use of conventional semasiographic scripts, developing these through a rebus based on letter and number names. The following message makes this clear:

C U 2nite or txt bk

X Jen

The message reads 'See you tonight or text back, kisses, Jen(ny)'. The first two words are obtained by a rebus on letter names 'C = see' and 'U = you'. Interestingly the third word revives the concept of syllabic representation with the first syllable represented through a rebus of the numeral '2' to mean 'to'. The second syllable 'night' is represented by a phonetic representation of the syllable as 'nite'. The phonetic spelling is probably used for reasons of economy and subculture. The economic reason is that text messages are charged by the number of letters used and 'nite' uses four as opposed to five for 'night'. The subcultural reason pertains to the use of a code to give a lan-guage-using community a sense of coherence. It is a clear instance of how practice and text shape each other. Implicit in this is the rejection of official, school-based forms of spelling in favour of the more consistent and rational use of a final 'e' to lengthen the vowel before the preceding constant. Equally interesting for the student of consonantal scripts is how users of English can ignore its dependence upon vowels to create semantic discrimination. If some-thing has to go, it seems to be vowels. Even a consonant cluster '-xt' is not reduced (to 't', for example). Again, this reduction operates out of a principle of metonymy, with the full word being represented through its most salient alphabetic components. A final nod at conventionality is given with the use of the quite old semograph for 'kiss' and its possible origin as a rebus of the letter 'x'. This is an instance of how language and its visual semiotic may evolve in lockstep, each extending the other's meaning and using the same metonymic principle to represent a word through its most significant sound, then to extend that representation into a large field of meaning (affection) through one of its physical signifiers (the kiss). A sign that evolves from a phonograph of a word with a quite specific meaning (X for kiss) is extended into a repre-sentation of the larger semantic field with which it is metonymically associated (X for love).

Many other iconic features can be identified both in contemporary texts and those of ancient civilisations. In the modern context, an international setting such as an airport will require signs that are transparent to people of different languages and cultures. They will therefore use icons with a quite low degree of conventionalisation to mark toilet, eating and restaurant facilities. The desktop of the computer on which I am writing this book also uses an elaborate set of signs which show varying degrees of conventionalisation and iconicity. The text-box sign on a Microsoft interface is an interesting example that will be well known to the millions of users of the Word software packages. It consists of a rectangle which is filled by horizontal lines except in the top left hand corner where there is a letter 'A'.

The sign is complicated on several counts. Like other icons in the desktop interface, this one reveals its meaning in letter form or as the metasign 't-e-x-t b-o-x' when the mouse pointer is drawn across it. The sign's salient iconic feature is the rectangle itself which resembles the larger box that a computer user can draw on screen after they have clicked on the icon. The rectangle's horizontal lines are supposed to resemble the written text which can be created inside the box that can be drawn on screen. The lines are metonymic in that they represent alphabetic writing through one of its facets, a horizontal linearity. It is also clear that the sign's designer regarded these basic features as unable to make its meaning sufficiently transparent. They therefore used another metonym, the top left-hand 'A', to stand for the alphabetic text that can be entered in the box. In this we see a revival of the determinative principle that we encountered in Chinese character script and will find again when we examine the ancient scripts of Sumeria and Egypt. When one sign risks ambiguity, another is used to assign it to a particular category of meaning. In the text-box case the ambiguity is analogical, with the lines possessing a wide field of meanings that they might resemble.

The unprompted resurgence of these ancient devices is unsurprising for a student of language and cognition because they represent solutions to the problems of sign-creation which are based upon fundamental and enduring cognitive processes. The processes manifest themselves as metaphor and metonymy but may have been more accurately described as *mapping* and *blending* (Fauconnier and Turner 1998, 2002).

Cognitive blend theory depends upon an earlier theory of *mapping and mental spaces* (Fauconnier 1997). In a metaphor, 'that man/woman is a horse', we can say that the domain of meaning represented by the horse is *mapped* onto that of a man/woman, where mapping means the transfer of meaning from one domain to another. Clearly the mapping results in the transfer of some features of a horse's meaning, 'outline facial features', 'strength and appetite', 'strong sexual desire' and not of others, 'having four legs' or 'foaming when exerted'. It is also clear that this mapping does not affect our construction of 'horse'. The horse can remain an animal even though it also transfers attributes of its meaning onto something else. This is made possible by a theory of mental spaces (Fauconnier 1997). A mental space is a zone of mind into which we can project attributes of meaning so that an operation upon them can occur. It is

Blend structure: the centaur

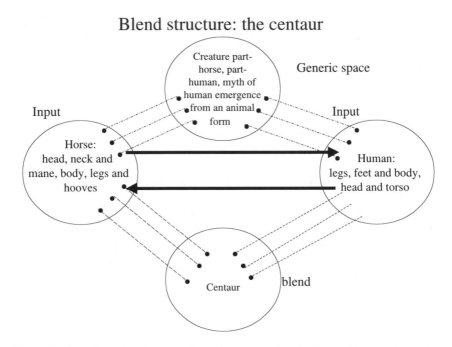

Figure 6.7 Blend use in totem creation: the centaur (Derived from Fauconnier and Turner 2002)

this act of projection into a mental space which allows the man/woman to be a horse while remaining intact as 'men', 'women' and 'horses' within their own zones of meaning. The mental space in which the two meanings are projected permits another cognitive operation. We can call this a *conceptual blend* or the blend of two domains of meaning. After this blend has occurred, the man/woman is neither horse nor human. They are a creature possessing the attributes of both, albeit with very different and often unpredictable weightings of these sets of attributes. For example, 'a woman' in aristocratic England may be demeaned by having the breeding capabilities of a 'thoroughbred' horse, while a man or woman may have the appetite of the same animal.

We can see these blend processes in early forms of record-keeping whether of myths and tallies (records of payment) or assertions of ownership. A popular mythic element represented through totems concerns the blend of human forms into each other in order to describe their semi-emergence one from the other in ancestral line. The Native American totem-pole records an ancestral lineage in exactly this manner. The carving of forms plots their emergence, one from another, on the same piece of timber or 'tree' providing a record against which an individual can situate themselves in society and time (Gaur 2000). Totems often fuse animal and human forms, as in Australian aboriginal myth or the Greek figure of the half-horse half-human centaur. It

Blend structure: rebus

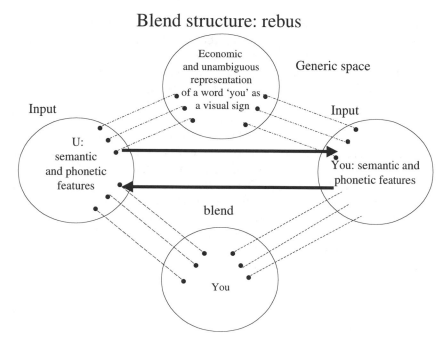

Figure 6.8 Rebus as a cognitive blend

is as if some totems represent a human struggle for disengagement from an earlier animal or semi-human form. A centaur may offer the clearest method of showing the blend process at work. This is shown in figure 6.7.

Figure 6.7 shows that for the blend to occur, three types of mental space are used. The topmost is the generic space. This is the space which guides and motivates the process, containing an expression of the blend's purpose. Beneath are the two input spaces, containing the concepts that will be blended. Shared features are mapped one onto the other, determining which will be retained and which will be eliminated in the final outcome. For example, from the man, the torso and head are mapped onto the head and neck of the horse ensuring the latter's elimination from the blend product. The opposite occurs with the body, legs and hooves of the horse and the body, legs and feet of the man. These mappings make the blend product what it is, a creature with the torso and head of a man, growing from the body and legs of a horse. Finally, the process is dynamic, ensuring that there is an information flow back and forth between the various constituents of the blend. The flow could be between the generic space, as this informs and is reshaped by the nature of the inputs and how they map between each other, and between these mappings and the form adopted by the blend product in the blend space.

In figure 6.8, we can now see how this blend process would derive phonographic sign-creation through a rebus. For the sake of transparency, I use a very simple example from text-messaging. However, this applies equally well to the type of process that underpins the ancient acts of sign creation in Chinese script or other ancient writing systems.

The generic objective of economical sign-creation involves our taking an alphabetical sign 'u' and the phonetic sign that we represent as 'you'. Because the two signs have the same phonetic values but different meanings, the visual representation 'u' maps onto that of 'you' and the semantic meaning of 'you' maps onto the letter meaning 'u'. This leaves a blend where the letter sign encodes a different semantic value, or where 'u = you' in other words, since this has not been incorporated into the mapping. A reverse use of the process enables us to decode this type of symbol. A rebus could not be classed as iconic in any conventional sense because it does not exploit any search for visual similarity. We can see, however, that a rebus exploits the same cognitive process that permitted the creation and interpretation of iconic signs before their conventionalisation as symbols.

Fauconnier and Turner (2002) analyse how we use the blend process to create and comprehend the icons used by the computer desktop. Their example uses the 'waste bin' icon. They point out how using a bin on a desktop and throwing something into it is a process that is quite unlike the physical process of throwing something away in real life. However, an obscure, electronic process is visualised through the iconic display used with its transfer of mina-ture papers from one bin icon to another. The iconography of the desktop is also created out of a blend process between the accoutrements of our physical world and the reality of the electronic process that actually occurs.

The users of writing systems created and increased their semiotic resources through a blend process. The earlier configurations of visual signs from which a full writing system evolved were rooted in human physical experience, or in its perception of the world. They were the iconic or indexical products of a blend process. Like the early Chinese pictograph of the horse, the icon created its meaning out of a resemblance to it. Like the Chinese compound indicative, the indexical sign pointed back to the sun and moon's most salient shared attribute, brightness. Through the process of conventionalisation, the iconic and indexical signs became symbols, and as they did so, permitted the evolu-tion of a larger and more complete system of representation of language.

Conclusions

In this chapter, I have applied our analysis of signs to the writing systems that produce and stimulate literacy practices. Harris (1996) criticises Peirce for his failure to provide a semiotic analysis of writing. I have argued that if we extend Peirce with a cognitive and diachronic examination of sign-creation such an analysis will start to fall into place. We will then see how iconic, indexical methods of encoding meaning evolve towards the symbolic while continuing to interact with the same in the scripts that we now use. With number as one example, we saw how conventional symbolic systems often begin with iconic or indexical modes of sign creation. As they develop, such systems may evolve towards a fuller representation of language but they will also exist in parallel with these linguistic systems. Their parallel existence will either encode the attributes of language that are unsympathetic to visual representation, or will extend the semiotic potential of language when it exists within a visual medium. Examples of the first function are the punctuation that give some clue to intonation or tone. An example of the second is manuscript illumination. This process is driven by our ability to deal in metaphor and metonymy, and finally by the blend process that underlies our metaphorical capacity.

Our first interest was to discuss the types of script that now exist and to consider how they may or may not differ from each other. We looked at the basic three types, the alphabet, the syllabary and the character script. The last is more aptly named a morphosyllabary, so that its phonetic components are fully understood. We looked at terms that pertain to each of these types, such as the digraphs and trigraphs that characterise alphabetic representation or the determinatives, compound indicatives and phonographs that appear in the character scripts. We also looked at how different script types may in fact relate closely to each other with consonantal alphabets overlapping with syllabaries, and syllabaries with the syllabic representations of character scripts.

Finally, we considered the core semasiographic/glottic distinction that is often used to analyse writing systems. We suggested that this should be re-examined by combining our current understanding of metaphor and blend structure with Peirce's analysis of sign. A stronger theory of how writing systems are developed and interpreted can then be put in place. In this last endeavour we only began to touch upon the potential of the tools that are being uncovered. However, I did begin to show how such an analysis could be pursued and will carry this further in Chapter 7.

Exercises

1. Discuss this statement: 'A full ideographic script would effectively be another language.' Try to think why the writer says this, then argue whether or not they are correct.
2. Take any icon from a standard computer desktop. Using your understanding of metaphor, sign-creation and cognitive blend theory, try to describe the thought process that led to that icon's development.
3. Imagine that the missionaries who brought writing back to Britain had not been Irish Christians who used the Latin alphabet but Chinese Buddhists who used the Chinese script. What kind of difficulties would these missionaries have found when they tried to use Chinese script to transcribe Anglo-Saxon? (For the purposes of this argument, you can assume that

Anglo-Saxon is similar to modern English.) Discuss why the type of solution developed by Japanese scribes would not have worked.

4. Try to describe each of these types of script: an alphabet, a syllabary and a morphosyllabary. Using reference books or the internet to extend your understanding of the Korean, Hangûl or the Arabic script, discuss whether there is any justification for calling these syllabaries.

5. Take an example of a text-message that you have received recently, or ask a friend to dictate one to you. Analyse the message using these terms: rebus, icon, indexical sign, metonym, glottic/non-glottic script, cognitive blend. Even if the message does not illustrate all such terms, you should explain why it does not.

7 Writing through Time

Introduction

Writing began in Sumeria, in the Tigris and Euphrates valleys and in the Nile valley in Egypt. Previously, Sumeria was thought to have developed the earliest full writing system. However, more recently, Egyptian hieroglyphs have been found which date back to 3500 BC. Estimates of how long human beings have been language users vary. However, if we consider that language probably dates back a minimum of 50,000 years, and the modern human 150,000 years before that, we can see that the evolution of parallel systems of sign use with the same semiotic capability as spoken language is a relatively recent phenomenon. In this chapter, I will try to summarise this difficult and complicated story. I will focus particularly on the development of the Greek alphabet, which is the forerunner of the Roman. I will also try to show the cognitive processes that were used in this development, discussing how these relate to the evolution of indexical, iconic, then symbolic types of sign.

From accidental to motivated sign-creation

As was made clear, the development of writing emerges from our wider semiotic needs and capabilities. Signs are both deliberate and artificial, or accidental and natural. The first type is created by us to encode meaning. Its final product is the symbol which encodes a meaning as a result of an agreed convention. The alphabet is thus an example of a symbolic system. The accidental type is represented by the hoof print in the dust that means 'animal'. We do not put the mark there but we create a sign from it by virtue of our capacity for indexical and iconic interpretation. Finding a hoof print in the dust, we decide that it resembles a hoof. The print then comes to mean 'hoof'. We see or hear a form, find that it has a physical or indicative connection to a phenomenon, then vest that form with the significance of the phenomenon to which it is connected, creating an indexical sign. Smoke issues from fire, so smoke 'means' fire.

The Russian psychologist Lev Vygotsky saw our capacity to deal in signs as fundamental to our nature. For him the need to find meaning in phenomena was intuitive. Yet a core moment in the development of a child is when that intuition is made subject to conscious control and put to use. Vygotsky (1978) takes the example of a child who knots their handkerchief in order to remember something. For Vygotsky, this action represents one of the first moments of intervention by the child in their semiotic environment. They create a sign to encode their need to remember. It seems plausible that all living creatures read signs. They exploit the semiotic potential of every sensory area. Bees move in ways that indicate the direction of flowers. Some fish use camouflage in order to hide from predators or pounce on prey. Others protect themselves by inflating themselves to an absurd size or declare their poisonous nature with an array of bright colours. Species of monkeys identify predators with alarm calls. Dogs mark territory with their urine. Infants and animals can use signs in this way. Vygotsky's interest is in how that capability is suddenly put to conscious use. The child is no longer simply reading its environment like a dog sniffing a scent, but creating an environment to be read.

A common distinction borrowed from life science by linguistics and other human sciences is that made between *phylogenesis* and *ontogenesis*. The phylogenetic processes refer to the historical or evolutionary development of a phenomenon. The ontogenetic refers to the development of the individual person. Thus, within our current study, phylogenesis refers to the development of sign systems in history and ontogenesis to the development and acquisition of these systems within the individual. The Vygotskian example is ontogenetic. It refers to how an individual reaches a stage of development where they can manipulate the environment as a semiotic system. One must be wary of looking for a simplistic overlap between these two approaches. For example, we might be tempted to see a parallel between the child's development of early literacy and the evolution of semiotic systems among pre-literate people. Such an approach could lead to naïve, and finally offensive, assumptions about the childlike innocence of primitive societies. However, Vygotsky's ontogenetic example does suggest a useful insight into a phylogenetic process. He identifies a core difference between the reflexive response to sign and the conscious attempt to enhance the semiotic potential of the environment. We can imagine such moments within the development of the sign systems that precede the emergence of literacy.

A core animal function is hunting and food-gathering. This also provides us with a basic act of sign reading and semiosis. An animal leaves a scent, a hoof print or other signs of environmental disturbance. A hoof print is both iconic and indexical. The hoof print is iconic because it resembles the hoof that it represents. It is indexical because it occurs as a result of the presence it represents. The sign also makes a larger indexical connection. The animal imprints the dust. Print and paw are *contiguously related*. They are joined in space. The track encodes the creature because the creature is momentarily in

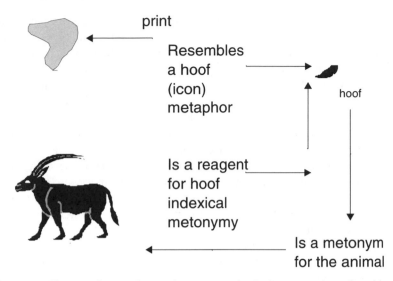

Figure 7.1 The use of metaphor and metonymy in the interpretation of accidental signs

the track. We must also connect the hoof to the larger animal that it is part of. We must interpret the hoof as a metonymy of the animal. Metaphor and metonymy thus underscore this act of sign interpretation and sign creation.

A second step would be the Vygotskian moment where we need a visual means of representing the animal when the creature does not oblige us by plodding across the canvas of our thought and leaving a trace. The hunters may then begin a conscious iconic or indexical representation of the absent creature. One consequence is our heritage of Stone Age painting.

In their use of totems, early literacies also suggest an exploitation of the blend processes that may underlie symbol creation. We saw how this might work in our example of that mythical creature, the centaur. Once they are conceptualised as signs, creatures become available for mental manipulation, we can mentally remodel them or mingle them with other things. When a phenomenon is no longer embedded into the context and identity through which it was first perceived, we can play with it, blending it into other forms.

Early writing systems

We can plot the conventionalisation of pictographic forms in the development of three of the best-known early writing systems, the Sumerian, the Egyptian and the Chinese. When a society evolves beyond a very small tribal group, there is also a need to record ownership and transactions. Very early forms of literacy and their proto-writing (Fischer 2001) revolve around the recording of transactions and the running of tallies. As we saw in the example of the quipu (Chapter 6), one of the more sophisticated tallies involves knotted strings. Unlike other systems of notches in wood or bone, knots can be easily erased and the nature of a transaction corrected or altered. Knots can keep a primitive diary as when the ancient Persian king, Darius, asked his Greek allies to guard a bridge and not leave until they had untied sixty knots in a string, one for each day (ibid. 2001: 14). The Inca quipu actually represented zero as an absence with a space on a string while revealing a decimal counting system where 'one overhand knot about two overhand knots above a group of seven knots recorded the number 127' (ibid.: 14). A further need in larger tribal groups is not just to record the transaction of property as taxation or whatever, but to register ownership. Brand-markings for cattle are a typical indexical mark of ownership. Their meaning lies in their attachment of an insignia to the object that is owned.

Tokens are a system of record-keeping that has been identified as leading directly to a concept of writing (Schmandt-Besserat 1992). Clay tokens have been found throughout the Middle East, but significantly not in Egypt. Some of these tokens stood for the object that was subject to a given transaction. The tokens were enfolded in a clay envelope to keep them together. The envelope was then marked with a representation of the tokens that it contained, so that it did not have to be broken open to verify its contents. Three things have happened that point towards writing. First, there is an act of indirect representation: the envelope bears a sign for a sign. Second, the representation is made as a set of marks on a surface not as a portable token. The theory therefore suggests that the wedge-like shape of the cuneiform script that developed in Sumeria could owe its origins to an imprint of the token, or to a representation of the same. The physical manipulation of objects or their words as tokens gives way to the arrangement of the tokens as an inscription on a surface. The third feature to suggest a more complete writing system is that the containment of tokens within a marked envelope suggests a method of gathering different signs into an interpretable text. Schmandt-Besserat's theory has been challenged however as not fully supported by archaeological evidence (Fischer 2001) and, although it offers an interesting glimpse into the forms of semiosis that precede full writing systems, it cannot be treated as their sole source.

Spurred on by the need for more elaborate records of ownership and property transactions, the Mesopotamian civilisations were some of the first to develop a writing system that could represent the core properties of language.

The system's pictographic base underwent the process of increasing abstraction and conventionalisation illustrated in the cuneiform for a star shown in figure 7.2.

By 2800 BC the system had developed a widely used set of signs that included semographs to encode word meanings, phonographs evolving from a rebus to encode syllable sounds, and determinatives to guide the reading of

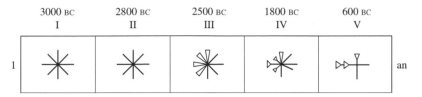

| 3000 BC | 2800 BC | 2500 BC | 1800 BC | 600 BC |
| I | II | III | IV | V |

Figure 7.2 The abstraction of cuneiform signs (Halliday 1979)

the phonographs. Another device to aid disambiguation was the use of what have been called 'phonetic complements'. This might follow a semograph to show how it should be read. An English equivalent would be to add 'nd' to the symbol '2' to show that it should be read as 'second' (2nd) rather than as 'two' (Barber 1974: 23).

The abstraction of the script into its characteristic and linear wedge-shape was doubtless hastened by the use of clay writing materials marked with a pointed stylus. It also evolved a 'nuclear' form, where much was not spelt out and its word order was sometimes haphazard and perhaps remote from the language it represented. We should not forget that the earliest tablets 'consisted of accounting notes written by book-keepers' (DeFrancis 1989: 79) and the script's cursive, abstract and conventional nature may have been motivated by this utilitarian function. Although the script became something of a cul-de-sac, its success should not be underrated. After the conquest of Sumeria by the Akkadians it was adapted to the Semitic language of the conquerors, but with some difficulty. There was an intermediary phase where Sumerian probably persisted as the language of literacy and had to be learnt in order to master writing. Although cuneiform can be considered a successful script that survived for a considerable period of time and underwent substantial evolution, it is something of a 'sideshow' in the history of writing because it did not evolve towards any of the writing systems that we now use.

Tokens do not seem to have played a significant part in the evolution of Ancient Egyptian writing, or hieroglyphs (meaning sacred carving). However, the script was similar to Chinese and cuneiform in that it derived from largely iconic and pictographic forms. Like cuneiform, it used a mix of semographs, phonographs derived through a rebus, and determinatives. For example, if we take the signs, shown in figure 7.3, we can see that the first indicates that we are dealing with a meaning that refers to man and his occupations. When this combines with the phonetic symbol for 's' placed above it, we can obtain the meaning, 'man'.

The second hieroglyph means 'god or king' and, on the left, it is used to show that phonetic symbols, equivalent to 's', 'k' and 'r', are spelling out the name of a god and not some other item. The third, 'sun, light and time', is clearly both indexical and iconic and metonymic in origin. The icon of the sun is a metonym for a larger field of meaning that includes 'light' and 'time' (as an item

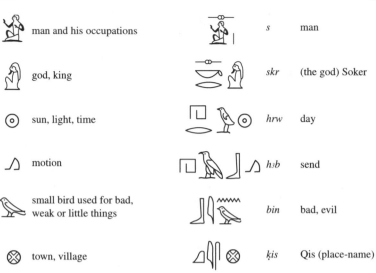

Figure 7.3 Egyptian determinatives (Collier and Manley 1998)

measured by the sun's progress). This combines with three symbols or phonographs that were derived from a rebus: 'hrw'. The fourth is also metonymic in origin, associated with an icon of the chief human agent of movement, the legs. The small bird, used in the fifth example, shows the overlap between metaphor and metonymy. Small birds do not even have a direct semantic connection to weakness, let alone to evil, though clearly in Ancient Egyptian culture their field was metaphorically stretched in order to incorporate that concept. The last is an interesting example of abstraction, from the village to a village plan as a crossroads, perhaps, then to this conventionalised symbol.

As in Chinese and cuneiform, the key Egyptian development was the phonograph which gave the script the potential to represent a language. This was derived by means of a rebus, but an important difference from other scripts lay in the fact that Egyptian was a Semitic, triliteral language. As in other such languages, consonants were key to meaning differentiation, and vowels only secondary. Therefore, whereas cuneiform phonographs had to incorporate vowels by representing syllables, hieroglyphs developed towards the representation of consonants. Hieroglyphs represented one, two or, more rarely, three consonants. Thus, a hieroglyph meaning water (shown in figure 7.4) came to

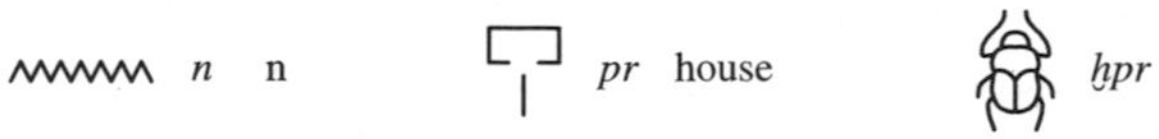

Figure 7.4 Consonantal hieroglyphs (Collier and Manley 1998)

represent its salient initial consonant, 'n'. The second, house or estate, came to represent its two salient consonants, 'p' and 'r'. The third, a beetle, came to represent 'h-p-r':

Again, we can see familiar cognitive processes at work here. Our ability to deal in metonymy means that triliteral languages may suggest a progressive reduction of words to what Fischer (2001: 83) calls 'consonantal skeletons', or their most salient phonetic features. They suggest this because they base their separation of meanings on consonantal differentiation. The consonant was the salient phonetic feature through which the larger semantic unit could be manipulated. Thus, the Egyptians could represent a word through the phonographs of the consonants and, by 2000–1800 BC, their scribes had begun to use a purely consonantal script for some less formal functions (Jensen 1969). Yet, Egyptian retained its decorative, pictographic nature despite its development of these consonantal forms and the cursive *book scripts*, *hieratic* and the later *demotic*. The proliferation of documents in the cursive script also owed much to the Egyptian invention of papyrus, a brittle but lightweight material made from reeds. This material could be scrolled and was easily transportable, allowing ancient literacies to develop some of the now familiar practices associated with the carriage of established forms of words through space as well as time.

Why the Egyptians retained other types of sign despite having a full consonantal system cannot be fully known. However, writing history reveals other examples of a cultural attachment to seemingly more cumbersome writing forms, long after the introduction of other types of representation. A notable case, mentioned in Chapter 6, is the continuing use of Kanji, or Chinese characters, in Japanese, despite the early development of two syllabaries, both of which can represent the entire language. Kanji even had greater status because they were difficult to learn. The script was thought to be a masculine challenge, with the easier syllabaries being used by women. In such examples of cultural conservatism and the preservation of ostensibly less efficient forms, we see how scripts intertwine with the literacy practices that they instigate. They are socio-cultural phenomena, and cannot be seen simply as the product of a Darwinian search for orthographic efficiency.

It took a shift across languages to force Egyptian writing finally to jettison its semographic heritage. There was contact between the Egyptians and other Middle Eastern peoples who spoke Semitic languages, the Canaanites, then their successors, the Phoenicians. This contact led to the development of an alphabet that represented all the consonants in the Phoenician language and which was based upon Egyptian phonographs. The Phoenicians were a trading people and may have been motivated by a need for a script that was better adapted to their mercantile life. Their development of a consonantal alphabet may be one of the most significant events in writing history, because it became the basis of the writing systems that evolved across Asia, towards the East and across Europe towards the West.

The evolution of the alphabet

The next crucial development in writing history occurred when the Phoenicians came into contact with the Greeks in around 2000 BC. As a mercantile and seafaring people, the Phoenicians traded out of the Levant, around the Mediterranean and into the Atlantic and as far north as the British Isles. Greek peoples had previously developed writing. The Bronze Age Minoan civilisation of Crete had developed a syllabary now known as Linear B. But this script vanished with the civilisation of which it was a part. The Phoenician contact was different because it introduced a fully-fledged consonantal alphabet into southern Europe. However, the consonantal alphabet faced a new challenge in the form of the Ancient Greek language. Ancient Greek was an Indo-European language, belonging to a group that includes almost all modern Indian and European languages as well as those from which they are derived. As any English speaker will realise, these languages have a complicated syllable structure and use vowels to differentiate their meanings. Some Indo-European languages, such as Ancient Greek, are highly inflected. We should remember that in a highly inflected language, other features such as word order might be less important as a method of encoding a sentence meaning. In the English sentence 'the slave loves the Lord', we know that 'Lord' is the object because it comes after the verb. In a more inflected language, such as Latin, the word for 'Lord', 'dominus', would indicate its object function through 'case' or the morpheme '-um' giving 'dominum'. This may allow the language more flexibility about where it places the object. We can now see how scribes who could not represent Greek inflections would lose much of the meaning of the language. We should further remember that in Indo-European languages, vowels, whether in the initial, medial or final position in a word, are important to both case and word identification. If English followed the Egyptian principle and wrote 'ten' with a consonantal skeleton 't-n', for example, we would be completely dependent on context in order to know whether we meant: 'tan', 'ten', 'teen', 'ton', 'tone', 'toon', 'tune' or 'tin'. In Greek, the problem might be even greater because a complex series of inflections must be represented as well. Clearly, vowel representation had to be an essential component of any phoneme-based adaptation of Phoenician script into Greek. The Greek solution was to use redundant Phoenician phonemes to represent the vowels of their language. They thus developed the first complete alphabet.

The alphabet developed as it moved across languages. Greek script evolved into the Cyrillic still used by many Slavic languages. It also evolved into the Etruscan script in northern Italy, before being developed into the Roman alphabet. The Roman alphabet itself evolved new diacritics, digraphs and trigraphs as it coped with different European, Slavic, Turkik and African languages. Yet we are talking about the adaptation of a common and enduring principle. In this sense, you, the reader, might pause and wonder at how you

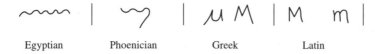

Egyptian   Phoenician   Greek   Latin

Figure 7.5 The derivation of the letter m. This shows how a pictograph for 'water' was conventionalised as a sign for water's initial syllable 'n' then developed into a Phoenician letter with a similar value before changing into the Greek mu then the Latin 'm'.

are decoding this book with the use of a semiotic principle that was developed 3,000 years ago. This is shown quite graphically in figure 7.5, which relates the Roman graphemes that we use today to the Egyptian hieroglyphs from which they evolved.

In moving eastwards, Semitic writing systems also changed when they had to represent other types of Indo-European language. The solution in this case was not an evolution towards an alphabetic principle but the development of a syllabic form. The original Brahmi script of India evolved into the countless syllabaries that represent the languages of the Indian subcontinent. In India, there has also been an interest in trying to trace Brahmi back to some indigenous forms of writing, such as the undeciphered script of the ancient Indus river civilisation. But this is now discounted by most scholars, who attest to its origins in the Middle East. In the Middle East itself, the consonantal alphabet was retained, evolving into the modern Arabic script discussed in Chapter 6.

Conclusions

In this chapter I have introduced the story of how writing systems came into being. The topic is important to our understanding of literacy because it reveals how our contemporary practices are steered by their use of systems whose evolution may be remote in time but contemporary in their use of familiar cognitive processes. If we take a device such as a rebus and the underlying blend process looked at in Chapter 6, we can see how this still drives the development of semiotic processes able to exploit cell phone technologies.

I looked first at the concept of phylogenesis and ontogenesis within semiotic systems. I suggested that although these two processes are distinct and that each will follow a separate course, they can be treated as metaphors of each other. One insight provided by this metaphor was the sense that both individual and collective human development can be charted as a process of gaining conscious control over our intuitive semiotic capability. The child's knotting of their handkerchief can act as a metaphor for the collective evolutionary development of techniques of conscious symbol use. Such techniques lead to early literacies or to practices that, for example, connect the social function of myth-making to the economic imperative of hunting by making the hunters' prey and predators available for cognitive manipulation as the totems of our ancestral history.

Next, I explored how the alphabet had developed after pictographic and semographic types of sign were squeezed out of the repertoire of writing systems by their movement across language. This showed again how core language differences and movement of scripts across languages will create different writing systems. Because Chinese is monosyllabic, a single character can begin as a pictograph then become a phonograph through a rebus yet still represent an entire word. In Chinese, in other words, an analysis of phonology does not have to go beyond the syllable. In Egyptian, however, the triliteral, consonantal root of the language made phoneme representation more important, resulting in the essentials of a consonantal alphabet. Yet it is significant also that although writing systems are to some extent a creature that must adapt to survive in a given linguistic environment, they also carry within them the older, less adaptive iconic and indexical modes of meaning representation from which they had first evolved. This is because iconic and indexical signs are the products of the metaphor and metonym-making; processes that, because they drive category representation and extension, must also underscore the creativity that made the rise of writing systems possible.

Exercises

1. Discuss the similarities and differences in the way the movement of scripts across languages will force the development of those scripts. Consider the examples Sumerian to Akkadian, Chinese to Japanese, and Phoenician to Greek.
2. All alphabets in current use have developed after contact with the Greek alphabet or its offshoots. Discuss whether this might be because of a unique movement of writing between two Semitic languages, then from the Semitic language of Phoenician to the Indo-European language, Greek.
3. Consult some writing histories and look for examples of how the evolution of scripts may have been driven by the cognitive processes with which this book has tried to familiarise you.
4. Consider how social or literacy practices may effect the development of script.
5. Design an alternative writing system for English. You should use your own pictographs, conventionalised semographs, determinatives, and phonographs that have been derived from them with a rebus. Discuss how well this script suits the structure of English.

8 The Nature of Writing

Introduction

Our discussion so far has raised three central points in respect of writing. All of these involve considerable controversy, which requires discussion and review. The problems can be summarised as follows:

1. whether writing systems are simply technological solutions to the problems of language representation or larger semiotic systems which both reflect and influence the larger nature of the practices by which they are employed;
2. whether a successful writing system is defined by its ability to represent speech;
3. the question of phonocentricism. How far writing is parasitic upon speech, and simply a system of metasigns.

All these are closely interrelated. For example, if we raise the status of semasiographic or meaning-representing writing systems, we might be implying that because thought and meaning are impossible without language, a successful writing system is not just a vehicle for encoding phonetic information, but has the status of sign rather than metasign, holding out the prospect of a route round language's phonetic representation. We might, therefore, see language as a property of mind that is given form by the voice, and writing as an expression of those mental processes of meaning construction. I will now look briefly at each of these questions.

Writing systems as technological solutions

As Street (1984) concedes, an understanding of literacy as social practices should not preclude our need to see those practices as bound up with the literacy technologies that make them possible. Technologies may arise as solutions to socio-economic need. Yet technologies also arise from a cultural process of experimentation, with some inventions being left to look for a social application. The processes of social and technological development are intertwined. It is impossible to imagine the Reformation of sixteenth- and seventeenth-century Europe and such associated practices as home bible study without the prior development of cheaper reading materials. Yet discontent with the Catholic Church and its corrupt practices preceded the development of printing. Heresy is almost a normal human reaction to an insistence on a single authorised version of the truth. Social practices and their supporting technologies are clearly bound up, one with the other.

As our discussion of scripts has made clear, a writing system cannot be treated as a technical solution to the needs of a given set of social practices. Writing systems emerge from a configuration of language, available technologies and social need. In considering language, different languages pose different representational problems.

We see the effect of language in the way the monosyllabic structure of Chinese meant that the representation of phonemes was unnecessary. Chinese script retained what could be called a 'conceptual residue', because to represent a syllable was often the same as representing a word and the concept that word encapsulated.

We find a cultural effect in how, in the scripts of both Ancient Egypt and modern Japan, efficient, phonographic types were discovered but were never totally used. Writing systems do not just express social practices, they are components of those practices. In Japan, despite the development of two syllabaries and the much later importation of the Roman alphabet, Kanji, the character script imported from China, survives to this day. The learning burden it imposes on Japanese school children is such that they continue studying it in secondary school. Kanji survives because writing is not just an efficient delivery system. Writing systems are repositories of social values and are, perhaps, value systems in themselves.

We find a technological effect in the way in which cuneiform's typical wedge-shape was a consequence of its being scratched into clay. In northern Europe, early, angular runic script was often scratched onto bone or wood. More flowing scripts needed the development of papyrus, parchment and paper. Yet while such technologies may facilitate change, they will not necessarily instigate it. Inherited practices retain their hold, becoming identified with the value-system of the culture itself. The development of papyrus, for example, did not deter Egypt's fascination for monumental literacies.

Successful writing systems must represent speech

Questions about the nature of writing were reformulated by DeFrancis's (1989) insistence on the separation of what he terms full and partial communication systems. According to this view, full communication systems are all built upon our capacity for speech. Behind such an assertion is Saussure's assertion that language is primarily speech. It is a view that accords superficially with both structuralism and Noam Chomsky's (1985) view of language. Yet in respect of Chomskyan linguistics, DeFrancis misses a basic point about the difference between phonetics and phonology. In Chomskyan analysis, language is not pre-eminently the phonetics of audible speech so much as the phonology of mental pattern creation which allows phonetic speech a consistent, interpretable form. In other words, it is about the plan of the speech-building more than about the fabric of the building itself. Though the primacy of speech is empirically beyond contest, Chomsky's interpretation allows us to express language through other media than sound. Language is finally not its phonetic manifestation but exists in the mental structures on which such manifestations are based. We see the problems that this raises most clearly in DeFrancis's (1989) earlier misinterpretation of the nature of American Sign Language (ASL).

Sign languages pose a challenge to those who want to limit the potential of a semasiographic literacy. They pose such a challenge because they suggest that a full non-phonetic communication system is a possibility. If we can communicate through visual gesture, then we can decouple writing from its more recent representation of spoken language and suggest that some larger visual sign system is possible, even if this is static and confined to the page. Accordingly, DeFrancis relegates semasiographic literacies to a category of partial communication systems but treats sign languages as a way of representing speech, rather as writing does. Our much larger contemporary understanding of the nature of these languages allows us to assert that this is simply not the case (see, for example, Uyechi 1996). If sign languages can be treated as autonomous and able to construct their own visual phonology, then we might hold out such prospects for semasiographic writing systems. Sign languages reveal how writing might have taken another direction, moving away from the representation of speech and towards an exploration of its potential as a visual form of meaning representation. Yet there are still two insurmountable problems with such a thesis.

First, according to much contemporary linguistic theory, language is finally a natural phenomenon, arising from the interaction of the infant's internal mental structures with whatever language input is available. In order to assume a fully-fledged existence, a language would have to pass through this infant filter, as happens with sign languages. We could not envisage such a process occurring with a writing system. Second, literacy practices do not develop their own language. Impelled by the need to replicate the communicative potential of speech, they develop their scripts towards the replication of speech sounds. If we treat language as a mental state, or knowledge, it may be possible to imagine it as entirely abstract, or as a regulatory system that produces and processes sound. Yet it seems unlikely that language really exists as a set of regulatory principles that are separate from the forms that they govern or produce. Once acquired through an auditory channel, language remains an aural or oral medium, one which evidently so dominates our semiotic processes that we are unable to abandon it entirely in favour of the visual medium. As changes in society required ever more complete communication systems, these had to be found in a representation of spoken language. Writing could not develop into sign language because its users' communicative systems were in fact dominated by their vocal tract. Writing had to represent speech even if the case of sign language reveals that we can conceive of fuller forms of semiosis, which are rooted in a visual medium.

The existence of sign languages, does, however, reveal a larger ability to develop our semiotic competence in whatever channel is available. Equally, we can see how, even as writing gravitates towards linguistic representation, it still seeks to circumvent that representation by contriving a direct evocation of the world. Lurking behind this aspect is the sense that iconicity proffers a form of semiosis that is more direct or somehow more sympathetic to the spirit of what is being represented, conveying its quality as well as its category. Proverbially, 'a picture is worth a thousand words' and the transfer of language into a visual medium tempts us with the prospect of iconity or of signs that look like what they mean.

One of the most productive manifestations of this tension between phonetic and visual semiosis lies in how writing development so often adopts a decorative strand. We find this in the interplay between abstract letter-forms and representative images in Japanese and Chinese painting, or in the exploration of the visual form of the grapheme itself that characterises Arabic calligraphy. We find it also in the earlier need of the Egyptians to retain writing's decorative principle. We find it again in our continuing employment and development of a wealth of semasiographic devices to elaborate upon linguistic meaning. We see this in the iconography of computer desktops and text messaging. It rests in the conventions such as spacing and punctuation which allow us to convey and elaborate upon a full linguistic representation of meaning. Writing, in this sense, represents a larger cognitive conflict between our need to tie signs to specific meanings, on the one hand, and to subvert the conventionality of the sign on the other, finding within it a metaphor to capture new sense. Because writing uses a visual medium, this impulse to iconicity takes a visual form.

The question of phonocentrism and the centrality of writing

When Derrida (1997) criticised the phonocentric nature of Western linguistic analysis, he was engaging with a wider current of philosophy, one which has put the nature of language at the heart of our intellectual dilemma. Language furnishes us with our only real instrument of philosophical enquiry. Yet most philosophical problems, those dealing with the nature of category, for example, arise from the nature of language. For Derrida, the problem lies partly in language's manifestation as speech, or its *phonocentricity*.

Phonocentricity relates to some larger reaction against human egocentricity (Spivak 1997). Derrida's concern is with how human expression is dominated by our own voice and that voice's fabrication of our world. It is as if a voice rephrases the world according to its producer's own constructions, isolating them within their own sound, and making their perception the victim of an enduring and inescapable soliloquy. Derrida's celebration of writing as somehow closer to the spirit of language than speech is partly through an assertion of a pre-writing, or a medium that is unsullied by the distortions of voice. Writing is celebrated because of how it puts language outside the voice. It gives language a fixed and visual form that is outside the writer. Although defective in its representation of language, writing carries a stronger trace of language's meanings than speech. Derrida understands writing as sign, but is reluctant to accord the same status to language, perhaps because he associates it more with the construction of meaning and the creation of category than with its representation.

At first sight, this type of argument seems not only difficult and imprecise but almost deliberately perverse, inverting the historical development of writing as a means to represent speech. Derrida's case is not well served by his deliberate obscurity and the accompanying sense that he is trying to dissolve the conventional boundaries of meaning. Yet his view is not altogether remote from the more accessible conclusions of linguists such as Halliday (1979) or Petterson (1996), who argue that theories of writing which stress its evolution into a vehicle that represented speech will under-represent how speech had to adapt itself to the constraints of writing. One can see this in the straightforward example of how some of our more elaborate semasiographic systems may constrain our use of language. For example, when mathematicians speak from mathematical texts, their use of language is constrained by the nature of the writing system with which they deal. When writing systems were more limited, they also limited the way language was used. Language therefore adapted itself to the sign systems that were designed to make it carry through time and space, even as these same systems adapted to language. By this argument, it was the convergence of two distinct forms of semiosis, language and visual sign systems, that produced what we now know as writing. How far this is true and how well it accounts for the nature of written language are topics that we will explore in Part III of this book.

Conclusions

In this chapter I have tried to summarise some of the outstanding issues concerning the nature of writing. Thought about the nature of writing involved some further reflection on language. A clear conclusion was that the questions we ask about the nature of writing systems cannot be separated from those that we pose about the nature of the literacy practices of which they were a part. Writing systems could not be seen as technologies fashioned by a Darwinian process that led us inexorably to what was easy and efficient. They carried within them the elaborate and contradictory values of the culture for which they were a vehicle. Less certainty surrounded my view of the nature of writing. Whilst I acknowledged that writing development was incomplete until it could represent the spoken word, I was also concerned to show how writing systems continued to carry within them concessions to the processes of meaning representation that were non-linguistic in nature. Finally, I looked at questions about the nature of writing as more faithful to the nature of language than speech. I found this argument difficult to summarise and sustain but stressed its insight into the manner in which writing systems did not just fashion themselves around the nature of language but demanded that language must rework itself in order to accommodate writing.

Exercises

1. Note down some literacy practices that use or produce some visually distinct texts types of text. Try to think of what makes the text reflect the needs of the practice. For example, you could think how the use of letter-head and its arrangement of the larger letter-text reflects the needs of bureaucratic or business literacy practices.
2. Think of how English spells the same sound in different ways (f, gh and ph, for example). Note down other instances. Discuss what this tells you about the impact of culture on literacy's sign systems.
3. Find a line from a popular comic for children or adults. Analyse its use of visual convention to convey meaning. Discuss how it may or may not justify some of the assertions in this chapter about the way in which giving language a visual form will encourage a search for parallel, non-linguistic forms of meaning representation.
4. The Peruvian quipu used an elaborate system of knots and strings to record Inca transactions. Try to imagine how the users of the quipu might talk to each other as they went about their work, doing what every community of practice does to develop codified ways of using language when they discuss their work. Decide what insights this might give you into the way speech must adapt to writing just as writing adapts to speech.

Part III

The Language of Literacy

9 Basic Differences between Speech and Writing

Introduction

A somewhat rough-and-ready approach to how reading and writing differ is to start from the view that they are somehow 'oppositional', and can each can be characterised according to a set of contrastive features. The list below makes one addition to a list compiled by Baron (2000: 21):

Writing is:	*Speech is:*
objective	Interpersonal
a monologue	a dialogue
durable	ephemeral
decontextualised	contextualised
scannable	only linearly accessible
planned/highly structured	spontaneous/loosely structured
syntactically complex	syntactically simple
concerned with past and future	concerned with the present
formal	informal
expository	narrative
argument-oriented	event-oriented
abstract	concrete
syntactically and morphologically complete	syntactically and morphologically incomplete
mediational	communicative

Such features may form a useful starting point from which to explore the difficult question of how to characterise or describe written language. But as Baron also attests, it will rapidly become plain that this type of dichotomous thinking fails because it does not recognise how people use written and spoken language differently to accomplish different tasks. Further, writing and speech are not always distinct categories of language use. We improvise upon a script, or use speech to prompt writing, as when we dictate a letter or take notes in a lecture. This *admixing* further blurs the concept of a spoken or written use of language. However, the above criteria are a useful means of summarising the debate about how written and spoken language do and do not differ. I will, therefore, use these topics as a starting pointing for my discussion, taking each in turn. I will come finally to Tannen's (1982) conclusion that text can be spread along a continuum that runs between a use of language that is loose and informal, typified by casual conversation, and a use that is highly formal and structured, expressing a conventional idea of writing.

Personal vs. interpersonal

Scholars since Plato have been bemused by how written language addresses the reader when its author is absent. Written language has no capacity to respond. Because the text may be read when its author is absent, the suggestion is that it leads towards a tradition of writing where the author absents themselves from their own text, recording events as if they had imprinted themselves upon the page. Science writing uses *passives* to do this, because passives hide the *agent* that instigates the action of the sentence and make the *patient*, the part that the action is performed upon, into the subject (e.g. Quirk et al.1985). We see this in the following passage where the passives are italicised:

> When aqueous NaCl solution *is electrolysed* under appropriate conditions, it *is observed* that hydrogen *is liberated* at the cathode and chlorine gas *is liberated* at the anode. (Sienko and Plane 1976: 286; author's italics)

'Aqueous NaCl solution', 'hydrogen', and 'cathode and chlorine gas' are all patients but also subjects. The agents of the actions are therefore hidden.

Banks (1994) maintains that the scientific use of the passive is more complex than simply this impersonal need to downplay the role of the observer and foreground the events themselves. For Banks, the passive is 'relational' in nature. By this he means that the past participles of passives should be treated as adjectives. Thus, they show the subject they describe as being 'in a state of' having an action performed upon them. For example, if we look at the two sentences 'Albert annoyed George' and 'George was annoyed', we should not interpret the second as a paraphrase of the first, but as a description of the state that results from the actions of the first. George is thus seen as being in a state of annoyance. Since science writing tries to describe 'states' that result from events, or causes from effects – 'the electrolysation' that results from 'electrolysis', to use the example given above – it drives its authors towards a preference for passive constructions.

Nominalisation, or the creation of nouns from other parts of speech, is another device that may result from the tendency of literacy to promote texts that veil the presence of their author. In a sentence such as 'walking made me tired', 'walk' is nominalised and functions as the agent of the sentence, or as the item which precipitates the events that it recounts. The first person 'me' is reduced to a patient or victim. An alternative sentence, 'I walked and I got tired', retains the first person as the subject and conveys their importance as an agent that precipitates their own fatigue. The nominalisation, on the other hand, makes the author into a victim of events. It is as if the events and not they construct the text. Also, nominalisation may respond to the need for a relational type of expression, where causes ensue from effects, without the mediation of an observer. Accordingly, Biber (1988: 14) observes how in scientific texts nominalisations and passives may have a dimension of co-occurrence. Halliday (1993) perceives these nominal forms as essential to the development of scientific thought, because science is finally about the discovery of relational sequences, or causes and their effects. A cause can be an event or action ('placing sodium in water') which precipitates another event or action ('a conflagration'). In fact, we perceive actions only through their effect on knowable phenomena, but in a nominalised cause-and-effect sentence we tend to cast the phenomena aside and treat the event or action as impacting upon another event or action as if each were a thing.

Consider this example from a medical text:

> *Miliary tuberculosis* is a generalised infection resulting from *haematogenous tubercle* dissemination. (Catzel and Roberts 1984: 326)

One process, 'dissemination', triggers another, 'infection'. We are asked to perceive the sequence as if events impact on events without the mediation of the populations they affect or of the author who witnesses them. The argument is that literacy promotes such a use of language because it distances the author from the record and, by implication, removes all actors from the events.

However, although this type of objective style may be encouraged by how written text removes the text producer from the text consumer, it is by no means an essential feature of written language. Written language can be personal in nature and has modes of address that make clear it is not for general readership, as when we address a note to a particular person. Written language can be personalised even as it seeks a larger readership, as when the author Rudyard Kippling addresses the reader as 'Dearly Beloved' in his *Just So Stories*. A text intended for a general child readership thus makes one child reader feel that the story is in fact intended for them.

Using such devices, literacy may well develop the metaphor of events as self-governing and unaffected by agency. It can therefore advance the scope for a scientific record that focuses on cause and effect. Yet, this is far from a universal product of written language. It does not result in a significant and discernible difference between the two modes of language use, but is more about the particular type of text that evolved as a vehicle of scientific expression. Biber

(1988: 16) points out how a written text such as the following has 'no passives' or 'nominalisations':

> She became aware that the pace was slackening; now the coach stopped. The moment had come. Upon the ensuing interview the future would depend. Outwardly she was calm, but her heart was beating fast, and the palms of her hand were damp.

This is not, of course, the same as saying that this text is more like speech than writing. In fact, it has other features which distinguish it as written – the short sentences and lack of conjunctions, for example.

Monologue vs. dialogue

Written text is arguably always monologic in the sense that it is produced in the absence of the reader. The writer hears only their own voice. But writing can also ask a reader to expect a response. This was always the case with letters and it is made more immediate with e-mail. There is also a more complicated way in which writing replicates a dialogic aspect of text. This is through its ability to record two voices or set one opinion against another. In the philosophical dialogue of Ancient Greece, this was done overtly by writing a text as a dialogue with two or more voices in discussion. For example, in Plato's *Timaeus and Critias,* the author prefaces a larger monologic discourse by saying that the text is to be delivered by a speaker or guest to his master Socrates.

> *Socrates:* One, two, three – but where my dear Timaeus is the fourth of my guests of yesterday who were to entertain me today?
> *Timaeus:* He's fallen sick, Socrates, otherwise he would never willingly have missed today's discussion.
> *Socrates:* Then if he's away it is up to you and the others to play his part as well as your own. (Plato 1971)

It is difficult for the author to contemplate delivering the treatise direct to an imaginary reader. It has to be offered to the character, Socrates, who is inserted into the text as a wise and enquiring listener. When the text moves on from the theme of the origins and nature of the world towards a discussion of the evolution of human society and the Atlantis myth, it is significant that the speaker also changes. New themes presuppose new voices. The second speaker, Critias, begs the indulgence of Socrates and his listeners because of the long and complicated text that he must unfold. This is almost an apology for the monologic nature of the text that will follow. Again, there is a sense that a writer cannot unfold ideas to a reader without recreating their presence as a listener in the text.

In the seventeenth-century dialogues of the scientist Galileo, we see a re-use of this classical genre. Galileo advances his support for Copernicus through an exchange of point and counterpoint between his discussants. Yet in other, near-contemporary examples we can see a more modern text starting to evolve:

> He that hath wife and children hath given hostages to fortune; for they are impediments to great enterprises, either of virtue or mischief. Certainly, the best works, and of greatest merit for the public, have proceeded from the unmarried or childless men, which both in affection and means have married and endowed the public. Yet, it were great reason that that those that have children should have greatest care of future times; unto which they know they must transmit their dearest pledges. Some there are, who though they lead a single life, yet their thoughts do end with themselves, and account future times impertinences. Nay, there are some others that account wife and children but as bills and changes. (Bacon 1969)

The text has the qualities of speech in the way in which it creates the illusion of a voice addressing a listener, or as a public oration. The use of connectors, 'Certainly . . . Yet . . . Nay', also makes it easy to recreate the text as a conversation. I do this here:

> *Speaker 1:* He that hath wife and children hath given hostages to fortune; for they are impediments to great enterprises, either of virtue or mischief.
> *Speaker 2:* [*agrees*] *Certainly*, the best works, and of greatest merit for the public, have proceeded from the unmarried or childless men, which both in affection and means have married and endowed the public.
> *Speaker 3* [*disagrees*] *Yet*, it were great reason that that those that have children should have greatest care of future times; unto which they know they must transmit their dearest pledges.

In modern texts the alternating voices are better hidden. This type of disguise may require substantial authorial skill, one which students attend university to acquire. Consider this academic text:

> Thus, Chomskyans have made a point of stressing that a grammar, as conceived within the formalist tradition, could not in principle be learned by any general learning mechanism. For this reason the basic architecture of the grammar has to be prewired into the human mind. The evidence for this claim is none other than linguistic theory itself.

Cognitive linguistics (with a capital C) approaches the relation between language and cognition rather differently than the Chomskyan tradition. Rather than regard language as an autonomous component of the mind (and expect cognitive science to incorporate this perspective), language study is shaped from the outset by what is perceived to be plausible. (Taylor 2002: 8)

The text is discursive in the sense that it juxtaposes two different points of view. But these are abstracted as arguments that seem to unfold as a consequence of each other and do not require two voices. The view of a single speaker is subsumed into the opinion of an intellectual movement 'Chomskyans' or 'Cognitive linguists'. When separate from their proponents, the schools of thought acquire the powers of *agency*. 'Cognitive linguistics', thus 'approaches' a problem. A deep use of metaphor is therefore essential, with people becoming their ideas, and ideas 'approaching' 'problems'. The schools of thought do not so much state opinions as accomplish them as if they were actions. The result is that although the text is a dialogue in its juxtaposition of views, it reads as a monologue in how it attributes these views to the same voice.

Yet we should again be wary of assuming that this is a general feature of modern written language. Consider this text:

The earth is flat. Did you not know that? The US vice president Dick Cheney, speaking on behalf of Boy George's administration, now insists this is so – and expects both the American people and the world to buckle under and believe it, or else. OK, so may be this is going a little too far. But the more hawkish members of the Bush administration still expect the world to believe things that not even the 25-member 'interim government' of Iraq expects any more: that the US occupation of Iraq is 'very successful'. (Andrew Stephen: America, *New Statesman*, 29 September 2003)

This text does not swing between opinions so much as attribute one body of opinion to the author and the other to an imaginary protagonist, the President of the United States. The President wants us to believe the world is flat. Well, not quite. But he does want us to believe in a successful occupation of Iraq. At first sight this contemporary example seems to harp back to the seventeenth-century one from Francis Bacon in that the switch between voices is clearly marked, even with the insertion of a tag to close one utterance with a mock threat, then an opener from the second line. It could be written as follows:

First speaker: Buckle under and believe it, or else.
Second speaker: OK.

This is an interesting example of a written text employing a repertoire of conversational effects inside what is in fact a highly literate monologue.

The dialogic versus monologic contrast raises some quite interesting issues about written language and how it has developed. It shows how literacy may help to drive language in a particular direction, subsuming many voices into one, for example. Since that development was not immediate, we might also suspect that it was achieved with some difficulty, a point that literacy teachers should keep strongly in mind when they search for ways to teach argument structures. The last text, however, shows how dialogic and monologic features may exist in a complex interplay in all extended texts and that this will vary more from one text type to another than from speech to writing.

Durable vs. ephemeral

Before the invention of technologies to record the human voice, all sound was ephemeral and a message could endure only if it was encoded in a visual sign system. Information technology can, of course, put combinations of words into indefinite storage but it gives written language a virtual existence and a more ephemeral impression than did earlier writing technologies. The concept of an original manuscript that endures through time has become tenuous when it is simply encoded as a set of digits and stored for unlimited future production. There has almost been an historical tendency to develop writing technologies to a point where the written word can be treated as being as disposable as the spoken one. It may be that this sense of an ephemeral script is already starting to change the way we write and how much we write.

The extent to which writing endures is affected by both the technologies on which it depends and by the practices of which it is a part. The ephemeral nature of speech cannot always be assumed, however. Goody and Watt (1968: 31) admit to the importance of 'assimilating mechanisms' that non-literate societies use to store information of continuing 'social relevance'. These 'mechanisms' employ 'mnemonics' which 'offer some resistance' to an interpretative process that will change a text in its retelling. 'Formalised patterns of speech, recital under ritual conditions, the use of drums and other musical instruments, the employment of professional remembrancers' are devices that 'shield the content of the memory' from 'the pressures of the present' (ibid.: 31). In this vein we should not forget how many societies have used the development of literacy to record remembered oral epics, such as those of the Babylonian Gilgamesh story, the Homeric epics, the Hindu Vedas or the Norse Sagas, and these came into existence long before the society had a means to write them down.

Writing, however, does preserve a form of words, even if orality preserves its content. Such durability affects our use of text and our development of literacy practices. It is the ability to make a form of words endure which allows us to assume that writing can encode promises and that written text in general may have a higher truth value as if the facts themselves have set themselves down. This is how literacy gives form to law and law to the practices of linguistic interpretation in which the legal profession must engage.

Carriage of a form of words through time reinforces the awareness that writing cannot always depend upon a shared context of writer and reader to help elucidate its meaning. When giving a spoken command such as 'get that thing out of here', we know what 'that thing' refers to because we share a context with our listener. In a written instruction, however, the writer may have to expound upon the identity of the thing as in 'remove the vehicle you left outside my house'. We will explore this topic under the heading of contextualisation and will find that the pressure upon written language to create a context is far from being a fact of written discourse.

Contextualised vs. decontextualised

One generalisation about spoken as opposed to written registers concerns the density of nouns and their modifiers, or *nominal elements*. Conversation uses fewer nominal elements but more pronouns, as in the following example (Biber et al. 1999: 231):

> Well *I* thought you were going to talk to *me* about [Christmas presents] (Biber et al. 1999: 231; author's italics)

The nominal element is in square brackets, the pronouns are in Italics. This can be contrasted with the following sentence which has three nominal elements:

> [Nonlinear systems theory] is of [great importance] to [anyone interested in [feedback systems]] (ibid.)

Pronouns or other terms that are *anaphoric* refer to items mentioned previously in the text and those that are *cataphoric* refer to items mentioned in the text after them. For example, in the first sentence below, 'she' is anaphoric, and in the second, cataphoric:

1. Jane ate a steak before she went out.
2. She, I mean Jane, enjoyed her food.
3. She's all right, she is.

Anaphoric and cataphoric reference are both endophoric because they refer to items or a context in the text. *Exophoric* reference is to a context outside the text (Halliday and Hassan 1976). For example, in the third sentence, 'she' might not refer to anybody in the text but to a person whom the speaker has seen leave the scene. The density of nominal elements in some forms of written language suggests that conversation tends to be more heavily exophoric than written language and less catophoric or exophoric. A high density of nominal elements in a text suggests that it is more endophoric because it has to build its own context by describing what it discusses.

Consider this translation of the nineteenth-century French novel, *Germinal*, by Emile Zola. He is describing the ascent of miners to their coal face:

> Etienne had to follow. The chimney was a private way left through the seam, by which miners could reach all the secondary roads. It was the same width as the coal seam, scarcely sixty centimetres, and it was as well that he was thin, for in his experience he hoisted himself up with needless waste of energy, pulling in his shoulders and haunches and moving up by sheer strength of arm as he clung to the timbers. The first gallery was fifteen metres up but they had to go on further, as the face on which Maheu and his gang were working was the sixth – up in hell, they called it. The galleries spaced one above the other at fifteen metre intervals, seemed to go on forever, and to climb up this narrow fissure was scraping the skin off his back and chest. (Zola 1968: 48)

Zola is renowned for his descriptive detail. This text is prefaced by a short sentence 'Etienne had to follow'. The rest of the text can be read as providing a context for the word 'follow'. It elaborates on what 'follow' in this context means. It must do this because it assumes that its readers will not be familiar with life in this particular coal mine or in any coal mine. The text constructs the context by using 'measurements': 'sixty centimetres', 'fifteen metres up', 'at fifteen metre intervals'. Our ability to visualise these measurements will vary from reader to reader but may be less important than the cumulative feeling they convey of a surveyor who is setting out a place before us with an aggregation of detail that makes it impossible for us to doubt its existence. This descriptive detail makes the text highly endophoric. However, this quality may not simply be a product of the fact that an author is trying to share a context with his readers that they do not know. There is also the pressure of interpretation, or of an author who is trying to convey a context as he has experienced it, thus making the reader live it through their eyes.

The following text was written seventy years earlier:

> They entered the woods, and bidding adieu to the river for a while, ascended some of the higher grounds; whence in spots where the opening of the trees gave the eye power to wander, were many charming views of the valley, the opposite hills, with the long range of the woods

overspreading many, and occasionally part of the stream. Mr. Gardner expressed a wish of going round the whole park, but it was feared it might be beyond a walk. With a triumphant smile, they were told that it was ten miles round. It settled the matter; and they pursued the accustomed circuit; which brought them again, after some time, in a descent among hanging woods, to the edge of the water in one of its narrowest parts. (Austen 1972: 274)

A notable feature is that this text probably 'describes' a larger and more varied topography than the first. Yet it does so with far fewer words. It is also significant that this text occurs in a novel where such descriptive detail is very rare. In the opening sentence of the text, the landscape is unfolded not as a context in which the protagonists will find themselves but as a product of their progression through it. The text does not build a context for itself but assembles a few pieces from the larger scene that we must assume to be there. This has an exophoric quality. There is a reference to 'many charming views', but the author feels no need to set out what such scenes must be composed of if they are to 'charm' us. There is thus an assumption that reader and author will share in their concept of what makes a scene beautiful, and beauty itself can evoke a shared physical picture. The writer is making a class assumption about a shared context. She lives in the world of her social group, assuming they share her notion of what makes a view charming, thus rendering a detailed description unnecessary.

On the basis of the difference between these two texts, it is tempting to speculate on how the first emerges from a growing understanding of how we can use language to control the context. The development of this endophoric capacity may relate to a growing understanding of how literacy can carry meaning through space and time, bringing the remote and unfamiliar environment of a coal mine into the middle-class drawing rooms of the period.

However, in speaking about the endophoric quality of written language, we should be clear that we are doing no more than attesting to a pressure that evolves out of the nature of certain literacy practices. As our above analysis shows, different types of practice will produce different degrees of endophoricity. Zola's *Germinal* may be highly endophoric, constructing its own context in painstaking detail. By contrast, a sign on the door marked 'Exit' is highly exophoric, because it is meaningful only if contextualised by its proximity to a door. As those who have been misdirected by a twisted sign post know too well, such texts take most of their larger meaning from their physical context. At a midway point between the highly endophoric and exophoric, we might find letters or e-mails between friends who are separated by a considerable distance. Some references will be contextualised by the shared experience of the reader and writer. Others will have to be clarified by the text because they may emerge from the different environments that the two correspondents inhabit.

Scannable vs. linearly accessible

Chafe's (1982) larger understanding of the differences between spoken and written languages rests in the view that this may not be a question of how a text is constructed but of how we relate to it. The consumer or producer of written text has more choice in how they interact with it. They have the choice of dipping in and out of spoken language but they cannot scroll a spoken text, home in upon key words and find the information they require. There are two consequences of this. The first is that literacy means exploiting the fact that written language can be scanned. Thus, writers arrange texts with headings, subheadings, numerical systems, paragraphs and clear sentence boundaries so that readers can find information quickly. They are no longer obliged to stay hooked up to an unfolding text or risk losing its continuity. They are free to reorganise the text in a way that is determined by the purpose they have for it, beginning with the conclusion, for example, then working back.

Allowing the text's user freedom to play with its order is a clear privilege of the written medium. The related concept of an index and an alphabetical order allows us to organise and retrieve information from text according to need. This order owes everything to an agreed convention about how we arrange the graphemes that encode the phonemes of a language; it does not root in any natural linguistic principle. The concept of an alphabetic order spawned a host of referencing and administrative practices. The use of alphabetic orders in indexes and contents pages has done much to reconstruct the reader's relationship to text. They can treat text as multidirectional, sequencing it according to their interest rather than just the author's. Related conventions exploit the spatial dimension of literacy in order to extend our semiotic capacity, using various tabular arrangements of data to let us create different meanings according to whether we read across or down a column. Tabulation is another tool of literacy that frees us from entrapment in a single temporal sequence, allowing us to participate in the ordering of a text and to vary our point of entry and exit.

Planned/highly structured vs. spontaneous/loosely structured

Again we are talking about tendencies here rather than absolute contrasts. Editing operates in both speech and writing. In speech we can monitor what we say to different degrees and will use words with different degrees of spontaneity and care. We can also practise what we are going to say, something speakers are advised to do before important and formal situations, such as job interviews. Yet we cannot unsay what we have said, nor do we have the same capacity to review and contrast different combinations of words. The planning capacity afforded by a visual medium may also account for the aversion of written text to elision and its emphasis upon complete sentences as if writing proffered a medium through which we can idealise language as complete units of sense, each with a subject and a verb.

The development of information technology has had two opposite effects on this quality of 'editability', and such polarity still lacks systematic exploration. On the one hand, the speed of exchange in e-mails and text-messages can simulate the informality of speech, though the use of semographs and abreviations means that we would be mistaken to see this as taking semiosis back to its heavily contextualised, oral form. On the other hand, the computer affords great scope for text editing. The nature of this effect on how we construct formal written language and how we should study it, however, has yet to receive full treatment. One area for exploration could lie in how we write introductions to reports, case studies, academic essays and research articles. Introductions to these *genres* may either *signpost* the content of the article to come by saying what it will contain and conclusions that it will draw, or, in the case of the report, they will preface the body of the text with its recommendations. Both practices mean that readers who do not need to grasp the finer detail of an argument or research project can grasp its essence from the first few paragraphs.

Consider the first two paragraphs of an introduction to an article on literacy pedagogy and the empowerment of children. I have placed these inside a *text-frame* in order to show the 'communicative' *moves* made by the text. The terminology for these moves, although partly developed by the author in order to describe this text, also owes much to Swales (1990) and his move structure analysis of research article introductions.

General summary of article	This chapter is based on a micro-ethnographic study conducted in a second grade classroom of a rural primary school in North India.
Elaboration of the summary	It describes and analyzes the means through which children appropriate literacy; the purpose that drove their development as writers; and the ways in which, as they enacted their purposes in this context, they grew as persons or were empowered.
Definition of terms	The term *appropriation* is used in this context to mean 'making one's own.' To appropriate literacy is to add to one's symbolic repertoire, aiding one in interpretative, constructive, creative interaction with the world and others in it. Appropriation is also used in the Marxian sense of appropriating a power-commodity or a set of practices controlled by dominant classes or cultures.
Reference to the literature	Empowerment has been conceived largely in political terms by critical educators like Freire, Giroux, Lankshear and others.

continued

Finding a research niche	In this chapter, I suggest that this conception of empowerment and critical pedagogy is more appropriate for adults than for children.
Giving the research outcome	The main thrust of this chapter is a presentation of a reconstructed definition of empowerment and power in children's terms.
Summarising research methods	This study centers on classroom life in general and four focal children in particular. In this chapter, I refer to only two of the children.
	Sahni (2001: 19–20)

After giving the structure of the article and its conclusions, the introduction recounts the methodology that was used to conduct the study. Whether it refers to the literature, the research niche or the research outcome, the larger part of this text is a signpost which guides the reader through the text by saying what is in it.

Such texts invert a traditional narrative order by placing their conclusions at the beginning. The traditional story mimics a concept of unfolding time where we are held in suspense as to what the future will bring. As Labov (1972) pointed out, the end of the story is a 'resolution' of the problems or 'complications' that arise within it. A structure such as the one above shows how literacy can free us from entrapment in the time-constrained linearity speech, letting us create a new narrative sequences.

One consequence of the potential for editing written language is to downplay the extent to which pre-literate societies may organise and give ritual form to speech, creating the practices that we can group under the notion of oracy. Oral cultures prize story-telling and ritualised performance. Such social practices are carried forward into literate societies. I have witnessed their durability among literate people in Central Africa, while in a formal study Stagg (1998) documented a drift away from the culture of oracy across the generations of West Indian family as they became acculturated to the more consciously literate environment of the UK. An important conclusion is that it may be more informative to document changes in social practices than to insist that one form is given greater structure than another by its literacy focus.

Yet the ritualised use of spoken language should not divert from the evident differences in structure between spoken and written texts. When one examines unedited transcriptions of speech, one of the most notable features is how transposing speech into the written medium makes its spontaneity and lack of form all the more evident, perhaps because writing sets up certain expectations about order and sequencing. Corpus linguists examine collections of authentic texts that are organised according to the register in which they operate and are also coded in a way that identifies the type of discourse being used. The corpus linguistic endeavour has done much to uncover how language is really used in both spoken and written registers.

Consider this example of part of a narrative, taken from the Lancaster spoken corpus:

> *Speaker 1:* He was a good arguer was he?
>
> *Speaker 2:* Oh, oh yes. I remember I went to Birmingham, I'd been out of work here and I went to Birmingham Carriage and Wagon Company they'd got five Pullman coaches for Chatham & South Eastern as it was then and they were in satin wood. Well they were only carriage finishers, they couldn't clean work veneer, no and clean it up and there were about six of us went from here. And while I went in February and while I was down there machinists were out at Waring and Gillows for about six week and they only got ha'penny an hour when it was settled. Ha'penny. Not this ere ten pound they're getting today, that was two shilling a week. Eh? (Extract from file 069, Lancaster SW & TP Spoken Corpus, http://www.ling.lancs.ac.uk/stwp/sample.htm)

The text is a narrative but the narrator makes no attempt to separate the events from himself and array them as a sequence upon a time line. The speaker eschews such linear organisation, embedding one anecdote inside a sentence dedicated to the expression of another, then embedding another clause inside this. For example, the larger purpose of the text is to talk about how the speaker's father led an industrial dispute. It is in answer to the question about 'being a good arguer'. This response is given in the form of a story about a trip the speaker took with his father. The speaker explains how they made the trip to do some work for a railway coach company. The explanation digresses into an anecdote upon the company's inability to put the appropriate 'finish' on the woodwork of their Pullman coaches. A relative clause without a relative pronoun ('they'd got . . .') is embedded to explain this. Another clause is embedded inside that one ('as it was then'), in order to explain how this company has undergone a change of name since. These multiple embeddings pull the text away from its principal objective, placing the narrator and not the narrative at the centre of the text. Such embedded structures are quite common in spoken language. Biber et al. (1999) cite several examples, which I will discuss in the next section.

We cannot assume that all oral narratives expand out from their original purpose and eschew linear progression in quite the way the Lancaster spoken corpus example does. However, the act of transposing this type of text into a written medium will provoke a bewildered response from many readers, because a written mode sets up the expectation of a better planned and more clearly focused narrative.

Syntactically complex vs. syntactically simple

At first sight this type of dichotomy seems based upon a clear misunderstanding of the nature of spoken language. Our examination of the text from the Lancaster spoken corpus reveals multiple embeddings and Biber et al., in their excellent *Grammar of Spoken and Written English*, find that speakers in conversation 'use a number of relatively complex and sophisticated relative clauses constructions with a deeply embedded gap' (1999: 7). We can see how this operates in an example drawn from an authentic spoken corpus:

There's so many things [that I want to learn < >]
That's the bit [that we don't tend to know so much about < >]

The gap where one would expect a noun phrase to occur is marked < >. One might, for example, anticipate an additional relative clause as in: 'so many things that I want to learn, that I just don't know where to start'. By contrast Biber et al. (1999: 7) point out that academic writers do not always live up to their reputation for using extended forms. Academics also omit relative pronouns:

Silicates are classified and named according to the way [the tetrahedra are linked]

Instead of:

Silicates are classified and named according to the way [in which the tetrahedra are linked]

It is a moot point, however, whether the omission of relative pronouns constitutes simplification in itself. Biber's overwhelming finding is that complexity in relative clauses is not a property of speech or writing but of a more specific way of use. Complex relative clauses are most common in conversation. The simplified version is more common in expository texts such as the science example cited above. We should also remember that many prose writers will deliberately look for a simple, muscular style, sometimes to unravel complicated issues. Such a style, with its use of short but complete sentences, is another way of using the opportunities that written text affords for editing. Arguably, it obtains a quite contrary result in syntactic complexity to the one that traditional views of writing might lead us to expect.

One way in which writing responds to its own capacity to endure is to try to predict the contexts to which it is likely to refer. Laws provide a prime example of this because they are written in order to regulate future events. *Binomials* and *multinomials* are sentences that employ two or more phrases in the same grammatical category. 'The good, the bad and the ugly came to town' might be an example, where 'the good', 'the bad' and 'the ugly' are all in same category. These expressions are also common in academic writing but rare in conversation (Biber et al. 1999: 1033). They are used by legal drafts-people to predict the future contexts to which laws will refer and are a common feature of legal texts. Gustaffason (1975, 1984, cited in Bhatia 1993). Bhatia (1993: 108–9) cites the following example from section 4 of the Indian Prevention of Corruption Act of 1947:

> Where in any trial offence punishable under [*section 161 or section 165 of the Indian Penal Code or of an offence referred to in clause B of subsection (1) of section 5 of this Act punishable under subsection (2) thereof*] it is proved that an accused person [*has accepted or obtained, or has agreed to accept or attempted to obtain,*] [*for himself, or any other person*] [*any gratification (other than legal remuneration) or any valuable thing for any person*] it shall be presumed unless the contrary is proved that he [*accepted or obtained, or agreed to accept or attempted to obtain*] [*that gratification or that valuable thing,*] as the case may be, [*as a motive or reward such as is mentioned in the said section 161, or as the case may be,*] without consideration [*or for a consideration which he knows to be inadequate.*] (Square brackets and italics inserted by the author)

In the above text I have used square brackets to mark out the occurrence of the bi- and multinomial expressions. For example, in the first occurrence these belong to the prepositional phrase that begins with 'under' or further down we find multiple verbs or verb phrases, 'accepted, obtained, agreed to accept, attempted to obtain' preceded by one common subject 'he'. If this were a spoken sentence one would also wonder if its complications might lose the reader. For example, after 'accepted' a listener would anticipate an object, but the object 'any gratification' is separated from the verb by a series of multinomial expressions, stretching our short-term memory to a point where we may have forgotten the subject or verb-phrase by the time we reach the object. Our ability to track back in written text means that this is not the problem it would be if spoken. Again, it is evident that simple contrasts between written and spoken language fail. Different types of language use encourage different forms of complexity. This is not an issue of writing being more complicated than speech. But it may be an example of certain literacy practices developing complexities that would not be operable in a spoken medium. The production and decipherment of these elaborate forms may come to characterise the practice.

Concerned with past and future not the present

Because literacy creates a textual archive it brings history into being, separating it from myth (Ong 1982, 1986). Literacy's carriage of language across time also pertains to its larger construction of a future. In the culture of Central America's Aztecs the calendar was so central that it was a major force in stimulating the development of writing. For medieval monasteries it meant treating their collective existence as a clock whose tick would measure out others' lives (see Chapter 3). By contrast the argument is that oral speech is situated in the here-and-now, fashioning its meanings from the present, shared context of its interlocutors.

In text, an expectation that speech is *situated*, or dependent, on a shared, present context would lead us to expect different patterns of tense use between speech and writing. Biber et al. (1999) find that the preference for the present tense is strong in conversation, giving some initial credence to the view that a speaker's focus is on the immediate context (ibid.: 457). But academic writing also has a high use of the present tense. This academic use of the present may result from the need to assert that a meaning will endure, for, as an unmarked form, the English present tense is used to situate meaning outside time (the problem *continues* to cause confusion, under such conditions it rarely *survives* for long).

A less surprising conclusion is that writers of fictional prose will use past tense verbs much more frequently than present tense ones. We should also note that the use of the present tense may be associated not with mode (speech vs. writing) but with the type of meaning that a verb expresses. Thus *epistemic verbs*, or ones that express mental states or mental attitudes towards a topic, will occur commonly in the present because they express the interlocutor's continuing stance towards the topic that they want to unfold: 'I bet he's starving for real grub' (ibid.: 459). On the other hand, words that report speech are commonly in the past, perhaps because we are often less concerned with 'saying' what we mean than recounting what we said. This indicates again that language is not simply controlled by its mode or medium, but by the larger pressures of the context in which it unfolds. Some language functions, such as narration or recounting speech events, require the past; others, such as expressing an attitude to what we say, use the present.

Formal vs. informal

The formality or informality of text will be an attribute of context. A text is not formal because it is written down or informal because it is spoken. It is formal because it is put to a formal purpose. One of the simplest ways to look at differences between spoken and written language is as an attribute of their function. Thus, while it is difficult to characterise context dependence as a consistence property of spoken language, it may be easier to decide that it is a property of certain types of text with a specific range of communicative functions.

A broad difference identified by Tannen (1985) is that written text is 'message-oriented' while spoken text is more socially directed. Thus we use speech to develop relationships with other people by engaging their attention and interest but employ writing to set out a scientific or historical record. A tendency towards this type of functional specialisation in speech and writing would mean that formal language is more a product of written language's message-bearing function and less related to its being written down. Bearing a message might, for example, place a premium upon accuracy and hence upon a considered use of language where meaning cannot be deduced from context. A social function, on the other hand, would put as much stress on feeling, tone of voice and supporting non-verbal strategies as on what is actually said. We should not forget, however, that writing also has a social function while speech will sometimes be dedicated to a formal, message-bearing task. Personal letter-writing has a motivation that is primarily social. The development of letter-writing towards e-mail and text-messaging has compelled some uses of language towards the informal forms associated with speech, but, as I noted in Part II, it has also exploited mechanisms of meaning representation that are purely visual and hence, literate, in nature.

Expository- and argument-oriented vs. event- and narrative-oriented

Olson (1994) has argued that the alphabet itself promotes analytic thought because it is by its nature analytic of the phonemic construction of language, isolating and representing the units of which language is composed. Alphabetic literacy fosters within it, therefore, an analytic approach to other areas of endeavour, expounding upon events and building a scientific record.

In Europe in the seventeenth century, the spread of printed material and a rise in levels of literacy was paralleled by a growing interest in both deductive or *Cartesian* approaches to philosophy and scientific enquiry. Cartesian method, named after the French philosopher René Descartes, builds its structures on the assumption that if one can find one statement which one knows to be true and deduce all subsequent thought out of it, then that thought will also be true. Descartes' famous truth was *cogito ergo sum*, 'I think, therefore I am'. The assumption behind such a method is that one can fix the value of words as if they were mathematical symbols. Thus one can say 'thought' = 'consciousness' just as one can say '$x = 2$' at the beginning of a mathematical calculation, and know that its value will remain '2' no matter what operation is performed upon it. The problem is that as every student of semantics or philosophy knows, words do not have strictly defined values in the way that a mathematical symbol does. The meanings of words will change according to the context in which they are used. Metaphor and other figurative devices such as simile or metonymy exert a highly subversive effect. They permit even basic terms such as 'think' to refer to a cognitive process at one instance, 'I think therefore I am', and to an expression of modality, in this case doubt about the action that when intends to accomplish as in 'I think I'll go'.

The problem is no less great for thinkers who are interested in developing a discourse of empirical enquiry. Empiricism finds its truths by observing the world. It therefore searches for a language that will represent real events without the mediation of rhetoric or other persuasive devices. 'Metaphor threatens the objectivity of rational argument with the involuntary interference of the mind that argues' (Holme 2003a). This deductivist and empiricist search for uncorrupt meaning finds a later expression in what Foucault (1974) characterised as the neo-classical aspiration to a univocal discourse. It was a discourse that searched for a one-to-one correspondence between words and categories of things.

The extract from Jane Austen cited above bears the imprint of this univocal aspiration. As shown, this text shows an exophoric tendency, or quite a strong context dependence. The writer assumes that her readers operate with a strong class and cultural consensus as to the field of reference of a given term. An ironic consequence is that the modern reader is in fact set free to construct the author's meanings more as they would wish. We have seen how words evoke larger categories and these categories are modelled by the individual according to the culture in which they exist and the experiences that they have had. An author who writes with an assumption that she is using a verbal currency of fixed meanings may in fact give the reader greater freedom to fashion those meanings in the way they see fit. A univocal style may therefore produce another need. This is to establish a firm consensus as to what words and sentences do really mean. A consequence is the strong eighteenth-century interest in dictionaries, grammars and scientific taxonomies. Dr Samuel Johnson, who provided a model for Jane Austen's prose style, was also the author of one of the most comprehensive early English dictionaries. The dictionary emerged from a growing interest in standardising English meaning which began with Robert Cawdrey's dictionary of 2,500 words in 1604 and Elisha Cole's 25,000 word effort in 1676 (Barber 1993: 204). Diderot had given the French language another model while Linnaeus had begun the vast task of producing a taxonomy of the natural world.

In the eighteenth century, an interest in a correct grammar was also widespread. In English, the appeal was to what constituted rational language and to the growing perception that a correct or 'literate' use of language conferred social distinction. On the logical side, grammarians legislated against double negatives, for example, on the mathematical assumption that two negatives would result in a positive. This was far from being a natural attribute of the language, as Shakespeare attests:

I have one heart, one bosom and one truth,
And that no woman has, *nor never* none
Shall mistris be of it, save I alone.
(*Twelfth Night*, cited in Barber 1993: 205)

Far from cancelling each other out, the three negatives in this quotation work together to add emphasis, yet the imposition of a logical principle makes two of them redundant. Such a mathematical approach to language is also a product of the expository role given it by literacy as well as by the manner in which literacy entraps discourse like a biological specimen, holding it up to scrutiny.

The use of literacy to capture language for analysis and re-engineering also overlaps with its function as a kind of linguistic 'deep freeze'. After the American War of Independence, the scholar Noah Webster wanted to present the new American Republic with a pure and democratic mode of expression. He also wanted to guard against the possibility of the political detachment of the United States from England being regarded as a licence to allow English to deviate from a standard form and devolve into a series of mutually unintelligible dialects. The American interest in language whose literate form could afford equality of access to all its citizens resulted in his semi-rationalisation and standardisation of English spellings, with, for example, the French influenced 're' in 'centre' being changed to 'er'.

In the eighteenth century, we can therefore see how American and European literacies fostered the interest of language in its own meanings, encouraging prescriptions of use and the development of a concept of correct language. Yet such practices do not amount to some broader expository or analytic tendency in literacy itself. It is evident that literacy allows the development of a scientific record, but this does not justify the assumption that alphabetic literacy leads inevitably towards the development of such a record. Scientific literacies should be treated no differently from other literacy practices. They arise from a complex interaction of other socio-cultural practices and their concerns. Among these one might number: the Greek tradition of philosophical enquiry; Arabic numerals, the use of '0' and the development of algebra; new literacy technologies such as paper-making and printing; the collapse of a centralised ecclesiastical authority; and a growing interest in textual interpretation fostered by legal and biblical commentaries. In their turn, science's expository needs may help develop expository and univocal discourses. But such a development does not preclude the use of literacy to examine language's figurative capacity within other genres and other practices.

Abstract vs. concrete

Removing language from its immediate context may arguably pressurise it into constructing more meanings out of itself and fewer from the world to which it at first referred. We saw in the previous section how in seventeenth- and eighteenth-century Europe the advent of mass literacy spawned sets of practices that were focused upon the definition of words. If language users stop making straightforward, shared assumptions about the meanings of the terms that they use and try to tie these down with other terms, then language consists less of meanings that are shaped by the world, developing a tendency to become a self-referential system. It is the difference between expressing the number '2' as '1 more than 1 and one less than 3' instead of simply pointing towards two objects of the same kind. According to the first definition, our notion of '2' is constructed out of its relation to other numerical terms. It supposes a language that is developing into an abstract system, able to shape its own meanings, if not totally to determine them. Some might argue that this tendency means that literacy encourages its users to engage in an act of huge self-deception. Numbers are relatively easy to define as parts of the relational system described above. We can determine what '3' is in relation to '4' and '4' in relation to '5'. Yet, as we saw in our brief discussion of Rosch, Lakoff and radial category theory, other categories are not defined according to the absence or presence of a fixed set of features, they exist as the groupings of the sometimes quite different phenomena into which we organise the world. By allowing us to stabilise and rework the meanings with which we deal, literacy may help us to foster the illusion that word meanings are more stable and consistent than they are.

Literacy's association with abstraction may actually be more basic still. If we accept writing as a series of metasigns, or signs of signs, then it is arguable that we are dealing with a more remote system of representation. Language represents one level of abstraction. When we combine the phonemes 'c-a-t' and agree that they refer to a category of animals, and not to an individual creature or 'token', we have already moved up to one level of abstraction. We are referring not to actual animals but to what Saussure would have termed a cat 'concept'. We may be ignoring the differences between lions, cheetahs and pet cats in order to treat them as one and the same. The act of ignoring individual differences presupposes an act of abstraction because it suggests that 'cat' does not actually refer to anything in the world but to a category we have inferred out of it. A further act of abstraction occurs as a consequence of our dealing in the 'c-a-t' symbol as opposed to the animal itself. We can, for example, place the 'cat' symbol on a 'moon' symbol even though no cat could ever get there. We can also understand this conjunction of objects while attesting to its impossibility. When we take the 'c-a-t' sign and represent it with another sign, then arguably we are moving even further from the reality in which that combination of phonemes is anchored.

It is one thing to suggest that written language has an abstract tendency built into it and another to say that this results in a more abstract use of language. One way to find out if this is what happens would be to look at the frequency of 'noun complement clauses'. Noun-complement clauses are typically 'that' or 'to' clauses which give us more information about a noun in a sentence:

These figures lead to *an expectation that* the main application area would be in office environments

Legal peers renewed their attack on the Government's *plans to* shake up the legal profession yesterday. (Biber et al. 1999: 645, noun and complementiser in the author's italics)

For our present purposes, an interesting feature of these structures is that the noun is generally abstract because it represents our feelings towards the topic under consideration. They express whether we have feelings of doubt, certainty or of how our information about it is sourced. Also of interest is that the noun structure often has an equivalent expression which uses a verb. Thus one could paraphrase 'lead to an expectation that' as 'we hope that'. An expectation might be that spoken language deals with immediate actions and representations of states of mind on the part of the speaker, resulting in a preference for the verbs. Yet again, this is not an issue of speech or writing. Conversation certainly has a very low use of noun complements and we tend to say 'we hope the story is true' and not 'the story leads us to the hope that it is true'. But written fiction also has a quite low rate of abstract noun complements, though more than treble that of conversation. The usage is much more common in news reports and academic texts (Biber 1988). In this small instance of language use, a drift towards an abstract, decontextualised form of language is again more a function of genre and register than of mode or medium.

Syntactically and morphologically complete

Because language is constantly changing we use a morphology that may have become redundant to our need to express a meaning clearly. Thus in the quotation below a speaker omits the morpheme '-ly' from 'previous'. According to the conventions of written grammar it is necessary to show that the adverb 'previously' and not the adjective 'previous' is being used. Yet we have absolutely no difficulty understanding this sentence, perhaps because the syntax, or the position of 'previous', gives us its function as a modifier of the verb. Morphology is no longer central to our interpretation:

Previous to that, he played for us. (author's data)

Many of the rules governing the morphology of the English language were imposed by eighteenth-century grammarians who used a classical language model of what a grammar should be. Their concept of grammaticality was largely derived from Latin, an inflected language with a quite complicated morphology. Latin needs inflections to distinguish between adjectives and adverbs, for example. Therefore one language with a complex system of inflections provided a yardstick of grammaticality for a language that was less dependent on them. The result was the construction of a written form which stipulated the need for features that were no longer common or necessary in speech, thus creating an artificial disjunction between speech and writing, one which owed more to a prescriptive principle than the functional or expressive needs of language. Because to be literate was a norm for the middle and upper classes and prescriptions for the use of written language also furnished a model for speech, the ability to apply this model to one's wider use of language evolved into a badge of class identity.

Another influence may come from the nature of writing itself. Because writing will hold a given sentence before us it affords more time to assess how it is formed. Ellipsis refers to the omission of words or parts of words; it is quite common in speech but less so in writing. Carter (1997) held that one of the most salient and constant characteristics of spoken language is its use of elided forms. Consider this exchange, for example:

Speaker 1: You going now?
Speaker 2: Yeah, just a sec. (author's data)

A written version of this text would require several insertions in order to satisfy the expectations that writers have for this medium. A complete version could be written as follows:

'Are you going now?'
'Yes I am going now, just wait a second.'

It is doubtful whether the entire verb phrase 'I am going now' would be repeated, even in written form. But the example shows how it is believed that we mentally complete incomplete forms so that we can *parse* their syntactic string, dividing it into components, according to a pattern we understand. Whether we actually do this is a moot point. It might be that we have schematised or stored phrases such as 'going now?' or 'just a sec' as meaningful patterns.

We can also note how we elide, or leave out, parts of the words themselves. We say 'sec' instead of 'second', thus eliding a syllable, '-ond'. We also say 'yeah' instead of 'yes', thus leaving out the phoneme 's'. It may even be that written language is helping to keep some 'complete' forms in being because even as we elide them we stand corrected by the complete model that is upheld as a correct standard.

Some of the factors that push a conversation towards syntactic incompleteness may lie in the way it unfolds. Conversation contains overlaps, as when speakers talk at the same time, with one trailing off as another takes the floor. Conversation also supplements itself with gesture or other forms of body language. Equally, it can make a calculated use of pauses where an interlocutor is meant to infer their own meaning or simply circle a meaning that is never spelt out and so never results in a complete sentence:

'I think you already know that . . .'
'Ok, but . . .'

'But?'
'Nothing. No, it's OK.'

Different spoken registers or genres also require different degrees of completeness. In courtrooms, for example, lawyers will press their clients to give full answers. But the fact that they must do this may reveal how an everyday use of spoken language may require disambiguation when transposed into a formal context; one which has been created out of the literacy-based practices of the law.

Conclusions

The above analysis reveals how when contrasting spoken and written language according to a set group of opposing features, we are unlikely to produce generalisations that are more substantive than statements such as 'writing is space constrained while speech is time constrained'. Nevertheless, the issues I discussed earlier are useful as pointers that can show some of the directions in which writing may develop language.

Every apprentice writer quickly understands how they cannot write the way they speak. Researchers must therefore provide teachers with a clearer sense of what must be taught when their students move from the spoken medium to the written. For this reason, the above discussion may be helpful if it points up the core issue that will be discussed in the next two chapters. This is that a given text configures and is configured by a given context. The medium of that text, whether it is written or spoken, is only one of the many ways in which it interacts with its context. We therefore need to think more closely about how other aspects of context and culture shape text so that we can discern the effects that writing has on language, then think how these can be formulated as a pedagogical tool. Such an approach means that we cannot assert that the use of the written medium does 'x' or 'y'. What we can do is consider how it may act as one among the many forces that configure a particular type of text. In Chapter 10 I will show how quantitative types of analysis can help us in that task. In Chapter 11 I will take a qualitative perspective.

Exercises

1. Consider this table of potential differences between written and spoken language:

Writing is:	*Speech is:*
objective	interpersonal
a monologue	a dialogue
durable	ephemeral

decontextualised	contextualised
scannable	only linearly accessible
planned/highly structured	spontaneous/loosely structured
syntactically complex	syntactically simple
concerned with past and future	concerned with the present
formal	informal
expository	narrative
argument-oriented	event-oriented
abstract	concrete
syntactically and morphologically complete	syntactically and morphologically incomplete
mediational	communicative

Working as a class or group, find some contrasting types of text such as: a poem from any era, science articles or treatises from different epochs, business or personal letters, academic essays, examples of writing from primary or elementary school children (age 9–11), laboratory experiment instructions or reports in science text books, broadsheet and tabloid newspaper articles, e-mails or text messages. Apply the above criteria to your text and present what this tells you about your text's use of spoken and written language. Retain these texts for question 2.

2. Thinking about Tannen's (1982) suggestion of continuum between spoken and written texts, draw this across the board as follows:

Figure 9.1 A continuum of difference between speech and writing

Using Blue Tack of something similar, place the texts on a suitable point on the above continuum. Note under it the features that have led you to place it there.

3. Use exercise 2 to make a study with examples of how spoken and written text may differ.

10 Dimensions of Difference between Spoken and Written Language

Introduction

It is now clear that we will obtain more useful information if we focus less on larger generalisations about the nature of spoken and written texts and more on the specific linguistic features that cause one type of text to differ from another. Second, the above discussion shows how we should look more at variations among different registers or genres of text and less at differences that simply depend on whether they are spoken or written. We can then consider the difference between 'natural conversation' in speech, for example, and 'the service encounter' that scripts commercial interactions such as the payment for services, finally asking whether these two forms show a consistent variation when contrasted with other genres such as narratives or academic texts in writing. In Biber's (1988) terminology, we can then look at 'dimensions' of difference between these different types of text.

In this chapter, I will explore what a *dimension of difference* actually means. I will then look at some dimensions that have been examined. Finally, I will assess the merits of this type of quantitative approach.

What is a dimension of difference?

For Biber (1988: 15) a text *'dimension* comprises an independent group of co-occurring linguistic features'. The absence or presence of these features shows how far a text possesses a given attribute. These attributes are referred to as *factors.* For example, his dimension 1 will show whether text can be categorised as having the factor 'involved' or 'informational production'. In other words, the dimension plots whether a speaker or writer inserts themselves into their text in order to take up a stance towards the meaning they unfold. When we produce a conversation, one attribute is how we are subject to the 'strict' 'constraints' of time. Time constraints mean that we cannot fully plan what we say, selecting the most appropriate noun to express a given meaning, for example. This may result in a lower density of nouns and nominalisations. In conversation we also position ourselves towards a given topic. This need to construct an attitude towards a topic means that we will make more frequent use of what Quirk et al. (1985: 1180–1) call *private verbs*. These verbs characterise our engagement with the world. They appear more frequently in conversation because we have to 'anticipate' events, 'reveal' hidden facts or 'think' about deep questions.

Writing tends to be less constrained by time, we can afford conscious thought to what is the right term, letting terminology do the talking for us. This results in a higher density of nouns and a lower use of pronouns that refer to things in our immediate physical context. By the same token, specific nominal terms or technical nouns and noun phrases are often longer orthographically, making word length another variable that comprises this factor. Further, we use prepositions to 'pack more information' into this *nominal*, or noun-dense, discourse. For example, in the following sentence, the preposition 'in' is used four times, first to position the topic, 'abnormalities', second to specify the topic's nature as 'abnormalities in personal relatedness', third and fourth to add information to the two adjectives 'onset' and 'degree':

> Having said this, there are also indications that at least *in* many autistic children, abnormalities *in* personal relatedness are early *in* onset and profound *in* degree.

We can hypothesise, therefore, that a genre such as 'official documents' or 'academic prose' will position itself towards the informational production end of *dimension 1* because of the frequency of such features as nouns and prepositions, the use of longer words, or the relative rarity of private verbs. The genres 'telephone conversations' and 'face-to-face' conversations, on the other hand, will position themselves towards the 'involved' production end. However, interestingly, there is not a clear split between 'writing' and 'speech' along the axis of the dimension. Written genres such as personal letters and even romantic fiction also score positively for features attesting to informational production, though to a much lower degree. They are therefore more akin to conversation than academic prose in respect of this dimension.

Narrative vs. non-narrative concerns

Another factor in Biber's approach appraises 'narrative vs. non-narrative concerns', with narration being marked out by such variables as the use of the past tense and reported speech and the non-narrative or expository by such variables as the present tense or other expressions of immediate time. Here the split is even less consistent, as between speech and writing. The degree of variation is much lower overall but romantic fiction has a strong narrative content as do other types of fiction, while academic prose and official documents will have a lower involvement.

Explicit vs. situation-dependent reference

The third factor has some correspondence to the Hallidayan endophoric/exophoric distinction, discussed above. The factor is described as 'explicit vs. situation-dependent reference'. A dimension that explores this is the frequency of relative clauses. Relative clauses elaborate upon noun phrases, situating them in a textually expressed context. If they are absent it may be because the text gathers its more precise meaning from its immediate context of use. The dimension 'explicit situation reference' would seem to favour formal written genres, fulfilling our expectations about the endophoric nature of literate language. Broadcasts are exophoric, on the other hand, perhaps because they refer to a scene unfolding before a broadcaster's eyes.

Persuasion

A fourth factor deals with 'persuasion' and the extent to which 'this is marked overtly'. For example, a head adjective or verb can persuade a listener as to the speaker's attitude towards what they are saying, as in 'I'd be happy to do it (adjective) or I'd love to do it (verb)'. The frequency of modals is another variable since these can mark 'the speaker's attempts to persuade an addressee that certain events are probable', as in 'you should go' (ibid.: 148). These features are therefore two of the variables used to show that broadcasts have a low coefficient of overt persuasion while that for editorials and professional letters is high. Many genres, such as telephone conversations, prepared speeches and official documents, occupy a mid-point, however, having neither a high nor a low coefficient.

Higher lexical varieties

A fifth factor expresses how 'non-technical informational discourse' has a much higher lexical variety than abstract technical discourse. Academic texts are high here but romantic fiction is lower, as is face-to-face conversation. Again, texts position themselves upon the factor according to their genre and not according to mode. The positioning is based upon a dimension such as 'type/token ratio', or the ratio of how often different words are used to express the one idea.

Informational elaboration under strict, real-time conditions

Another factor looks at 'informational elaboration under strict, real-time conditions'. Such oral genres as prepared and spontaneous speeches or interviews scored high here, while most written types showed less evidence of the need to use such subordinate features as the 'that relative' which are used to elaborate upon the noun as in 'the warning that he gave'.

Conclusions

Biber's larger conclusion is that we cannot make a simple distinction between spoken and written texts that is based upon the mode factor alone. As the above summary shows, different genres will vary differently along a given dimension. However, this does not negate how some genres such as face-to-face conversation or academic prose will typify the constraints of their mode, showing more consistent differences to each other than others such as romantic fiction.

Though Biber completes one of the most systematic studies of the differences between spoken and written language we cannot forget the self-confessed limitations of his type of quantitative approach. The approach assumes a strong relationship between the quantifiable features and the dimension of which they are a variable than may be fully justified. For example, a relative clause may indicate how the text is endophoric, placing a sentence inside the context that it creates as in the non-defining clause below:

> The child, who had lived all his life a few miles from the sea, had still never seen it.

Doubtless, there is reasonable statistical support for this, but it is does not mean that relative clauses with an exophoric reference are implausible, as in this extract from a dialogue:

> Who do you mean?
> You know, the one who I was with last week.
> Oh him!

Second, a major difficulty with Biber's type of quantitative analysis is that although it may have some success in identifying grammatical features, or variables, that are commonly associated with a given register, it will be less successful when it comes to giving reasons for their use. Swales (1990) made this point well in respect of the use of the word 'given' as in a 'given variable'. His point was that an analysis based on quantification might show that in a scientific register this word had a higher frequency of use than in other types of text. However, such knowledge gave us no indication of how or when to use it. To provide this information the teacher needs to relate the use of the word to the text's larger communicative purpose as this is served by its larger organising principles. We would use the word 'given' to describe a variable when we wanted to make clear that while we are not talking about any variable we are not talking about one that is known to us either. It is a variable that our textual purpose has decided to select. Such a constriction of purpose in the selection of a given item needs to be related to the text's larger communicative purpose and the discourse structure that this imposes on it. If we are to look more closely at the nature of communicative purpose and the selection of language within a given register as this is affected by context, then we need to look more closely at this issue within the frame of communicative purpose and the construction of register. We will do this in the next chapter.

Exercises

1. Use the ideas in the chapter to decide how you would show dimensions of difference in respect of such factors as:
    Involved or informational production, narrative vs. non-narrative concerns, explicit vs. situation-dependent reference, persuasion, higher lexical varieties, informational elaboration under strict, real-time conditions.
2. With other students, brainstorm a list of text genres – for example, laws, fairy stories, student essays. Discuss how you think they might show the types of differences that are discussed above.

11 Written Language in Context

Introduction

In Chapter 2, my discussion of critical literacy looked at Halliday's understanding of language as existing inside a social context and thus as having evolved to convey the meanings that are a response to our social existence. A consequence of this view of a language as a social semiotic is that the structures of its 'system' reflect its need to fulfil social functions. In this chapter, I will consider how text is affected by social context, summarising the mechanisms through which that effect is transmitted as register and genre. I will then raise how an understanding of genre will identify other ways of differentiating one type of text from another, looking particularly at how some written genres configure parts of text as a language use known as grammatical metaphor. I will argue that this view of genre again shows how we should differentiate speech and writing not according to a general appraisal of spoken and written language, but according to genres or categories of text.

Understanding genre

Martin (1997) shows how we need context to understand text with a straightforward example taken from sport. We can see how this works in a simple sentence, 'He hit sixty'. In very general terms, the speaker or writer of the sentence 'he hit sixty' is realising a need to recount a past event where somebody performed an action and something changed as a result of that. This means that they formulate an expression where they represent themselves as a being that carries out an action, or an *agent,* and where a word represents the actions as a *process,* 'hit' (as scoring), and an object expresses the purpose of the action or *goal.* Thus, in this sentence we can say that 'he' is fulfilling the function of an *agent,* 'hit', of a *process* or action, and 'sixty' of a *goal.* A more general point is that this sentence is probably operating in the context of an event that seems to require this form of expression.

If the sentence 'he hit sixty' were removed from its context, it might become a puzzle. We might ask how we can 'hit' a 'number' and even if the 'number' is perceived as a goal, we do not know what it refers to. In Australia, India or the UK, the meaning should be clear. In the US, it might also be transparent, but differently. The phrase is meaningful because it refers to 'cricket' and the interlocutors who exchange the sentence will probably know that. In the US, it might refer to baseball, but since a score of 60 is unlikely in a single match it would refer to a score achieved over a longer period of time. Therefore if we remember our discussion in Chapter 2 of how context can be analysed according to 'field', 'mode' and 'tenor', we can see that by itself this sentence does not operate with a very specific concept of field or tenor. To understand it, we do need a very strong sense of field. We need to know that we are operating in the field of sport, and more specifically cricket.

Now let us suppose that this remark is merely part of a longer text which we watch unfold between two interlocutors on television:

> Yes, John, he clearly looked uneasy when he came out after tea and twice nearly lost his wicket to some very accurate bowling but then he began to establish himself and he hit sixty before the close of play.

We now have quite a lot of information about tenor and mode. The tenor is complicated. It is nominally an informal dialogue between two individuals, yet the speakers are not the intended audience; they are speaking in order to be heard by people who are unknown to them. This probably constrains their choice of language to some extent and will mean that they will avoid informalities or private jokes. The mode configuration is also quite complicated. The dialogue is a spoken broadcast. If it is televised, this will also afford some visual contextualisation, meaning that the language has to carry less weight. The audience may assume that it is improvised or unscripted. But in reality it may refer to notes made by the speakers with the points they have to cover.

Outside register there is another attribute of context which is affecting how this dialogue unfolds and the direction that it takes. This is generally called 'genre'. For Martin (e.g. 1997), genre is set up 'above and beyond' the metafunctions of field mode and tenor, representing a confluence of social processes that not only affect these but also focus particularly on the structure of the discourse, or on what kind of meaning we want to communicate at a given point within it. This is modelled in figure 11.1.

First, a given level in this model will affect another level, moving both up and down. Thus, it is inaccurate to think of context determining language. Context and language construct each other. Genre is a more abstract and more general determining principle than register, but it is also affected by register. For example, if we return to the cricket dialogue above, we can see that this takes place within a genre of informal conversation. Yet we can also see that the field, 'cricket', and the mode, 'sports broadcast, written and spoken (semi-scripted)' both affect the genre because this belongs to something less general

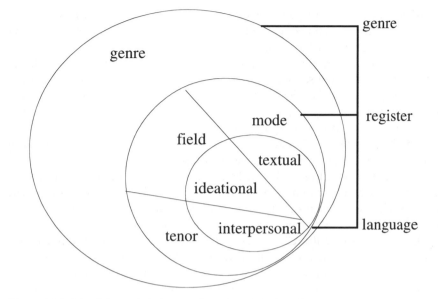

Figure 11.1 Martin's model of genre (based on Martin 1997)

than simply conversations, concerning broadcast sports conversations. The genre, however, also exerts an independent effect because it is a repository of social practices and establishes expectations as to how the text will unfold. For example, we will expect a strong element of both narrative and critical comment. The narrative may come more from a commentator as they summarise the sporting action. The commentator may then defer to an expert colleague in order to encourage criticism. We will also expect a conclusion, which may mean the commentator handing back to the newscaster in the main studio.

Martin's concept of register and genre differs considerably from that of Biber. Apart from the quantifiable features from which Biber models a genre, Martin also sees a genre as spawning less general categories of text, or what he calls 'agnate' forms. For example, in analysing the genres that secondary school history students have to deal with, Coffin (1997) identifies a general narrative form which she calls 'prosodic appraisal'. This is basically the core narrative function of history, or of telling how a sequence of events has unfolded. The second strand is 'periodic appraisal'. This takes us towards a more critical examination of the unfolding narrative and a more focused searched-for cause and effect. The most specific category is called 'thesis appraisal' where discussing events and mounting challenges to a given point of view are perhaps the writer's principal objectives. In this genre events are not the cornerstone of a narrative but are treated as 'evidence' to support or challenge a point of view.

What is also interesting about Coffin's establishment of agnate forms is how they are arranged as a pedagogical sequence. The broader narrative function is the genre through which children can be apprenticed as writers of history. This is 'easier' because it corresponds to oral narrative genres which will not be unfamiliar to most school children. A first stage therefore involves getting children to recount historical narratives. In this way a literacy practice that is unfamiliar, producing a written account of historical events, is embedded in familiar linguistic ones, telling stories, listening to read stories or reading them aloud. Many skilled primary teachers will also access critical appraisal through another genre, that of the 'eye-witness account'.

For example, children will be asked to look at the Norman Conquest of England through the eye of a 'high-born' Saxon child who must suddenly lose their privileged social position. This account, by its nature, starts to shape a critical challenge: 'Why have these Normans come here and taken our homes and destroyed our culture?' (Sandra Thompson, personal communication). Two contrary eye-witness accounts can be juxtaposed, that of the Norman and the Saxon, engendering critical dialogue and a search for cause and effect. Over time these can be abstracted towards the more difficult task of thesis appraisal where the writer absorbs two voices into one, juxtaposing opinions instead of characters. An ontogenetic process mirrors the phylogenetic one characterised in Chapter 9, where different opinions are first expressed through different characters in a dialogue, then subsumed into a more modern discursive form. The three genres of prosodic, periodic and thesis appraisal also show how a more communicative view of genre can spread written genres upon a continuum of distance or proximity to spoken forms. This is in the spirit of Biber's own conclusion but the use of Coffin's narrower, agnate-based view of genre means that we can use it to shape a more useful sequence of writing instruction. We can also achieve a better understanding of how register, through its mode metafunction, can interact with genre in order to shape text differently.

We can see how this operates at the level of language when we consider its effect on another phenomenon identified by Halliday, that of grammatical metaphor.

Grammatical metaphor as an expression of how register and genre affect text

I summarised how a language itself should be perceived as a representation of the meanings that the members of a given society wish to represent so that they can communicate them to each other. Thus, the grammatical system of a language will be wedded to the expression of different types of meaning.

Let us take the example 'I watched her at sunset'. Traditionally, we would analyse 'I' as a subject, 'watched' as a verb, 'her' as an object and 'at sunset' as a prepositional phrase or adjunct. However, if we look at another, but quite

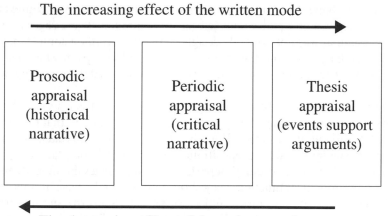

The increasing effect of the written mode

| Prosodic appraisal (historical narrative) | Periodic appraisal (critical narrative) | Thesis appraisal (events support arguments) |

The decreasing effect of the written mode

Figure 11.2 History genres and their proximity to spoken forms (based on Coffin 1997)

similar sentence such as 'I shot her at sunset' we will notice that this sentence has exactly the same structure, but we will also see that the subject is initiating an action in a much more direct sense than in 'I watched her at sunset'. 'Shot' is clearly an action with a direct physical impact. 'Watched' is not an action at all but a mode of perception.

We can say that the subject in 'I watched her at sunset' is a *senser* because it is sensing something that occurs, and that the subject in 'I shot her at sunset' is an *actor* because it is accomplishing an action. We can now make a further judgement that a senser will typically be an animate subject. This is because animals have the capacity of seeing, hearing and feeling, whereas objects do not.

Another SFL term is *congruent* (Halliday 1985). The example 'I watched her at sunset' shows a congruent use of language because a senser is typically an animate creature that senses events and, in this sentence, it is. Equally, 'watched' is normally an expression of a mental process, or of our perception of a 'phenomenon'. This usage is 'congruent' because the grammar and the lexis work in harmony with the social objective by which they were spawned. According to Halliday (1985), then, congruent language is in some sense 'natural'. Congruent language will closely reflect the physical relationships in which language is grounded. 'I shot her at sunset' recounts a set of events that we can observe and may need to communicate. The structure of language arose from the need to express this set of physical relationships.

A problem is that language structures and roles will evolve in one type of context yet may have to adapt to another very different one. Arguably, literacy, with its profound impact on the mode metafunction and on genre, will do much to reshape that context on its own. This means that new contexts may pressure a given group of language users to communicate messages for which their grammar was not explicitly designed. In other words, a context may start to detach language from the set of physical relationships in which language begins. If we take another sentence, 'The sunset watched their meeting' we can see how this happens.

Congruently, the verb 'watch' requires a subject that is a *seeker*. A seeker should also be an animate being since 'seeking' is a function that presupposes the ability to initiate an action. Equally, 'sunset', as an event that marks a time, might normally require a prepositional phrase, or adjunct, 'at sunset'. 'The sunset watched their meeting' departs from congruency because items in it assume grammatical functions they should not normally have. In this case an adjunct, 'at sunset', becomes a subject, or perhaps a *locative subject* since it is positioning the person in time. We could therefore call this *an adjunct to locative subject metaphor* (Downing and Locke 1992).

Literacy's separation of the author and reader is advantageous if we want to create texts such as laws or moral diktats that can be put beyond challenge. In other words, we disguise 'the source of a modality' to 'make it more difficult to query', making it part of an established order that compels agreement (Thompson 1996). We can see this in a sentence such as:

Discussion will bring disagreement.

Here, the nominalisation of the verb 'discuss' ensures that a process is not expressed congruently as a verb but as a noun-subject. An instruction is made part of an established order that tries to compel obedience.

Consider another example:

The disenfranchisement of ex-felons in Florida gave the election to George Bush.

In this sentence, the process, disenfranchise, should naturally be expressed by a verb, while the subject of give should normally be an actor or a being capable of action. Thus a congruent version would be: 'because the authorities in Florida disenfranchised ex-felons, George Bush won the election'. Yet we can see how the congruent version obstructs the expression of the cause-and-effect relationship that is expressed by the incongruent 'disenfranchisement'. In the version that is not congruent, 'disenfranchisement' is a noun-subject which impacts directly upon another process 'the election'. Processes are being made to behave as if they were things so that we can see how one affects the other.

We can look at another example:

Oil price rises may inflict some damage on the prospects of economic revival in the Far East.

Again a process, 'rise', is functioning as a noun-subject, 'rises', so that we can construct a causal relationship that seems as credible as if we had seen one object strike another and make it move. We can see how a genre of 'thesis appraisal' combines with mode and field to shift text away from a congruent or natural language. The genre does this because it treats events not as part of the unfolding sequence that we perceive but as existing in the networks of cause-and-effect relationships that the historian is trying to help us understand. In a genre of thesis appraisal, the real interest is not, for example, in when and where oil companies or oil-producing nations raised prices. The objective is to understand what the effect of this price rise might be and to challenge any alternative hypotheses about such effects. The written mode promotes this objective because it disguises 'the source of modality', foregrounding the events and not the narrator's observation of them.

Perhaps our most obvious perceptual boundary is between 'actions' and 'things'. 'Actions' can be represented only as an effect upon an object. 'Objects' are indubitably there. 'Actions' and 'objects' therefore have a different status that is encoded in language as verbs and nouns. A grammatically congruent use of language implies that verbs primarily represent actions and nouns primarily represent objects. In the sentence above, two actions, 'rise' and 'revive', impact upon each without the mediation of objects. They impact upon each other as if they were things (Holme 2003b).

One possible thesis is therefore that language at its oral inception is contextualised within the here-and-now. Congruent language begins in this everyday relationship of objects to objects, people to objects and objects to things, respecting core divisions between phenomena, states and actions. Literacy creates an endophoric pressure, reinforcing the tendency for texts that refer beyond our immediate shared experience to build their context out of themselves. Literacy may also reinforce what we can call a conceptual shorthand. The conceptual shorthand involves our use of the language to bypass the more long-winded sets of events that we actually perceive. For example, when we are discussing the water cycle, we might have observed how when clouds rise and cool, rain will fall. This observation is rooted in the 'here' and 'now' of an observer watching clouds. Yet our major interest is not in what the clouds do but in which event causes which. We therefore use a grammatical metaphor and nominalise the processes that are involved, giving:

'The cooling of the water vapour causes rainfall.'

The sentence is now lifted from the 'here-and-now', expressing a deduction that cannot literally be observed. Certain literate genres pressure the removal of the text from a real-world context. They encourage language to be more self-referential, or to draw its meanings out of itself. Literacy thus encourages our ability to conceptualise actions and events as if they were things, thus allowing us to focus on what things do.

Grammatical metaphors are in no sense a product of literacy; however, the more frequent appearance of their nominalised manifestation in some written genres may be a product of how those genres have evolved to express such literacy practices as 'thesis appraisal'. We can represent this as in figure 11.3. Here, a given social practice will produce a particular configuration of text. The genre is about the understanding of events and seeks to explain why they occur. The need for a record establishes this as a literacy rather than a speech practice. The genre pressures the text towards an expression of cause-and-effect connections and thus away from a congruent relationship with the world of things. It also suggests an engagement with specific meanings which the text must define from itself with a diminished dependence on the external, physical context. The mode, which is the writing of scientific text, must transmit meanings through time and space, further enhancing the endophoric effect. The science field involves the analysis of cause-and-effect between events rather than the recollection of the events themselves. Field and tenor also combine to focus upon the topic itself, taking the author out of their text and creating an impersonal style. In this way we can see how genre and register operate in order to configure a segment of text as a product of its literacy practice. The result is an incongruent use of language, or one separated from the straightforward representation of everyday events. This type of grammatical metaphor shows how it is a useful way to examine how literacy affects language, but only as an attribute of the genre in which it operates.

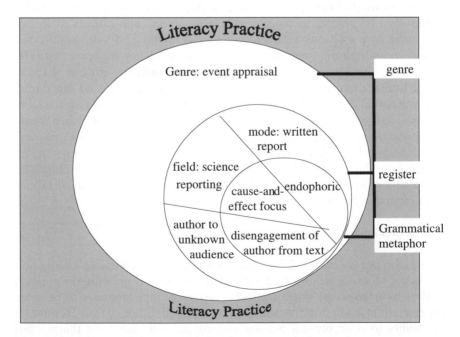

Figure 11.3 Literacy and context configuring grammatical metaphor

Looking at text

The above treatment of a genre helps us understand further how we should look at written language not as a distinct form of language use in itself but should see the use of writing as one aspect of the larger configuration of context which determines the way a text represents the meanings of a given practice. I will conclude by showing briefly how we now have the means to analyse a written genre not simply as a way of using language but as a text that uses non-linguistic forms of semiosis.

The sample text is an informational letter genre, or, if one can speak of an agnate form, it is perhaps 'information about enclosures'. The text reconstructs a genre but has been written for this book in order to exemplify its adopted approach:

Your reference PISB 171134

Our reference Ow230104/0

Mr. S. Owen
65 Railwood Terrace
Lanchester
DURHAM
DH7 6DJ1

Dear Mr. Owen,

Public Investment & Savings Bank

Public Investment and
Savings Bank
Glasgow G2 1EG
Enquiries 033-756-3145
Fax: 033-756-3145
Date: 23 January 2004

Investment Bonus Bond number Z -63216589

I am pleased to enclose the certificate of investment for the Bonus Bond for your investment account.

The certificate confirms full details of the investment including the amount invested and the guaranteed value if held until maturity.

The value of the Bond will continue to grow for the duration of your account, during which time further bonuses will be added.

If you have any questions about this bond, please call us on 033-756-3145, or write to the above address, quoting the bond number. We will be delighted to help.

Yours sincerely

Joan Westerness
Account Manager

The text exists within the literacy practices that develop from various forms of commercial activity, most notably, saving money and banking. Its format, visual semiosis and language are shaped by the larger practice of commercial letter-writing and the specific legal and fiscal literacies with which that is often intertwined. The practices express themselves through the text's letter genre, giving its discourse structure (what is said when), format, and visual semiotics as well as through how the components of its register select particular forms of language. For example, at a basic level, mode (writing), field (banking) and tenor (formal client relations) combine to select the written, formal opening salutation 'Dear Mr. Owen'. The text emerges from a network of practices with concerns that go far beyond the letter's expressed purpose of conveying information about an attached document. When we understand the practice's association with a nexus of other legal and fiscal literacies, the letter's real objectives become clearer. The purpose is less to explain the contents of the enclosure and more to situate these in a legal framework by explaining and limiting the customer's rights in respect of the bond purchased by their account. The letter returns us to the early literacy practice of assigning property rights. The assignation of such rights requires a sign unique to the individual who confers them and a method of attesting to whom they are assigned. The sign that is unique to a person was once the seal, and its imprimatur was an act of authorisation. Its modern equivalent is the signature of an individual who is authorised to represent the organisation.

This convergence of practices in the information-giving genre sets up various semiotic expectations, both at the linguistic and visual level. First, the letter must attest to its authenticity. This is not simply through the act of signature as that amounts to no more than the individual's authentication of their text. In this instance the individual authentication commits a corporation and they do this by signing on paper that bears a series of corporate signs. In the top right corner, the corporation names itself and draws attention and hence significance to that semiotic by using a different font and colour. The name 'Public Investment and Savings Bank' is written with one of the few logographs allowed by mainstream English literacy conventions, the ampersand, '&'.

The name is a caption to the semograph, or company logo that is written beneath, 'pi&sb'. Although logos function as semographs, they are generally built out of an alphabetic and phonemic principle, representing an interesting case of how we would be unwise to see literacy as passing through a semasiographic phase then discarding this when it was able to represent language. Writing cannot be said to be developing directionally in this sense when the logo reveals a reverse process where a glottic system regresses into semiography. Such devices show we are engaged in an on-going exploitation of a wide range of semiotic resources. Although we need to represent language to fulfil our larger communicative need, a visual medium tempts us back towards a predominantly visual form of semiography. The letters of an acronym are metonyms where part of the word, the salient initial letter, stands for the whole. In the example, in question, the graphemes 'i', and 's' and the logograph '&' are combined into a single grapheme. The device is iconic and metaphoric in that the ampersand draws the other two graphemes together to create one meaning from them. Harris (1996) calls this *syncretism*, and the example here is associated with another, where the semi-circle on the 'b' encloses a coin to create a pictograph of the banking function. This gives graphic form to the metonym 'coin' for 'bank' and a metaphor where the letter 'b' assumes the function of the word it stands for by enclosing (or storing) the coin. We can analyse this syncretism as a cognitive blend. The circular form of the coin maps onto that of the semi circle of the 'b', creating the conceptual blend between the drawing of the coin and the graphological symbol.

The text also uses conventional semographs in its use of reference numbers, telephone numbers and bond numbers. Our use of numbers as identifiers rather than as expressions of quantity shows how we can play with a system of symbols in order to give it new meanings. The use of bond and reference numbers also serves the intertextual function of associating this document with another.

In the top left-hand corner, the address of the addressee, placed there by convention, also shows a conventional and alphabet-derived semasiographic device with the first letter corresponding to that of the town.

The use of space evidences the effect of this formal letter genre. The opening salutation, 'Dear Mr. Owen', is set up in a largely conventionalised act of semi-osis that is also iconic in origin because of how it isolates the opening phrase as a kind of verbal handshake. The letter's subject is also isolated in bold for easy reference. Until the closing message, each of the text's sentences is given its own paragraph. This highlights its information-bearing function by isolating each point as a component of a generic pattern, giving the reason for writing, providing information (about the enclosure) and closing with a message of re-assurance. The message 'we'll be happy to help', which concludes a form letter that is generated by a machine, signifies a shift in the tenor, employing a contracted form in order to make the writer sound accessible. This contrasts oddly with the opening passive, 'I am pleased', which places the fictional writer on the periphery of their text, framing them as the object of an emotion generated by duty or employment function. This process of removal had also been further reinforced by the grammatical metaphor 'the certificate confirms', where a document acquires the incongruent function of an agent and speaker.

This letter is no different from thousands of other machine-distributed texts which are posted daily throughout the world. Our analysis makes plain how grounded in one practice such texts also express a complicated social dynamic, one which in this case involves law, property and corporate identity, as well as the glottic and other types of sign use that the practices have developed and in which some of their facets are encoded.

Conclusions

In this brief introduction to genre I have tried to show how it is an important factor in determining the type of text that is often associated with written language. To show how this operates, I took the example of grammatical metaphor, not just because this has been associated with literacy by its proponents, but because it shows so well how language can respond to pressures that certain written genres impose. Grammatical metaphor shows how language responds to its own contextual needs taking it away from forms governed by naturally occurring physical boundaries. Returning briefly to our discussion of sign, it therefore shows how language, and above all written language, exploits its symbolic nature to achieve a new conceptual freedom. The achievement of that freedom is not a semiotic response to literacy but to the needs of a given practice, as these are mediated by the configurations of genre and register. I showed how this operates by analysing how a common letter genre uses linguistic and non-linguistic devices to represent the meanings of its practice.

Exercises

1. Take any complete text of 300–500 words or more and decide how you would describe its genre or its register.
2. Look carefully at the text and see if you can identify any ways of using language that you would identify with that genre and register. For example, if it is narrative, you might expect it to have co-ordinators that link one sentence to another in order to unfold its story in time. Do you find many? How would you describe how they are used? Look at features like tense and aspect. If you find passives, for example, would you associate that with its use of a written mode, or do they reflect field in some way? NB. Do not worry about finding the correct terms here, just choose the language that will make your findings clear.
3. Look at the text again and see if you can identify a move structure. Decide what function the text has and when. For example: Does it begin by saluting the reader or citing recommendations? Does it follow this with a statement of purpose? Decide how far you think it would be justifiable to associate this move structure with the genre of the text and how far it is simply a feature of this one example.
4. Imagine you had to teach a group of students who wanted to write in the genre of your text. How would the answers to questions 2 and 3 help you to do that?
5. Discuss whether there is a way in which the structure of the genre can be described as a response to the nature of the literacy practice of which it is a part.

Part IV

Literacy as Mind

Marxist philosophy risks becoming an unstable victim of social forces. It offers no set of characteristics that we can aim to uncover.

A solution is to understand mind as a product of a society and its history, and therefore to accept that psychologists will largely examine the social manifestations of mental processes. A problem here is that we are left without a way to account for how society arose in the first place, since, if mind is manifest only in society, it cannot pre-exist the social arrangements that it has brought into existence.

Lev Vygotsky was one of the most influential psychologists of the twentieth century and his ideas can be framed as a response to the dilemma posed for the psychologist by a Marxist world-view. More importantly for our topic, Vygotsky understood literacy as a central manifestation of the interaction of mind and society. Vygotsky's view of literacy expressed how he responded to the problem of building a Marxist theory of mental development. In this chapter I will to outline what that view of mental development was, and how literacy emerged as one of its core components.

A socio-historical construction of mind

Vygotsky did most of his significant work just after Russia's Bolshevik revolution. His response to Marxism's intellectual challenge was to treat society and mind not as independent entities but as interpenetrating each other. Society is finally an interaction of different minds, and the mind is finally a social product. While the mind is shaped by the society of which it is a part, society reflects the actions of the mind. Society and mind are thus 'mutually constitutive' or mutually developmental (Wells 2000: 54). It is therefore misconceived to think of the mind as using the environment to educate itself. We should think instead of the mind as reshaping or redirecting the confluence of social forces that make its education a possibility. These social forces are manifest in the groups and institutions of which the individual became a member. A more modern perception of these groups might be to characterise them as communities of practice.

A term used by many commentators on Vygotsky, but never used by Vygotsky himself, is *scaffolding* (Blanck 1990). Coined by Bruner (1975), the term means creating one social structure in order to build another mental one. It involves maximising the developmental potential of an individual at a given moment through an act of social organisation. To develop the mind, society scaffolds it in pedagogical institutions and their interventions. The scaffolding metaphor also exposes how mind is not simply the product of the communities and cultures in which it is located. Just as scaffolding adopts the shape of the building that rises within it, so a social intervention should be reshaped by the mental structures that it surrounds and supports.

The scaffolding metaphor also shows where Vygotsky's thought contrasts

12 Social Practice and a Socio-historical Theory of Mind

Introduction

A core debate in Western thought has been between those who hold that knowledge is largely constructed by us from our contact with our environment and those who ascribe it more to an internal mental state, or between *nature*, knowing things simply by dint of who we are, and *nurture*, obtaining most of our knowledge from the environment.

A quite recent expression of this long-standing nature–nurture debate was between the *mentalist* linguist Noam Chomsky and *behaviourist* school of psychology represented by B. F. Skinner (1957). Skinner's strong nurture view held that the infant acquired language from its environment as a series of habits or observable forms of behaviour. Chomsky (1965) argued that the infant's linguistic environment was incomplete and thus unable to account for the complete knowledge that was finally acquired. This supported the mentalist or 'nature' assumption that the key structures of language were hard-wired into the human brain as a Universal Grammar. These universal principles would both organise and be reorganised by the input received from the infant's linguistic environment, becoming the different types of language knowledge that characterise human communication.

A more traditional philosophical exposition of the nurture view can be found in the thought of the nineteenth-century socialist philosopher Karl Marx. For Marx, 'mind' was a product of its socio-historical environment. Therefore, a corrupt capitalist society created a corrupt mind. After capitalism had been destroyed by its internal contradictions, the communist society that would follow would create a different type of mind, one that was in tune with the socialist goal of selfless commitment to a common good.

One can see that a psychologist would find the Marxist view of mind difficult. Since what we do with society is crucial to how we reshape mind, psychology largely becomes a form of social science. The route to psychological understanding and re-engineering was social understanding and re-engineering. Like any scientist, a psychologist needs an entity to study. Yet the entity delivered by markedly with that of another famous developmental psychologist, Jean Piaget (1954). Piaget imagined mental development as proceeding in fixed, biologically determined stages. For example, very young children possess a very limited capacity to conceive of their own identity as a being that is capable of reflective actions. They simply respond to a given situation, for example, crying when deprived. The construction of a sense of identity marks a predetermined stage of psychological development, which is universal and fundamentally unaffected by the kind of cultural environment in which we exist. One can recognise the mentalist strand in Piaget's thinking. The child's development is determined by innate features of mind, and environmental or 'nurturing' effects take second place. Vygotsky's view was very different. The child's developmental progression was treated as more fluid and as susceptible to interventions by caregivers, educators and educational institutions.

If we accept that the mind shapes society just as society shapes the mind, we still cannot understand how this *mutually constitutive development* has been so much greater in human society than in that of any other species. Understanding this meant identifying and understanding the instruments through which that development was achieved. Broadly, Vygotsky perceived two kinds of instrument, one technological, the other semiotic. Tools facilitate the operation of mind on society. For example, the mind learns to make, then to use, a chisel. Through this mechanism the mind changes its environment, chiselling out a sign from wood, for example. The process of semiosis is more complicated. In Part II, we ascertained that human beings are intuitive users of signs, but at some point in their development they gain conscious control over that usage. We examined Vygotsky's own example of a child who knots a handkerchief to remember something and so exercises control over their semiotic environment by making a meaningful object. The consciously constructed sign, therefore, becomes a mechanism through which the sign-maker manipulates their thought processes. The child makes themselves remember. This is how the sign becomes a mechanism of self-development.

I illustrate this two-channel model in figure 12.1. Tool use permits an environmental effect. One of these effects can be the construction of signs.

The child thus begins a fourfold process of assisted self-development through the means of signs (Díaz et al. 1990: 135). First, society and its caregivers use 'auxiliary signs' to 'regulate the child's behaviour'. The child is then a passive consumer of its semiotic environment. Second, the child begins to use the signs to 'influence' others, as when they ask for 'milk' instead of just expressing their need through an unconscious, indexical yell. Third, the child understands that language, with its socially shared meanings and its access to an elaborate symbolic system, is the most useful way to exert an environmental effect. Fourth, because the child now commands an elaborate symbolic code, they can use this to cause a larger transformation, of both the environment and the symbolic processes through which their knowledge of the environment is mediated. They no longer just respond to the stimulus of their

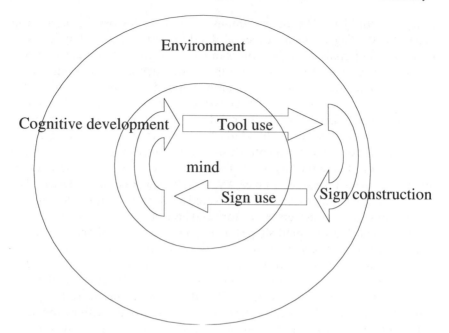

Figure 12.1 Vygotsky's two-channel model of psychological development

environment but can construct and control how that response should unfold. They can in turn use that capacity to design and construct new tools through which to achieve more radical environmental re-engineering. As part of this process. speech is itself a tool that transforms what we do, giving rise to 'purely human forms of intelligence' (Vygotsky 1978: 24, cited in Díaz et al. 1990: 135), and speech is also a system of signs which can combine to exercise a cognitive effect

Yet this theory still does not account for the rapidity and scope of individual human development. To understand this, Vygotsky required what he called a *genetic approach*, one which understood how we are born into a society which has the means to transmit the knowledge of past generations, and so relieves us of the animal burden of learning everything anew (Wells 2000: 50). The mechanism of transmission is a culture and its language, as these have developed through time. Here, we can again see the influence of Marxism on Vygotsky's thought. The mind's socio-cultural landscape is a repository of historical forces. We can thus interpret a culture and its society as an accumulation of historical knowledge which exerts an active and formative effect upon our ontogenesis and can, therefore, explain our unparalleled capacity for self-development.

Literacy provides one of the clearest examples of the socio-historical view of mind that was outlined in figure 12.1. First, we should remember that society builds mind through sign and that language is a pre-eminent sign system. The development of literacy affords the mind a tool with which they can rework their semiotic environment, and, through that environment, restructure itself. Again, the example of the child's knotted handkerchief is relevant here, affording an ontogenetic illustration of literacy's phylogenetic effect. Literacy represents a much larger development of our semiotic environment. It surrounds us with new modes of signification, all of which are susceptible to conscious development and control. In Vygotsky's model, we should remember, it is through signs and not through tools that our socio-historical environment will develop the mind. Because literacy makes such a large extension of our semiotic capacity, it constitutes a restructuring of our cognition itself. In other words, literacy augments our mental ability to develop other forms of knowledge and other ways of thinking.

One might find support for such a position in the straightforward example of mathematics. We have already suggested that the historical development of mathematics and literacy cannot be separated. An advanced mathematical culture involves forms of semiosis that put many new cognitive and technological tools at our disposal. Mathematics underpins much deductive thought and suggests ways of thinking that underpin science itself. If we accept this, we can also argue that it is not so much science but an ability to engage in scientific thought which should be treated as literacy's by-product. The inverse will also hold. Those who are illiterate will lack the cognitive structures to think scientifically.

The zone of proximal development

We can obtain a closer understanding of how this would happen if we look at another plank of Vygotskian theory, the *zone of proximal development* (ZPD). ZPD is basically an ontogenetic theory. It is about individual development, in other words, though, as we have seen, phylogenesis and ontogenesis are really aspects of the same process in Vygotskian thought. The concept of a ZPD also rejects Piaget's concept of individual development passing through fixed and biologically triggered stages. It suggests that such development is a dynamic resulting from a fusion of external social effects and internal cognitive activity. In figure 12.2, we must imagine a child's mind that is at stage 'x' in its development. Exactly what that stage involves will vary from individual to individual and according to the previous development that has occurred. A child at stage 'x' has the ability to reach stage 'y' in their learning provided the right environmental triggers are present. However, the child does not have the ability to reach beyond the zone, to 'z', for example. The zone should be understood as existing in a state of dynamic interaction with its environment, and its scope will depend upon the type of inputs that arise from it and the response to the inputs that the individual makes into it.

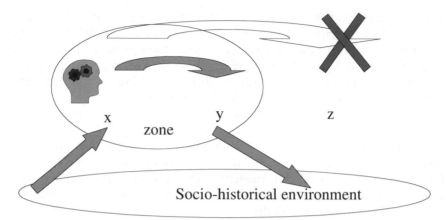

Figure 12.2 Vygotsky's zone of proximal development. A child at stage 'X' in their development will have the capacity to reach 'Y' but not 'Z' because Y falls within the zone.

We should remember that for Vygotsky (1978) the primary means of cognitive development was through sign and its associated socio-linguistic activity. For teachers, a core interest is in the type of socio-linguistic intervention that has to be made and in how well it targets the zone, maximising the child's development instead of ensuring pedagogical failure by moving outside its capacity and under-exploiting the same. A successful intervention will also ensure the child's own ability to rework their socio-linguistic environment and lay down the grounds for a further subsequent intervention from it, thus ensuring a learning progression.

Vygotsky's socio-historical approach to mind blurs the boundaries between ontogenesis and phylogenesis. 'Mind' is a socio-historical construction that is scaffolded by the interventions and educational practices that a society evolves throughout its history. Society is built around the way in which the mind fashions its use of signs and tools from those interventions. One can perceive this, ontogenetically, as the individual developing their own mental capacity throughout their life; of becoming educated, in other words. One can also perceive this phylogenetically, as a process of the collective mind evolving its intellectual and technical capacity within society over time. However, each is finally a facet of the other, since the development of the individual mind is as an attribute of the knowledge that is banked in our social environment.

If we were to perceive the ZPD in a phylogenetic context, we could see how this works by taking the example of the Greek alphabet. The alphabet can be understood as a tool through which Greek society was able to reshape its perception of language. The alphabet's analysis of language nurtured the Greek intellect with a new analytic interest in what a given statement really said (Olson 1994). Arguably, then, the alphabet can be understood as a tool that affords the Greek mind a new analytic capacity. This capacity means that society produces new types of sign, or new linguistic possibilities, and these in turn scaffold the mind's development. In other words, the new literacy affords extended semiotic possibilities and these restructure cognition. We might next suppose that this restructuration awakens our collective mind to further new possibilities, perhaps within the domains of logic, mathematics and analytical philosophy. As these activities reshape the social domain, the impact upon the mind is further increased. In this way we can see that the ZPD is not just a definition of the scope of an individual's cognitive development at a given moment. It further reveals what a society can accomplish at a given moment in its history. The zone is a dynamic that is subject to constant movement. We can also understand how we can see literacy as shaping new methods of sign-use which open greater cognitive possibilities.

Conclusions

In this chapter, I have introduced Vygotsky's socio-historical theory of mind, showing how this emerges from a Marxist view of history and society. I have explained how Vygotsky saw tool use as the method through which mind achieves its impact on society, and sign as the mechanism through which society scaffolds the mind. I have then suggested how writing can be seen as a tool that exerts a significant social effect. That effect is literacy, which then scaffolds the mind with its enhanced semiotic potential, affording new cognitive possibilities. I have explained how Vygotsky's theory of a ZPD charted an individual's potential for further cognitive development at any one time. I have suggested that one might map this ontogenetic theory onto the larger historical development of mind in society. I used this as an example of how a Vygotskian could argue that literacy restructured cognition, permitting the new realms of intellectual possibility in which mathematics and science took root.

Exercises

1. Imagine a society of hunter-gatherers with language but no literacy. That society evolves a system of precise visual signs which makes it easier for them to hunt in groups. Use Vygotsky's theory of mind to describe how this might help that society to dominate other groups.
2. Describe Vygotsky's view of how the mind develops in society. Suggest why literacy should have such a strong interest for this view.
3. Explain what is meant by a ZPD, deciding whether it should be characterised as a dynamic, or static, view of cognitive development. Reflect on your own life and its learning. Try to identify any moments where care-givers or

teachers suddenly extended your understanding in a way that allowed you to do new things, making what was once hard, seem easy. Analyse one of these experiences through Vygotsky's theory of ZPD. Explore whether the experience was in any way literacy-related.

13 Great Divide Theory

Introduction

The Vygotskian vision of a cognition that is progressively developing its capabilities through the medium of literacy has given rise to the concept of *a Great Divide*, where the impact of literacy upon the capabilities of mind is seen as being great enough to mark a key development in human history. The Great Divide stands between non-literate and literate societies and is marked by the cognitive possibilities that literacy allows. As the socio-historical theory of mind implies, the Great Divide should exist at both the psychological level, within the difference between a non-literate and literate cognitive structure, and the historical level, within the changes that occur in society when literacy is introduced. Each aspect, however, should be treated as a reflection of the other. I will now look at each in turn.

The historical Great Divide

Scholars such as Goody (1977), Havelock (1963), Ong (1982), Illich and Sanders (1988) and Olson (1994) have looked for the cognitive effects of literacy within the differences between literate and pre-literate societies or between societies possessing very limited literacy and mass literacy. According to Goody and Watt (1968), it is literacy that separates history from pre-history. On the surface, such a view is really a circularity, since literacy gives voice to the past and thus creates history. Yet, the view has also triggered some significant research into the historical effects that literacy has really had.

Ong (1982: 16–57) offers a succinct categorisation of how literacy may separate societies that possess literacy from those that preceded them. Oral societies differ from literate ones because they:

1. Associate words and actions.
2. Limit knowledge to what could be remembered.
3. Are homeostatic.

4. Are aggregative rather than subordinative.
5. Are aggregative rather than analytic.
6. Use language in a manner that is redundant or 'copious'.
7. Are conservative or traditionalist.
8. Stay close to the human lifeworld.
9. Have discourse that is empathetic and participatory rather than objectively distanced.
10. Can be agnostically toned.
11. Remain situational rather than abstract.

We can treat these as the components of a historical divide, and I will now consider how they are constituted.

Because speech is rooted in time, oral societies are *associative of words with actions*. Ong surmises that primitive societies give inordinate power to words or names simply because they perceive words as actions that beg an immediate response. Primitive people see words as 'power-driven', evoking the need for a response in action, as when we run towards a cry for help. Because words have the power to trigger actions they may become over-associated with the events they stimulate. This over-association endows words with a 'magical potency' (ibid.: 32), giving them the ability to summon up the person or object which they name. Giving away a name can be dangerous because it confers power on the person who comes to know it. In the Old Testament, uttering God's name was considered blasphemous, perhaps because it represented an intrusion on his power and a presumptuous limitation of his identity. The larger outcome is a failure to distinguish between words and their meanings. In this vein, Finnegan (1979) noted when trying to write down an oral version of a Limba poem in Sierrra Leone, that her informants held two versions to be 'the same' because their stories were the same, not because their exact words were (cited in Olson and Astington 1990: 710). For her part, Finnegan could not convey the concept of a verbatim rendition. If the meaning was repeated, the words were also seen to be, because words and their meaning were effectively one and the same.

The *limitation of knowledge* to what can be remembered gives us a different view of what knowledge is. According to Vygotsky, cognition operates with two kinds of memory. The first of these is characterised by the 'non-mediated impression of materials' and events (Vygotsky 1978: 38). This is held to dominate in 'non-literate peoples'. The second kind is characterised by the mediated impression of events or language. It is dependent upon 'self-generated' simulation (ibid.). We bring back the past, not as in a reflexive moment of recognition as when we know we have seen a person or place before. We rebuild it in language, sometimes in response to a deliberate act of remembering. Concomitantly, we force ourselves to do things to remember and reconstruct the past, using mnemonics, for example. Literacy encourages the development of this second type of memory because it permits our construction of the past as an archive which we can reconstitute, access at will, reinterpret or ignore. The anthropologist Claude Lévi-Strauss may have rejected a concept of historical progress, but he marked out the invention of writing as a watershed because it enables us to archive the knowledge of one generation so that the next can use it as their 'working capital' (Charbonnier 1973, cited in Scribner and Cole 1981: 4). This suggests a larger construction of knowledge as something outside the self. By this argument, the scope for reinterpreting knowledge in oral societies is limited because their members cannot alter the words in which that knowledge is framed. They vest knowledge in the knower, threatening the difference between knowledge and wisdom. Wisdom is in the interpretation of knowledge, but without our modern sense of archived knowledge, we interpret as we recollect, finding no difference between interpretation and understanding. Because oral societies must devote so much cognitive effort to knowledge conservation, they have less scope for reinterpretation. They reject the knowledge that seems to be irrelevant to their current existence, re-using only that which supports the current social order (Goody and Watt 1968: 31–4). Existing without an archive of alternative thought from which to challenge custom and convention, oral societies are *homeostatic*, or gripped by tradition, and impervious to change.

The limitation of knowledge to what we can remember also vests it in sets of formulaic utterances because these make easy mnemonics. The poet Homer made an early use of the Greek alphabet to found a recreational 'literature'. Parry (1971) observed that his poetry was not the startling act of inventiveness that might be associated with later seminal figures such as Shakespeare. In fact, his poetry was an act of rhetorically sewing together formulaic utterances which the Greek traditions of oral narrative would have passed down to him. Homer's images may have been developed from an inherited stock that acted as narrative prompts for his memory-dependent predecessors. Havelock's (1963) implication is that orality has to base itself upon the use of these repeated mnemonics and that this encourages a repetitive use of language and the consequent adjectival stereotyping of character evident in such phrases as 'the beautiful Helen' or 'the mighty Achilles'. In the evolution of Ancient Greek culture, Homer can be perceived as orality's last throw of the dice. Later, Greek drama, which is perceived as a product of a literate age, offers an evolved, critical and, hence, introspective view of character, one that is a far cry from Homer's presentation of cutout, one-dimensional heroes and heroines (ibid.). For Olson (1994) literacy's extension of our capacity for knowledge extends this capacity for self-analysis into a larger propensity for a more objective representation of reality. In fiscal literacies and their search for an unassailable value, or in the visual exactitude of Flemish painters such as the seventeenth-century Jan Vermeer, we see a growing desire to endow the people and objects which compose our reality with an identity that resists individual interpretation just as literacy postulates texts that exist independently of both author and reader.

As touched upon in the previous section, there is a hypothesis that writing tends to evolve syntactically complex sentences with multiple embeddings. The complexity may be lexical also. Traugött (1987) put forward the view that some more complicated uses of verbs in English evolved from how literacy influenced the spoken discourse of the law courts. Thus, the need to express an opinion about written material may have helped develop the use of verbs that perform this function. The result was an increase in the borrowing of verbs from Latin to help clarify claims, promise, assure or assert rights. Because these verbs use indirect speech, they subordinate what people say. 'I am innocent', for example, becomes 'He claimed *that he was innocent*'. Such borrowings support the contention that oral language is *aggregative* and written, rather than *subordinative*. By contrast, an oral, *aggregative* use of language piles one memorable chunk upon another and is shaped by a bard's need for formulaic, adjectival chunks: 'brave soldiers', 'beautiful princesses' or 'sturdy oaks'. The text's structural coherence emerges from the dead weight of one rhetorical chunk being heaped upon another and not from the fabric of an argument.

Excessive *redundancy* is another identifiable feature of oral discourse. Speakers talk round a topic, searching for the apt phrase with which to nail it down, producing redundant language as they do so. Speakers also revert to stock phrases in order to remind themselves and their listeners of exactly what they are talking about. Writers have the capacity to edit text down to the few words that are actually needed to convey their meaning. They can assume that they have readers who can also track back over a text if their recapitulation is too sparse to hold it in the readers' minds. They too can be their reader, editing their discourse until it conveys their desired meaning, neither more nor less.

Ong argues that, because oral discourse needs a framework of repeated prompts and conventionalised images, orality creates a *conservative* or *traditionalist* cast of mind. In oral societies, all knowledge exists in collective working memory and is a scarce commodity, limited by our cognitive capacity, and seen as precious. Innovation in oral societies is highly limited because their rhetorical resources are dedicated to hanging on to what they already know and not to using that knowledge as a platform for reinterpretation and augmentation. Accordingly, Havelock saw the alphabetic literacy of Ancient Greece as driving this analytic principle in two directions. First, in the work of the historian Heroditus, we see the development of a concept of history, or of a human narrative susceptible to interpretation. Second, we see the development of a more static, analytic and abstract language with the Greek philosophical tradition and the work of such figures as Socrates and his interpreter, Plato, or of Aristotle. To express this change of emphasis, Greek syntax started to downplay notions of 'doing, acting and happening', and focused instead on the stative relationship between things. Heraclitus declared that 'is' should replace the use of all other verbs. It was as if we should replace our frenetic attempts to respond to lives and languages that unfold in time with a static universe where all things endure, bound like writing by unchanging logical and spatial relationships. Our notion of being is then itself removed from time. Platonic thought, where every category has an ideal and enduring form, can be constructed as literacy's perfect product.

Ong perceives literacy as the technology that releases knowledge from the limitations of memory. By contrast, an oral society lacks the capacity to keep hold of the knowledge that falls from memory. It therefore follows that we have less need to interpret language as a subject of comment and therefore fail to develop the vocabulary and grammar through which such comments are expressed. We call this capacity to comment on what we say a *metalanguage*. A precondition of a metalanguage is that we differentiate language as a subject of comment from meaning. In orality, some research suggests that this differentiation is not made. Arguably our metalinguistic vocabulary is enhanced by the spread of literacy. Olson and Astington (1990) note how metalinguistic expression in English was assisted by a huge influx of Latin verbs during the sixteenth century. These verbs were often borrowed by the translators of classical texts, and disseminated by the increasing use of printing. The seventeenth-century translators of the King James Bible prefaced chapters with glosses that contained many Latinate *epistemic verbs,* or verbs of recalling, accusing, justifying and exhorting.

A richer epistemic vocabulary also developed our sense of separateness from what we know because it confirms knowledge as a separate archive, or a text outside ourselves, upon which we can pass judgement. By contrast, orality, for Ong, is *empathetic and participatory* rather than *objectively distanced,* inhibiting our capacity to examine our own use of words and the knowledge that we have invested in them.

Failing to evolve a diction of self-scrutiny and reflection, oral discourse remains strongly rooted in the here-and-now, responding to what Ong calls 'the human lifeworld' (1986: 42–3). This *attachment to the human lifeworld* inhibits the development of a strong religious conviction in the abstract, monotheistic sense. Oral discourse remains tied to the struggle of daily survival, spirits are vested in natural phenomena and subsumed by the identities and states of the same. Evidence for the association of oral speech with a struggle is found in the primitive customs of boasting, or speaking of one's own prowess, a habit common among the plains Native Americans, for example, but also receiving a considerable amount of text in Homer's *Iliad*. A related instance that allegedly keeps orality grounded in the human struggle is the engagement of two protagonists in ritualistic exchanges, where each tries to outdo the other in insults. This custom has evolved a more literate form in the rapping contests of contemporary African-American youth culture. However, the custom's origins in orality supposedly attest to a culture too bound up with the expression of a daily struggle to develop a conception of God as an overarching, invisible and finally abstract force, which is held not in a chunk of statuary but in an unalterable form of words.

The attachment to the human lifeworld makes orality situational. The implication is the exophoric tendency discussed in Chapter 9. Oral discourse gathers meaning from its immediate context. The exophoric nature of oral texts supposedly ties them into the 'here-and-now' of our physical world. The endophoric pressure upon writing means that language is rebuilt as an entity that can to some extent create meanings from itself. This promotes abstraction; it also makes a more sustained logical argument possible. In the Cartesian system, we have noted how a single fact rooted in human experience becomes the basis for a large logical structure. The structure is not vindicated by the degree of its correspondence to the facts of the world but by how each of its ideas is contained in one on which it rests, creating a deductive chain that can be traced back to the first incontestable fact: the *cogito ergo sum*. This is a mathematical wisdom, which in its pure form is endophoric, creating structures where the meaning of one proposition is deduced from another. This argument should not be taken as a denial of the logical capacity of pre-literate peoples. They understand cause-and-effect well enough. Where they fail, according to the Great Divide argument, is in their inability to extract that principle from the events through which it is observed. Pre-literate people supposedly fail to make cause-and-effect into an organisational principle of discourse, and so will lack the means to build an extended deductive text.

Proponents of the Great Historical Divide provide a fascinating insight into how the rise of literacy in many societies has been accompanied by the development of new forms of knowledge and new approaches to problems. We should remember, however, that if one phenomenon makes another possible – literacy leading to symbolic logic, for example – this does not mean it can be set down as its cause. What is surprising is that none of the studies that attribute such a vast range of innovations to literacy actually presents data which show how individuals in non-literate societies process information differently from those in literate ones (Scribner and Cole 1981). That issue is explored next.

The psychological Great Divide

One of the first people to try to understand literacy as a state that might affect our larger structures of mind was Alexandr Romanovitch Luria (1976), who began a series of studies in post-revolutionary Russia at the suggestion of Vygotsky. Luria's method involved giving Russia's illiterate peasantry tests on logical reasoning and abstract thought, then comparing the results with those of tests made on their literate peers. One test instrument was the *syllogism,* a form of logical argument derived from Greek philosophical tradition. A syllogism has two propositions or premises. These are statements which we know to be true:

Animals are creatures that have physical substance.
Humans are animals.

And one statement that is derived from the other two:

Therefore humans have physical substance.

Or more famously:

All men are mortal.
Socrates is a man.
Therefore Socrates is mortal.

The interest in the syllogism is in how it encapsulates logical deductive method.

Luria tested groups of literate and illiterate people in Russian villages by giving them the two premises of a syllogism then asking them to provide a deduction by answering a question. In a well-known example, he asked:

In the far north where there is snow, all bears are white (proposition 1). Novaya Zembla is in the far North and there is always snow there (proposition 2). What colour are the bears? (to deduce: Therefore the bears of Zembla are white). (Luria 1976: 104; insertions in parentheses are the author's)

Great Divide theory argues that speech is deeply embedded in its physical context. Illiterate thought will therefore depend on that context. It is rooted in the conviction that we know only what we can see, and cannot reason out a picture of how things stand in the far country of Zembla. The respondent can therefore do no more than admit their ignorance of this far country: 'I don't know. I've seen a black bear. I've never seen any others.' As Ong observes, the response of a collective farm manager with the bare bones of literacy is steered by an 'awareness of formal intellectual structures' (1982: 53) when he says: 'To go by your words they should all be white.' But the phrase 'to go by your words' indicates that the speaker may feel some discomfort at having taken this step into abstraction. Propositions deduced from 'words' convey none of the certainty of observed facts.

Another area of enquiry concerned definition. Literacy's removal of language from its immediate physical context and the consequent endophoric pressure upon it meant that written text developed a concept of definition as part of a process of creating more meanings out of itself. Luria's conclusion was that the illiterate assumed that language could only be used with an immediate context to which they could refer. Asked to define 'a tree', one respondent, not unreasonably, treats the question as ridiculous because everybody knows what a tree is. They can see it with their own eyes and do not need anybody to tell them. Another respondent replied in a way that would be predicted by many students of cognitive linguistics. We create meanings by taking a salient category member and making that stand for the category as a whole. Thus we often use a brand name to name the larger category – hoover for vacuum cleaner, for example. Using this metonymic process, the respondent described a tree as the category's subordinate members: 'apple tree, elm, poplar'. By contrast, even those with quite minimal literacy gravitate towards a more abstract, classificatory approach. They try to define an item according to its function or its core features. 'Cars' according to a subject with minimal literacy, 'use fire, are made in factories and travel fast'.

A related measure of abstraction concerns the identification of shape and its distinction from the type of object through which it is identified. Thus Greenfield (1972), who also argued that a knowledge of written language pro-motes abstract thought, gave children experiments in which they were asked to classify common objects according to their shape or some other attribute, such as colour or number. Greenfield's findings were that schooling – and hence, arguably, literacy – improved children's ability to classify objects no matter what the criterion. However, the improvement was most significant in respect of the most abstract property, namely shape. The wider suggestion is therefore that literacy enhances our ability to deal in abstraction.

The work conducted by Luria and by Greenfield indicates that those who have been in school and acquired even basic literacy may learn to extend their cognitive capabilities in some sense. However, because Luria's higher-performing subjects acquired their literacy in school, we have no way of knowing whether their superior cognitive performance is a result of education or of literacy itself. The larger claim of such scholars as Ong, Goody and Watt, and Havelock is that it is literacy itself which so altered the semiotic potential of our socio-historical environment that it induced new cognitive capabilities within us. Yet all they may really be able to show is that literacy was a key element in a culture of education that has allowed us to extend our intellec-tual capacity as never before.

The obvious problem with trying to disengage literacy's cognitive effects from those of schooling is that reading and writing are generally acquired in school. Even if taught in the home, these skills will generally be delivered within a framework of general education. For such studies to show the differ-ence between literacy and schooling, one would need to find a population that had acquired literacy in school, another that had acquired literacy outside school and a third that had not acquired literacy at all. It is difficult to imagine where one might find such a scenario since literacy is so closely associated with schooling. However, such a set of different coexistent states of literacy and oracy was found by Scribner and Cole (1981) among the Vai people in the West African state of Liberia.

Literacy rates among the Vai were quite low but the proportion of the pop-ulation who were literate had knowledge of one or more of three scripts. Those who went to school studied in English and acquired Roman script. The region was predominantly Muslim and literacy in Arabic served their religious life. Rote-learning and reading the Quran at the fireside made Arabic a 'visible, audible part of everyday life'. The Vai language also had its own indigenous syllabary. This last literacy was particularly useful for Scribner and Cole's purposes as it was acquired outside school as part of a socialisation process, or an induction into Vai life and culture. As they put it, 'learning Vai script is more or less an invisible activity that fills the interstices of people's lives' (1981: 70). Vai was used for letter-writing and Scribner and Cole describe how one subject learnt it informally from workmates so that they could send and receive letters when they were away from home. Another recalled learning the script from a parent in adulthood because the parent had become worried about how their failing sight would leave the household isolated from the literacy traffic of Vai society.

Scribner and Cole tested the Vai for their ability to deal with abstraction and categorisation through shape definition, logical ability and language understanding. To separate the effects of literacy from those of schooling they found samples that had school-based literacies in English and informal forms in Arabic and Vai. Their conclusion was broadly that although schooling exerted an effect on some areas, literacy itself could not be associated with such effects. In the area of classification, for example, they found that all groups, including non-literates, could achieve at least one successful abstraction (the dimensional sort) and all were equally good or poor at breaking up one classification and achieving another (ibid.: 121). More surprising was the absence of both strong literacy and schooling effects on categorisation and abstraction tasks, though this may have been affected by how the schooling had rarely been of more than a few years' duration and may have taken place some time in the past (ibid.: 124). It was in logic that the literacy and schooling effect showed itself most clearly, with a significant difference between those who had a school-based English language literacy and the others (ibid.: 127). Tasks intended to find differences in how language was seen and understood were more problematic. There was 'no evidence that literacy in Vai script (or other literacies) led to an understanding of "word" differing in any noticeable way from nonliterates'. Their results cast doubt on the notion that 'learning to read and write in any writing system will heighten awareness of lexical units' and make it 'akin to the grammarian's'.

Such research is supported by Karmiloff-Smith et al. (1996) who challenged Ong's (1982) and Malinowski's (1952) assertions about how our concept of the word derives uniquely from literacy. Vygotsky (1986) had maintained that preliterate children fail to understand how signs or words, and the categories that they represent, are distinct. Karmiloff-Smith et al. concluded, however, that under certain test conditions pre-literate 3–4-year-olds can identify word boundaries. *Closed categories of words*, such as the articles 'the' and 'a', require particular metalinguistic effort because they do not actually refer to anything in the world. But pre-literate children also showed some ability to recognise these when using a particular test format.

Overall, Scribner and Cole's conclusion was that 'literacy affected performance only on tasks whose requirements were linked directly to requirements of specific literacy activities among the Vai'. For example, if Vai literates were interested in discussions about what was correct Vai when writing letters, they did this not because literacy itself promoted a concept of correct language but because it was part of the social practice of letter-writing. Another more certain effect was that of the proximity of the school experience. For example, those in school showed a more fluent mastery of terminology associated with the expression of abstract thought than those who had left some years before. Again, there seemed to be few grounds to maintain that literacy's reshaping of cognition was other than an influence in a wider educational process.

Literacy practices and Vygotsky's view of mind

Scribner and Cole's work among the Vai attests to how we cannot talk about literacy as a cognition-building technology. It is not meaningful to search for a wider literacy effect upon cognition. Instead we should discuss the cognitive nature of the practices that make literacy what it is and which literacy will itself develop.

If we take the area of logic and the larger spectrum of philosophical enquiry, we can perceive the emergence of one social practice from others that may have been grounded in a pre-literate culture. For example, we have alluded to the practice of competitive boasting and character assassination in some oral societies. Such practices promote the concept of point-scoring in a competitive argument. Points may be scored according to an argument's competitive appeal, but the scorer may also see a more objective set of criteria from which to garner a judgement about how well they have done. In short, they may start to appeal not to the intuition that something is right or wrong but to a definitive set of criteria that hold it to be so. At root such criteria may be embedded into a simple assertion of belief, one that writing lets us set down as an unalterable form of words, the biblical or Quranic commandment, for example, or in its more recent and more modern form, a Bill of Rights. Often these texts come to underpin and justify a larger legal framework with its growing consensus about how some more fundamental moral stricture such as the biblical commandment, 'thou shalt not kill', should be interpreted within a given context. A concern for interpretation results in a search for the criteria against which the truth of falsity of a meaning can be established. Because they thus produce a larger industry of textual interpretation, legal literacies may redirect their larger enquiry into the nature of meaning towards the linguistic forms through which such meanings are conveyed. Motivated by the implausible goal of a definitive interpretation such enquiries still defer to the idea of some set of immutable regulatory principles or laws whose truth they will elicit but not corrupt. Finally, because laws must govern human actions, and are at root god-given, 'self-evident' and natural, nature is itself perceived as governed and now sustains an enquiry into the principles of its government. The enquiry defers to legal principles of evidence and testimony and to the theological insistence on an immutable law from which all other truths must be deduced. Thus it may be that theological and legal literacies will furnish the cornerstones of a philosophical and finally a scientific culture. Cultures that promote the idea of government by an authority that receives open counsel and advice are also more likely to foster the practices of debate, discussion and the weighing of evidence than those that vest the powers of decision making in a single authority. In Ancient Greece, it is no coincidence that the practices of philosophical and scientific enquiry emerged against the larger background of a political debate fostered by class conflict between small farmers and larger, wealthier landowners.

The above picture of the origins of rational philosophic practices is speculative. The only certainty is that philosophical practices do not always evolve where there is literacy. Nor, having evolved, do they always survive and flourish. Throughout the early medieval period, spurred on by Quranic exhortations about the value of learning, Arabic culture absorbed Greek knowledge and developed a scholastic tradition that brought about advances in the study of mathematics, language, science and medicine. The dwindling away of this spirit of learning can be attributed to a number of factors, not least among them the expansion of the Ottoman Empire and its development of an ethos of bureaucratic despotism. Yet it did not amount to a sudden flight from literacy, which remained a religious duty throughout the Islamic world. Arguments about the superior analytic capabilities of the Greek alphabet and its ability to promote such modes of thought are based on a misunderstanding of the Arabic alphabet. To this day, and notwithstanding its principled omissions of short vowels, the Arabic alphabet provides a more accurate representation of the phonetics of its language than the applications of the Greek and Roman writing systems to such Germanic languages as English. We should further remember that the consonantal alphabet on which both Arabic and Greek are based partly evolved from the mercantile culture of its people. Its larger analytic capacity did not trigger a grand philosophical tradition in Phoenicia, and the fact that this took place in Greece must have been due to the convergence of many practices and not to the nature of the adopted literacy technology itself. In sum, we need first to understand how the literacies that supported science and philosophy emerged from a coincidental confluence of other socio-linguistic practices, some fostered by the new alphabetic writing and some rooted in much older traditions. Second, we need to understand a literacy as first and foremost a grouping of socio-historical practices. We need to view it not as something we do with reading and writing, but as a configuration of social activities that form and are formed by the literacy events to which they give rise. Such a perception will allow us to see the social practice as one way in which the mind reshapes its semiotic environment through the use of reading and writing. It will then position the literacy practice as the means through which the mind achieves an unfolding reorganisation and development of itself.

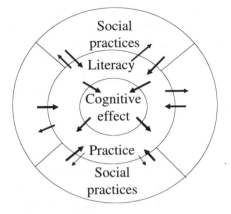

Figure 13.1 Accommodating a social practice view of literacy within a socio-historical model of mind

The Vygotskian model does not view cognition as waiting in a limited but stable pre-literate state before it is finally edged over into a creative ferment by the sudden introduction of literacy's new forms of sign use. Cognitive development, according to the instigator of the ZPD, is a fluid response to how the mind is scaffolded by its socio-cultural environment. The scaffolding is erected out of an induction into socio-cultural practice. For its part, the practice will endure only if it can scaffold a creative dynamic within the cognition of its users. We can therefore see the symbiotic nature of the relationship between a practice and the state of mind that it fosters, and on which its perpetuation depends. As Scribner and Cole put it:

> The general construct of practice offers a possibility for integrating socio-cultural and psychological levels of analysis and achieving explanatory accounts of how basic mental processes and structures become specialized and diversified through experience. (Scribner and Cole 1981: 13)

In figure 13.1, I model this view of a literacy practice as both a consequence of a cognitive operation and its cause whilst remaining a confluence of other social practices. Essentially the practice is both its cognitive effect and the consequence of adjacent or similar practices, and we can see how this would operate in some of the instructional models that have been implemented.

Scaffolding with literacy practices

Heath (1983) revealed the indirect effects of home discourse on children's emerging literacy skills. Literacy development of children from privileged backgrounds, was, by implication, scaffolded within a deep and varied discourse and the type of interactions that it fostered. Yet the practices that engender such discourse can be recreated within the school. Heath and Brandscombe (1985) plotted how one could develop writing among remedial students through the practice of exchanging letters, first with people in their own age group, then with a higher class. The letters from the higher class help the remedial students to notice, then to use, the units of which a letter is composed. The example provides a model of how one can activate the model shown in figure 13.1. Letter-writing provides an example of a literacy practice as a confluence of other practices involving different types of social interaction. It was once central to how literacy could operate the socialisation function of language across space and time. It gave concrete form to many of the practices of greeting and leave-taking with which people facilitate their contact one with another, confirming their common membership of a social group or class. In Heath and Brandscombe's study, scaffolding for the remedial group was constructed out of the responses of their audience of seniors. The letters that they wrote in reply provided an example of more appropriate textual moves which the remedial group started to analyse and apply to their own writing. Heath and Brandscombe (1986) showed how the book and the narrative can help educators scaffold the wider process of literacy and language acquisition. Nystrand (1997) makes the larger point that one cannot advance the acquisition of literacy if one perceives it as decontextualised knowledge which less privileged students can simply be brought to know. In focusing 'comprehensively on children's interactions with others', one has to place learning inside the social context of learning. Composed as it is of the practices of the children's home and school life, it is this context 'which sanctions' children's 'reading and writing and consequently promotes the values and expectations essential to literacy' (Nystrand 1997).

Brodova et al. (1999) advance the interpenetration of practice and mind inside the activity of learning to write in kindergarten using the three Vygotskian techniques of *materialisation, private speech* and *shared activity*. Materialisation, described by Gal'perin (1969) and Haenin (1996), is when teachers use physical actions or objects to symbolise the technique they are trying to put across. For example, in the study of Brodova et al., the teacher asks the child what they want to write. They then help the child to draw a line on their paper that will represent each word they want to use, thus giving physical form to the concept of the word itself and helping the child to internalise it. Private speech exploits the way children and adults quite naturally talk to themselves when confronted with a difficult task (Berk 1992). This conversation with the self can be used as a method whereby the teacher hears how a student formulates a given learning strategy and can thus help them to reformulate it in the most useful and powerful manner. Brodova et al. used the technique when children were asked to comment on what they were doing when giving words a material form as lines. A shared activity is crucial to the Vygotskian concept of learning. Because learning begins in our manipulation of the world outside the mind, or as social intervention, we must externalise the knowledge that we wish to convey as activity amongst other people. The sharing in Brodova et al.'s study was between the child who materialised the words as lines and the teacher who guided the activity. The project was between two groups: an experimental one, which was subject to the scaffolded procedure; and a control group, which learnt in a more conventional manner. The results found significant differences between the groups in such areas as the complexity of written language used, spelling accuracy and the number of words produced.

The perception of literacy acquisition as social, and finally about how one scaffolds development within the practice, entails a need to counter the routine devaluation of the language practices of disenfranchised groups by mainstream education, which has been recognised by researchers such as Cook-Gumperz (1986). Showing how one can use a vernacular practice as a way to extend her students' ZPD towards a school-based one, Lee (2000) takes the example of signifying in the AAL speech community. Signifying involves ritualised and sometimes competitive use of word-play and figurative language. This becomes a means through which to access school-based literary criticism.

A practice interpretation of Vygotskian theory also makes the multicultural classroom central to how we think about literacy acquisition. A perception of literacy as a singular, measurable entity that permits the performance of a social function results in the construction of the wrong scaffolding for a given cultural minority (Laughlin et al. 2001). It means that the learning experience of the school may become too remote from the practices of the home, establishing literacy as more culturally alien than it is. The gulf can also exist within pedagogical methods as well as literacy, an insight that made Raphael et al. (2001) realise how their students also needed to understand how the 'important customs' teachers brought to the classroom could add 'passion to the curriculum'. This insight could help literacy educators understand how they needed to scaffold their students' development within the types of practices that they themselves took for granted because they were provided by their social background. For example, they could re-establish book clubs, helping them develop the discursive discourse that surrounded some literacy practices while using such shared activity to foster a stronger interest in critical reading (Raphael et al. 2001: 379). In this way, we understand that literacy is no longer an imparted technology which the student is left to discard or use at will. Literacy is the social manifestation of the cognitive process that it fostered. To be fully literate is to engage in literacy practices, and to become literate is not simply to acquire a predetermined set of skills. It is the acquisition of the desire to participate in certain socio-cultural practices and an understanding of the skills that these require.

Conclusions

In this chapter, I have discussed how we can use a Vygotskian view of mind to examine the relationship between the literacy practice and the cognitive structures it employs. I stressed the symbiotic nature of the relationship between these forms of cognitive and social activity, arguing that we should not look for the effect of literacy upon cognition but should instead understand cognitive development as scaffolded by social practices, and these practices as engendering cognitive effects that are peculiar to them. I then cited some of the many examples of literacy education that show how this can be done. I would also emphasise that one of the dilemmas in literacy education concerns a concept that has been expressed as *post-literacy*, or the issue of how to sustain literacy once basic reading skills have been imparted. The understanding of a literacy as practices means we can put aside the post-literacy concept, because learning to read and write constitutes an induction into practices where writing and reading occur. In this sense, we can perceive literacy as self-sustaining, provided that an induction to the practice has been successful and a participation in it is sustained.

Exercises

1. List some of the uses of literacy as these have evolved over time. Try to decide if these uses of literacy could have exerted a specific cognitive effect. For example, think about the evolution of dictionaries, the much earlier process of word separation or the use of the alphabet in the Arab development of algebra. Justify your decision and expose the weaknesses in your argument.
2. Imagine that you had to design a research project which had to link one or more of the cognitive effects described above to a literacy innovation. Say how you would design the project and discuss its potential flaws and weaknesses.
3. Scribner and Cole's study has been interpreted differently by different commentators. Some, such as Barton (1994), consider that it makes arguments about a literacy effect on cognition unsustainable; others still think it is possible to argue that literacy, or more specifically alphabetic literacy, introduced real and powerful change in our cognitive capacity (for example, Olson 1994). After reviewing the historical and the psychological evidence, discuss whether or not you could still maintain that there was a Great Divide.
4. This author treats the Great Divide as both a psychological and a historical theory. Discuss whether that dual approach is justified by Vygotskian theory.

14 Literacy and Patterns of Mind

Introduction

If literacy practice and mind are mutually constitutive, then we should reflect further on the mechanisms through which that cognitive effect is achieved. To advance that discussion, we need to consider some of the cognitive theories that deal with how we store meanings, patterns and ways of doing things. Some of the more recent versions of these theories have already been touched upon, as when we looked at metaphor deconstruction and critical literacy in Chapter 2, or symbolisation and sign in Chapter 5. Here, we will elaborate on these ideas and place them in the larger discussion of the literacy practice and its cognitive effect.

Although we must make allowances for improvisation and change within a given social structure, a practice will, by definition, constitute a forum of repeated activity. Such a patterning presupposes a conscious or unconscious grasp of event orders and events on the part of the practitioner as well as of how the events' meaning should be framed within a given cognitive predisposition. In order to understand this we need to look at three concepts in cognitive theory. The first is the theory of frames, the second is that of scripts, and the third is the larger and more general idea of a schema, which can function as a broader superordinate name for the first two. I will consider frame theory first.

Frame theory

When we considered the concept of a category in Chapter 5, we learnt how a given category can group quite a large number of sometimes disparate phenomena. A related but earlier concept is that of the frame (Minsky 1975). A frame is put forward as a structure through which we build knowledge. Memory therefore 'comprises millions of frames' that arrange data in a hierarchy which determines how central they are to the idea being described (Sandford and Garrod 1981: 31). Thus when we think of a child's birthday party, we identify it with certain 'necessary and fixed' features, 'the hosts and the guests', then with normal but optional features, 'the presents', 'the games' and 'the décor' (ibid.). The first set is essential to our concept of a child's birthday. The second will normally contribute to our understanding of this idea. However, if we move to another culture we might recognise a child's birthday even though it had no games or décor, simply because there are hosts and guests. It is only when the last two elements are missing that the frame collapses.

We can see the relevance to our topic of Minsky's frames when we consider how they organise almost any structured situation or phenomenon. There are frames for objects and, significantly, these allow us to complete and hence recognise something of which we only have partial sight. For example, if we saw the silhouette of a man or woman moving in the darkness of our home, we could construct from this fleeting impression a larger picture of a human intruder. We could attribute to the silhouette a host of composite but unseen features, such as the 'ears nose, face, limbs, etc.' as well as the more abstract, 'a capacity for speech, sensation and emotion'. We can do this because we carry a cognitive frame for a human being and use this to complete the very sketchy impression that we actually obtain using our eyes. Writers can assume that they will share frames with their readers and that the same phenomena will evoke similar features, but they must also allow for how different cultures and personal histories will frame the same concept differently.

Our participation in a given literacy practice may establish certain shared frames. It may also make assumptions about the type of frames we carry within us. We can see this within a concept called *mind style* (Fowler 1996). Halliday (1971) argued that attributes of text can be used to convey how a character may have a more limited understanding of the world than we. Thus a restricted vocabulary can convey a character's limited vision, and a use of language can be wedded to the way a given character sees the world. Fowler's elaboration, mind style, refers to the world-view, or the way of seeing of the narrator or character in a story. This view is conveyed through the ideational structure of the text.

Semino (2002) uses Fowler's notion and frame theory to elaborate this point. She takes as one of her examples, a character in Louis de Bernière's book, *Captain Corelli's Mandolin*. Semino uses de Bernière's setting of wartime Greece to show how the simple-minded shepherd, Alekos, cannot make sense of a military parachutist, who, after landing, tries to use a radio. She argues that the author treats Alekos as having no frame for parachutist, and therefore as needing to map the descent of the person onto that of the only frame for a flying humanoid he possesses. This is the frame of an angel. Alekos therefore interprets the whistles and crackles of the radio as 'angel speech' and thinks that God has 'modernised' his messenger's armaments by giving him a pistol instead of a spear. This type of authorial play with a character's limited frames is far from uncommon. A popular literary and cinematic device is to create comic effect by using the mind style of a child narrator to misinterpret adult mysteries. It reveals how 'mind style', rather than being a conscious stance of an author or character towards the world, is built out of their own knowledge frames and is dependent on these. It also implies how writers make assumptions about the frames of their readers and use them to complete the text. De Bernière's intended humour depends on a reader who can frame parachutists as parachutists and angels as mythical creatures who do not carry guns.

We can see, therefore, that we interpret text through the cognitive frames that we bring to its language. We can also understand how authors will play upon discrepancies in the way these frames are constructed to create a certain mind style. Such devices work because the text and reader are situated inside a practice that can assume such common frames while anticipating an authorial play with them. A given literacy practice, such as novel-reading, will make assumptions about the cognitive frames shared by its members. It may also establish others that are peculiar to it, as when a technical or academic text tries to build a new term in its readers or re-embed a familiar one in a new context of use.

Script theory

Temporal or programmatic frames have been called *scripts* by Schank and Abelson (1977). Scripts give us the expectation that events will unfold according to a particular sequence. For example, if we want to travel to a given destination overseas, we know that we will have to go to a travel agent or an airline office, or use the internet, to find out the most convenient or cost-effective time, make a reservation and purchase a ticket. We know this because we hold a script of the relevant sequence.

Schema theory and narrative frames

As sequential orders, scripts can be related to what Minsky calls *narrative* or *text frames*. Like other types of frame, these relate to the concept of a schema as it was conceived by the psychologist F. C. Bartlett. In one of Bartlett's experiments (1932) he learnt folk-tales from Native Americans, then recounted them to British students in exactly the way that they had been told to him. Bartlett's contention was that we would remember a story in a certain way and according to the narrative structures which we have heard since childhood. These culturally shaped and repeated patterns build schemas (Greek plural: schemata) which organise our knowledge for us, determining where we will put a narrative phase, and also, perhaps, the emphasis we accord to it and the way we talk about it. Bartlett's observation was that after some time had elapsed, his students would reorganise the Native American narratives along European lines. His conclusion was that they did this because from birth they had schematised Western narrative patterns and would use this to reorganise any relevant data, whether or not it was delivered in that way.

In Chapter 5, we mentioned how the linguist Propp (1968) had sought to identify typical narrative structures as these existed in text. We now understand how folk stories will typically have an orientation phase, where they introduce the reader to the characters and the 'setting' in which they live. They will then have a problem-raising phase where events occur that require a 'solution', though solutions may fail and beget other complications. Finally, the problems meet a 'resolution', which is sometimes carried towards the present by a coda, or a comment that things have been like that ever since, or the protagonists lived happily ever after (Labov 1972). A genre is in some measure a realisation in text of this type of schema. However, a given discourse schema may be shared by different genres, as when certain types of academic research papers also contain an orientation, raise problems and posit solutions. A genre will therefore also be identified by other frames, such as those which store its linguistic formulations and the sense of how appropriate they are in a given context. Therefore, reading in a given genre may create a relevant schema while employing those that are already there. But a discourse structure and a script or narrative frame should not be treated as the same thing. Genre is an attribute of text and a schema is a property of cognition. Genre and schema could be seen as mutually constitutive, however.

Genre, schema and literacy practice

We can now start to place genre as a dimension of the ongoing interaction of mind and practice. This is illustrated in figure 14.1.

Genre is a defining attribute of a literacy practice as this is manifest in the texts upon which a practice will focus. For example, romantic novels belong to a quite private practice of silent, recreational reading. A dimension of the practice could be the exchange of views about the novel's plot, characters or qualities between readers. This exchange is steered by the expectations that the genre gives the reader. They may require a certain kind of ending, for example, and be disconcerted if it does not appear. The practice of writing romantic fiction will acknowledge the transformational power of the genre, allowing it to produce a gripping narrative from a loose collection of events. Whether it transforms material or sets up reader expectations, the genre transmits a set of social expectations about the nature of a given text. That act of transmission is central to the practice, affecting its shape and ensuring its perpetuation. A genre may carry modes of expression from one practice to another. Writing love poetry was once the quite public expression of some of the larger practices surrounding courtship between certain class members. Recently, it has

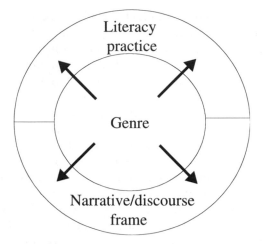

Figure 14.1 Genre as an attribute of practice and frame

become more private, a way for the author to express their own emotions to themselves, perhaps to control them better. What may have begun as the poet's use of a quite public genre to understand their own emotions may result in a modification of the genre, bending it away from a public, declarative tone towards a private dialogue with the self.

As a social product, genre draws together the principles that constrain how meaning will be represented. Yet a practice and a genre cannot simply be placed 'out there' in society because finally that location exists only as a property of the mind of which that space is composed, and of the interactions in which they are engaged. A genre is therefore the textual identity of a frame or schema, just as the schema is the cognitive identity of the genre.

Image schema

Another type of mental pattern that has been more recently exposed is the image schema. This is the cognitive frame that underpins the conceptual metaphor. In Chapter 3, we learnt how much of our discourse about everyday topics was organised by related metaphors, with time always being discussed as if it were space or an object in space, for example. More significantly, all abstract language evolves from metaphor, and generally from metaphors which are constructed out of physical or visible phenomena (e.g. Lakoff and Johnson 1999).

Image schemas are the mental images that we have of ourselves as embodied creatures and of our embodied interactions with the physical world. We use these images to form the conceptual metaphors through which we grasp abstract ideas. If we consider how we express the emotion anger, we talk about being 'hot under the collar', 'letting off steam', 'exploding with fury', having a 'pent-up' or 'bottled-up wrath' then 'letting it all come out'. We notice how we think about the abstract emotion as if it were a physical essence held within us, with our bodies as its container (Lakoff and Johnson 1980). This gives us a conceptual metaphor 'the body is a container'. We also understand how 'containment' is essential to the way we conceptualise many abstract ideas, reaching beyond our perception of the body itself. For example, it underpins how we conceptualise thought itself as when we talk about our *inner* life or of our bafflement at what is going on *inside* somebody's head. When, in logical argument, we 'deduce' a statement from others, as in the syllogisms discussed above, we are using a Latin term, *deducere*, whose literal meaning is 'lead out of' and are therefore treating the deduced proposition as actually 'contained' in those on which it is based. It becomes apparent, therefore, that our bodily experience of ourselves as a kind of container of blood and heat has developed a very deep schematisation of the idea of containment. The container is therefore an image-schema which is used by conceptual metaphor. Without these conceptual metaphors and their schemas we would not be able to think about abstract ideas such as emotion, thought and logic at all.

We have already outlined how the processes of metaphor-making and interpretation are crucial to the development of writing. Iconic signs underpin early writing systems and, even after their conventionalisation as symbols, new forms of iconicity continue to develop the communicative potential of our graphic systems. For example, graphs use the schema of vertical orientation, or the metaphors 'up is more' and 'down is less' to express quantity. The visual arrangement of text equates size with importance, or importance with spatial isolation. Most fundamentally, when we give language a visual representation, we are using a 'time is space' metaphor, perceiving the language that unfolds in time as language unfolding in space. It is evident then that literacy begins in the exploitation of certain image schema. Furthermore, these schemas are not isolated and inviolable semantic frames but are parts of a developing network of cognitive frames that can enhance our ability to grapple with abstract ideas. Learning to use one schema in a new way – perceiving speech as a spatial entity for example – will provide us with an enhanced cognitive resource, one which will stimulate our exploration of other topics.

We have already questioned how Great Divide theory connects the development of logical and deductive thought to the development of alphabetic literacy, arguing that such processes were scaffolded by a combination of social practices, such as political debate or speech competitions. However, the development of a philosophical literacy will further scaffold our exploration of deductive thought. It can do this by exploiting the image schema whose fuller potential is uncovered by writing. We can understand this if we consider the use of horizontal and vertical space, or the associated schema that Johnson (1989) calls 'the path'.

Writing is given existence by our use of various spatial schemas to represent meaning. Most fundamentally, we see time as space, unfolding language upon a horizontal or vertical line. By giving language a spatial existence, we enhanced our understanding of it, and may have also triggered a wider interest in how we can use the schemas of spatial orientation to explore other types of meaning. Logic, and cause-and-effect relations in particular, may provide one example of this.

Like all abstract ideas, cause-and-effect relations are conceptualised through an image-schema. One of the vehicles used is the 'path', or the concept of a spatial connection. Lakoff and Johnson (1999: 170–234) analyse 'cause' as a point in space that is connected to an effect, which is another point in space. Thus a statement 'leads us to' a logical conclusion as if from location to location along a path. If we see a cause-and-effect relation, we talk about establishing a 'connection' between two events, as if they are two points in space that we have tied together. Writing itself isolates words, and by implication meanings, as locations, which we may or may not use other words to connect. In short, the schematic bases of writing and logic are sometimes the same.

Cause-and-effect is conceptualised through a variety of image-schemas, among which spatial connection is only one. Another cause-and-effect schema, which relates more closely to our bodily existence and our genetic origins, is that of procreation and pro-generation (Lakoff and Johnson 1999). Causes produce or generate effects out of themselves as when we say that an effect is produced by a cause or brings it about. Yet pro-generation is itself conceptualised through spatial metaphor. We 'come from' a family in the more literal manner that we 'come from' our mother. We also retain family 'connections' and in the past talked of our lineage. Furthermore, we cannot overlook our parents and their lineage as our biological *raison d'être*. Therefore, we treat procreation as a prototypical cause, using pro-generation as a metaphor of causation, but we express this through spatial connection. We come from our parents rather as one idea is led out of another. Because establishing a connection between two events as if they were locations can be used to attribute cause, the connection's discovery also confers an idea of rectitude. This metaphor fashions the concept of family in many societies. Children inherit the goods, the titles and even offices of their parents. Those who are not gifted with the legitimacy of a direct connection become insecure and need to establish the prospect of their own line.

Lineage also has a wider ontological significance. It locates people within time, giving them the sense of being more than creatures who are simply stranded on their own island of allotted life, but of creatures who can exist as part of an unfolding pattern. This infuses them with purpose and reinforces another common conceptual metaphor; that of life as a journey (Lakoff and Johnson 1980), one which again exploits the ubiquitous 'path' image-schema. Journeys are goal-directed and afford the sense of one life as being given purpose by its becoming a platform for the next.

Some of our earliest visual texts express this ontological need to express lineage and legitimise our current existence by connecting us to a pro-generative *raison d'être*. Totem poles are pre-literate texts that locate tribal members within an unfolding sense of lineage. They may also permit an onto-logical location as a pathway back from our present, material existence towards the spiritual and mythical existences of our ancestors. We have seen how the development of writing cannot be separated from the need to assert ownership over property and to confirm identity with seals, then signatures. Our sense of identity and the associated claim to legitimacy rest in our estab-lishment of lineage. In some Native American tribes, the need for a genealogy and its associated practices may have carved text from the trunks of trees to connect a present life to its ancestral past, creating the totems that we can still see today. In late medieval and Renaissance Europe, we can again see how lit-eracy kindled the search for cause and legitimacy in the obsessive construction of family trees. These documents exploit the capacity of literacy to create an interaction between diagrammatic symbolism and language. Some late Renaissance versions of the tree, such as the Spanish example shown in figure 14.2, treat their subject with a decorative literalness, nesting family members amidst their bowers as if they were the cast of a woodland fantasy. This example, from *circa* 1530, further legitimises the claim of its subject, Ramero, by showing his victory in battle over his half-brothers in the border below. Some of these documents draw the bloodline as a more straightforward line of descent, and claim the unfolding cause-and-effect sequence that legitimises Henry IV of England in the *Tabula Regum Anglie ab Adamo usque ad Henricum IV*. This presumptuous document gives Henry IV a biblical legiti-macy by unscrolling his ancestry from Adam, the biblical first man. The line of kings is itself the document's organising principle, running down the centre of the parchment and attaching to each descendant a Latin text that describes their achievements.

A second and much earlier example from the twelfth century, shown in figure 14.3, reverses the concept of descent to one of ascent by showing the lineage of Christ as a process of ascent from his earthly parentage towards a moment of infusion when the seven gifts of the Holy Spirit emanate from him.

The text exploits other attributes of literacy's spatial schema, detailing the gifts in writing whilst connecting them to the halo of a visually represented Christ, the halo forming part of a spiritual mansion, or vessel from which the text emanates.

The tree-form and its supporting schematisations of cause, lineage and legitimacy have now evolved into more diverse, abstract and ubiquitous schemas, supporting the identification of organisational principles and the analysis of cause-and-effect connections. We now see tree diagrams developed as instruments of symbolic logic and adopted into the analysis of transforma-tional syntax. We see the evolution of the tree as a flowchart showing the con-nections between the phases of an operation. The tree is an organisation chart,

Figure 14.2 Exploiting a metaphor of spatial connection *circa* 1530 (by permission of the British Library)

Figure 14.3 Genealogy, spatial metaphor and lineage as an ascending spatial order: 'the house of wisdom' (by permission of the British Library)

illustrating corporate hierarchies or reporting structures. All these create new sets of meaning relations and analytic possibilities. For example, figure 14.4 shows how a tree diagram is used to reveal the syntactic organisation of a sentence. This device exposes a surface form, the sentence as it is written or uttered, while uncovering the phrases of which it is composed, as well as the categories of parts of speech of which these are made up. In a metaphor of generation and analysis, it shows a sentence at four levels simultaneously, as if taken outside time:

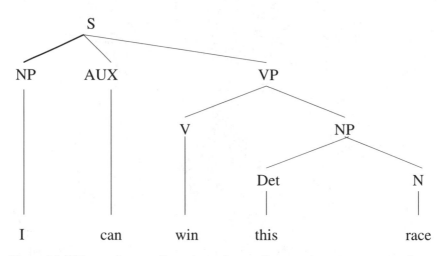

Figure 14.4 Literacy's many dimensions: the tree diagram shows a sentence at four levels of analysis

There is the sentence itself, S, then three phrases of which it is composed, NP (noun-phrase), AUX (the auxiliary), and VP, the verb-phrase. While the NP and the AUX are each instantiated by one word, the pronoun 'I' and the auxiliary 'can', the VP phrase itself divides into two components, a verb, 'win', and a noun phrase (NP), 'this race'. This is again subdivided into its components, a determiner, 'this', and a noun, 'race'.

Figure 14.4 is one example of how literacy proposes methods of extending the spatial metaphors through which we grasp and analyse abstract meanings. As we have described, it exploits a tree schema that is used to analyse the components of a given entity as if providing them with their own genealogy. As in an order of descent, the sentence spawns its constituent phrases which in turn produce their own constituents. This is not to say that all of these diagrammatic methods have a close chronological or developmental pedigree. My argument is certainly not that syntactic tree diagrams, whilst being evolved out of the tree diagrams of symbolic logic, can also claim direct descent from genealogical trees. It would be even more absurd to suggest that the metaphors of space and procreation that underpin these modes of analysis are a product of the literacy practices in which they are employed. We therefore cannot even claim that cognitive metaphor theory gives new strength to the Great Divide hypothesis by suggesting that literacy extended our conceptual possibilities by offering the new image-schematic resource of language arranged in space. Rather, our objective is to show how image schemas are, like Minsky's textual frames, another channel through which mind and literacy practice develop each other. They also lend themselves to many different purposes, whether it is the illustration of a line of descent or the analysis of a corporate structure. They therefore put the conceptualisations developed within one practice into the service of another, developing the potential of the written medium, and implicating the exploration of new forms of analysis. Image schemas make themselves available to the constructions that we wish to explore, becoming the vehicles through which one practice will influence and help establish another. The schemas may also stimulate the act of exploration itself by furnishing us with an extended cognitive resource. Giving language a spatial existence opens a new diagrammatic resource, allowing us to map the connections between names, then concepts, and thus gain a better understanding the components from which a given entity has evolved.

Conclusions

In this chapter I have tried to go a little beyond the standard way of looking at literacy and social practice as these are reflected in mind. I have looked at the channels through which literacy practices exert their mental effect. I looked first at Minsky's frame theory and its assertion that we use frames to complete the incomplete perceptions of reality that our sensory systems afford us. I saw how this transfers to literacy texts. Practices construct their frames and schemas. These schemas pertain to both the structure of discourse that is associated with a given practice, or its genres, in other words, and to the larger pattern of social interaction, or the manner in which it unfolds. Such schematisations were the cognitive representation of a text's generic structure. They are in a mutually constitutive relationship with the practices of which the genre is a part, showing how the practice takes a cognitive form and how this will generate a certain type of text.

I then turned to the concept of an image schema. I suggested that literacy's transposition of language into a visual format had put new image-schematic possibilities at the service of thought. I showed how this might operate with the metaphor of a 'tree'. I also saw such schemas not as a method through which we separate practices, associating a tree metaphor with one practice, and an 'up' metaphor with another, but as a device that ensures their cross-fertilisation and mutual development.

Exercises

1. Review the passages on mind style in this chapter. Find an editorial in the popular press. Show how the writer creates a 'mind style' through their shared assumptions about what some of the language means. Use cognitive frame theory to do this. For example, if the article were about gun crime, consider the assumptions about how writer and reader frame the word 'gun' and how this contributes to the article's mind style.
2. Take a text of 300–500 words from any source. Review the literacy practice the text is part of, suggesting what its central features are and how it unfolds. Profile the frame with which the text operates from the perspective of its own organisational schema and from that of the practice.
3. Try to think of other metaphors and their associated image schemas that are produced or reinforced by literacy's spatial representation of language. Describe how these might affect our larger perception of the world.

Part V

Conclusions

15 The Social Nature of Literacy

Introduction

In this book I have explored literacy as a skill required by society, as a level of understanding of society and our place in it, and as a social activity. I have considered the manifestation of literacy as text, first from the perspective of its visual existence as script, then from that of a use of language or discourse. Finally, I have turned to literacy as a cognitive state, asking about the mental patterns with which it is associated. Through this exploration, I have sought to embed our understanding of literacy in a sense of its history and its international, multicultural nature, thinking not only of its contemporary texts but those of the past also. My final objective is to draw these different strands of thought together and leave the reader with a more coherent understanding of our topic.

Literacy as skill, practice and socio-economic function

On the surface, an advocacy of literacy as a state of knowledge that allows a social function is not compatible with an understanding of literacy as the social practices in which we engage. The one tries to objectify it as a socially defined goal, the other places it inside the society of which we are a part, associating it with our own subjectivity by identifying it with the activities from which our sense of self is constituted. Yet we have also concluded that we may need all of these apparently incompatible modes of understanding to make the literacy phenomenon complete. Thus, functionality gives us literacy as a planning target, criticality reveals literacy as an educational process and the practice view integrates it into our social existence.

Perhaps, first, we should consider that the process of becoming literate is central to our understanding of the state that is attained. Yet this educative process cannot be separated from the activities by which the attained state is defined. The only literacy function is the practices in which we engage and the only literacy state is the level of knowledge that such an engagement requires. For the purposes of educational argument, a 'cognitive state' supposes a stable condition for the mastery of skills and hence a condition that educators can target. Yet, this model also acknowledges that when educators take such states as a target, they are effectively 'freeze-framing' a dynamic of our social existence. One result is that literacy education is placed elsewhere, put into an academic holding-pen, where, reconstructed as a process of skills acquisition, it leave its students with no sense of what these skills are for. Yet all complicated social activity requires an apprenticeship, establishing the necessary rites of passage. We cannot, like the subjects' of some ill-applied whole-book method of literacy acquisition, simply plunge students into a complicated practice such as novel reading, and leave them to swim through the problems of interpretation that it poses. In other words, we need to wed the literacy function to our ability to engage in the practices that may constitute our wider existence. We also need to learn how to understand these zones of activity, appraise what their students need to know or question how they came to be.

It should be self-evident that education has as its objective the attainment of different cognitive states by the educated. If literacy reveals itself as social practices, then these practices both shape and are shaped by the cognitive state that is their prerequisite. The educator's understanding of these states of mind, as they exist in others, will in turn determine what they teach. But pedagogy is not only about a straightforward induction to accepted forms of activity; it is also about a parallel development of a stronger critical disposition, and, hence, a more creative engagement with the practices to which we are inducted. Only then does the literacy student become a practitioner in the real sense of entering into a critical dialogue with a prevailing cultural ethos and thereby developing its future forms.

Finally, we must distinguish between local and global practice. What literacy does is an attribute of the types of community with which its users engage. Communities can now be local or global, or both. A community should no longer have a geographic meaning. The term might make better sense if we define it according to a larger and common communicative goal. Academic literacies, for example, now reach beyond the linguistic frontiers within which they first took shape. Yet academic literacies express a common community interest in knowledge formulation and transmission. According to Swales (1990), a *discourse community* is a group of language users who have common communicative aims. They also possess genres, or ways of linguistically structuring knowledge that are specific to them, share terminology and accompanying forms of expression whilst possessing channels through which they can communicate information with each other. Spatial congregation, whether or not it occurs, is irrelevant to the establishment of such communities. Some communities, however, do have a local geography. They have a vernacular and use it to express an indigenous culture. Such communities must underpin the strong sense of identity that is essential to a critical foray into the literacies that our global media now make available. Such global practices may entail the use of global languages, but when multilingualism is treated as the normal condition and divested of its association with social exclusion and under-achievement, a global and a local language are no longer necessary opposites.

Participatory appraisal: the model in practice

Towards the end of the twentieth century we saw the emergence of literacy approaches that take the larger eclectic view of literacy that the above discussion appraisal (PRA) grouped a series of techniques that were used for analysing the needs of rural communities in order to ensure that development aid was properly directed. A core understanding of PA is that the community should be treated as owners of the information concerning their development needs. Therefore, the objective of the needs analyst was not to enter a community, survey it, identify a missing commodity such as water for crop irrigation, recommend the construc-tion of a tube well and the importation of pumping equipment, then depart. Such methods failed to recognise the nature of the community in which they engaged. Typically, the newly provided pump might breakdown because maintenance skills were not to hand, or the pattern of local landownership meant that the digging of irrigation ditches linked to a common water source was impossible.

The PA solution was to devise a series of activities through which the commu-nity would identify their needs. For example, the needs analyst could ask com-munity leaders to engage in values clarification, ranking in order of importance the improvements that they would most like to see. The analyst might then con-struct a matrix which listed the improvements to be made on one axis whilst exploring the factors that prevented their implementation along another. Other activities involved semi-structured interviews or mapping the community with its members, not simply to discover such features as who lived where and who owned what, but also to understand the social relations that were involved.

The deeper understanding was that a community might require a package of inventions in quite different areas to ensure a holistic development process. One aspect of this development might be literacy. Archer (1994) revealed how a lit-eracy intervention could itself take the form of a PA exercise. The process of becoming literate also uncovered the wider community that the literacy inter-vention intends to address whilst shaping the practices into which it would be embedded. The type of literacy offered, and the way in which its provision is structured, responds to the needs that its instructional process uncovers. This development will, in its turn, feed the larger process of community develop-ment. Literacy might begin with the identification of a mapping ground, or an area of the village where community members draw the plan of their village. Those who understand Freirean methodology might find here a sense of how literacy can be approached through visual literacy. One thus moves from the concrete village to its semi-abstract and still iconic representation, the map, to its highly abstract symbolisation, the literate representation of the word. There is also a strong critical and dialogic element. The map can reveal a disquiet about inequities in land distribution or the control of production by the transport companies that take produce to market. Yet the analysis does not proceed from the patronising assertion of the inequities that are known to exist. The analysis emerges from the participants' own understanding of their community.

In a further stage of abstraction the map is labelled and transferred to paper. It is as if, by lifting it from the ground, the literacy teacher further removes it from the reality it represents, pushing it further into the representational and symbolic realm from which literacy evolves. Labelling the map introduces writing. Written language is now introduced in order to enhance the community's growing capacity for self-expression, embedding literacy in the language practices of the community.

We can see mechanisms that engage people in literacies that do not emerge from any misinformed sense of what they need to do. These mechanisms do not impose a vision of socio-economic relations that is either so abstract it is unreal, or of such rigid construction that it fails to understand the intricacies of the cultures with which it has to engage. We should not assume that such approaches should be confined to the developing world. The sense of literacy activity as beginning in a community's use of language and in its closer understanding of itself may inform all successful literacy education, beginning, for example, in familiar narratives of family life with which teachers know they can engage young children. Thus early writing expresses their family and community existences even as it extends this map of localised existences into a larger fictive, story-telling realm.

However plausible such an approach may sound, one might argue that an integrative model of literacy will fail because it does not understand the contrasting nature of the ideas with which it has to deal. Thus, functionality evolves from literacy as a collection of socio-linguistic and socio-economic competences, whilst a practice theory of literacy derives from a mode of social description. However, when we deepened our understanding of literacy as a mental state in Part IV, we looked at Vygotsky's view of society and mind as mutually constitutive. Within such a model, a practice is a product of the mental schemas that we possess, and those schemas are built by the practices in which we participate. In this sense, we can start to understand how we can see literacy as a confluence of social activities, the mental states that these induce, the texts that they produce or interpret, and the functional level that these schematisations and interpretations require.

Text as a forum of the literacy practice

If we integrate the literacy state, the literacy function and the literacy activity within a Vygotskian concept of the social construction of mind, we can then perceive written texts themselves as a zone of this socio-cognitive interaction, at once a method representing the expressive needs of the literacy practice and of giving voice to its cognitive existence. Texts are thus a vehicle which can enhance our understanding of the practices of which they are a part. Such understanding also helps us to achieve a more practice-focused literacy education. In Parts II and III, I described how we might analyse the semiotic components of written text as attributes of the context in which the text operates and of the social practices out of which that context is constituted, as well as of the cognitive processes that we bring to bear. I considered the early semiotic systems of Charles Peirce and Ferdinand de Saussure in order to find a framework through which we might analyse writing as sign. I also showed how we can use the work of scholars such as Deacon (1998) to study how these earlier systems evolved as expressions of the socially embedded cognition that characterises our humanity. I recounted metonymy's illustration of how signs can represent categories while stimulating their evolution from indexical to symbolic form. In Part lll, I turned to the question of how we determine the nature of written language and the way it might differ from the spoken form. I looked at some of the features of written and spoken language that have been characterised as oppositional. This discussion brought us to the view that texts do not differ consistently according to whether they are spoken or written, but through the ways in which they are used to accomplish different purposes. These differences exist as much between different written genres as between spoken and written ones. I found support for this by looking first at Biber's quantitative analysis of the dimensions of difference between spoken and written language, then at how Martin developed Halliday's systemic functional analysis of language in a way that includes a stronger concept of genre. The view expressed was that the text's genre can be perceived as an expression of the common attributes of its schematisation within a community of users. In a given community we agree on what constitutes a fairy story, for example, because the practices of reading and writing such texts are consolidated by a collective, tacit understanding of what the fairy story genre is. The genres of literacy have a semiotic identity that is both visual and linguistic. They may evolve that identity from common frames, scripts and conceptual metaphors, becoming the mechanism through which literacy practices and their schematisations will develop each other.

Conclusions

My conclusion is not that textual analysis can expose the larger practice that produced the text, for this could only be the result of a more sustained ethnographic engagement, and a deeper understanding of its community of users. My interest is in clarifying how even a mundane text will employ a complicated and enduring set of semiotic devices. These devices are understood only after our induction into the relevant practices and after the practice's schematisation of the necessary knowledge frames. In short, text, practice and the facilitative cognitive schematisations are all mutually constitutive. It is this interaction of social practice and mind through the medium of sign which constitutes the literacy vision of this book.

Glossary

AAL   African-American Language. According to some, the dialect spoken by African-Americans has the status of language, or a Creole that underwent a process of decreolisation, becoming more like one of the language's (English) out which it evolved in the first place.

Actor   A term used here to describe a grammatical function in systemic functional linguistics. An actor is a part of a sentence that precipitates an action. Thus in 'she hit the boy', the subject 'she' is also an actor.

Admixing   Where the mode or medium of text, as between writing and speech, is overlapping or confused. Reading a written speech, for example, or writing in a way that represents how people speak.

Agent   The part of a sentence that produces the action in a sentence. In 'I bought a boat', 'I' is the agent.

Agglutinative languages   Agglutinative languages are languages which have a tendency to create words by combining other shorter words.

Aggregative   A description of a type of text structure that simply adds one statement to another without analysis of discussion: the opposite of subordinate.

Alphabet   A type of writing system where signs represent individual phonemes.

Anaphoric   The use of a word or phrase to refer to a word or phrase that has occurred earlier in a text.

Behaviourism   A school of psychology which considered that the study of mind can take place only through its observable forms behaviour. Mental structures were deemed unobservable and thus unavailable for scientific study. The mind was therefore treated as an organism that simply responds to the external stimuli of the environment and these stimuli were studied.

Biliteracy   Literacy in two languages.

Binomial expression   Two expressions in one sentence with the same grammatical role. Thus in the sentence 'Jack is tired, and doomed to remain so', 'tired' and 'doomed to remain so' are binomial. A multinomial sentence would have more than two expressions.

Cataphoric   The use of a word or phrase to refer to another word or phrase that occurs later in the text.

Category, superordinate and subordinate category members   Used here to refer to the cognitive groupings of the phenomena that make up our world, Thus beeches, oaks, birches and palms, etc., collectively constitute a tree category. Different types of palms constitute the palm category. Palms are a subordinate category of trees and trees are the superordinate category of palms.

CDA (Critical discourse analysis)   Discourse analysis is the study of how sentences in language create larger, meaningful units. Critical discourse analysis tries to deconstruct how this process reflects the kind of power relationships in which we are engaged and meanings that our social roles require us to convey.

Code (of signs)   The principles that differentiate one sign from another. Thus Roman letters are differentiated by different uses of vertical, horizontal and curved lines.

Cognitive surplus/deficit   Theories of bilingualism which consider that having a native speaker knowledge of more than one language can have an adverse (deficit) or beneficial (surplus) effect on other types of knowledge acquisition.

Community language   This may be an ethnic minority language. More rarely it might be a language that is not the national language which is used by several minorities living in one urban community.

Community of practice   A community that is defined by its sharing of common skills and activities. Carpenters, authors and coin collectors would all form different communities of practice.

Compound indicative   Creating one sign out of two or more others to indicate a shared part of their field of meaning – sun and moon to mean 'brightness' in Chinese, for example.

Conceptual metaphor   A term coined by Lakoff and Johnson (1980), it refers to how we use metaphors to cognitively grasp an abstract topic such as time, anger or argument, then produce all other relevant metaphors out of the conceptual one. Thus we talk about 'taking the high ground' or 'defeating an opponent' in an argument because we perceive it through the conceptual metaphor 'argument is war'.

Congruent language   In systemic functional linguistics, congruent language is language which serves the original grammatical function that it was evolved to express. Thus in 'I know you are crazy', 'I know' is the expression of the mental process it has always been, where as in 'Thinking destroyed my brain', thinking is no longer a process but an agent; it is therefore not congruent. *See also*: grammatical metaphor.

Consonantal alphabet   An alphabet that represents the consonants of the language but under-represents or does not represent the vowels.

Contiguous   Adjoining spatially. In a metonymy we can say that the topic of the metonym is contiguous to the metonym. Thus we represent a boat through its 'sail' because the sail is contiguous. There is also a concept of semantic contiguity which refers to two items that come from the same area of meaning. Thus 'teachers' and 'school' are semantically contiguous.

Creole   A language formed out of the fusion of two or more other languages that has become a native language for its speakers.

Cultural literacy   The term cultural literacy was coined by E. D. Hirsch (1987) and suggests that a people need a knowledge of the core events and symbols of the culture where they live in order to be literate in it.

Decreolisation   A process where a Creole loses some of the features that make it a distinct language, so that it starts to become more intelligible to the speakers of one of the languages from which it first evolved.

Determinative   A sign used in some writing systems to indicate the area of meaning in which other signs operate. According to DeFrancis (1989), there are also phonetic determinatives which are used to show that a phonograph is representing one sound and not another if there is likely to be an ambiguity.

Diachronic   Unfolding in time, thus the diachronic study of writing looks at its development over time.

Diacritic   A mark attached to a letter either to distinguish it from another or to show that it has a different phonetic value.

Diglossia   The existence of two languages or dialects that are used for different purposes within the same community.

Digraph   The use of two letters to represent one phoneme, 'th' in the, for example.

Dimension (A linguistic)   A term coined by Biber (1986) to mean a co-occurring group of linguistic features in text. For example, written text may have a factor that is oriented towards giving information. This will result in the dimension of a higher density of nouns, since these name new ideas and concepts.

Diminishing marginal productivity   The economic idea that the use of more of a variable factor such as labour upon the fixed amount of another factor such as land will achieve a diminishing return.

Document literacy   The knowledge and skill required to locate and to use information contained in such texts as job applications, payroll forms, transportation schedules, maps, tables and graphics.

Empowerment   Here: the use of literacy as way for the individual to take control of their life through greater understanding of their social circumstances.

Endophoric   A type of text that constructs its context out of itself. Thus most historical novels are endophoric because they try to create an historical context within their text.

Epistemic verbs   Verbs which express a state of mind towards a topic: 'I know', 'I understand', 'I wish', for example.

Ethnic minority languages   The first language of a minority emigrant group, when this is not the national language of the country they inhabit.

Exophoric A type of text that is meaningful only through its reference to a context outside itself. Road signs are exophoric because they are made meaningful by their pointing down a road. Without the road as a context, they are meaningless.

Factor (in textual analysis) A term developed by Biber (1986) from statistical analysis to show the way in which one type of text might differ from another: 'Involved' versus 'informational' production, for example.

Field *See* register.

Frame A cognitive frame includes the larger mental image we have of phenomena. Thus we can understand that an object is a cube with four equal sides without seeing all the sides at once because we use a mental frame to complete the phenomenon in question.

Generative linguistics Originating with the linguist Noam Chomsky, a generative grammar tries to show how the infinite variety of utterances that we can understand and produce is generated by the fixed series of rules that form our mental knowledge or competence. This competence is a transformational grammar of a language.

Genre A category of text, or a group texts, that will have a common communicative purpose and common expectations in respect of audience and structure.

Glottic/non-glottic scripts Scripts that represent language through its phonetic values or sounds. Non-glottic scripts make a more direct representation of meaning as opposed to language sound. *See also* semasiographic script.

Grammatical metaphor Using a grammatical form to express a meaning when it originally evolved to serve a different kind of meaning. For example, in 'Thinking destroyed my brain', 'thinking' is originally a process or an act of mental predication but is here an agent which is accomplishing an action. *See also* congruent language.

Grapheme Sometimes used to mean the graphic equivalent of a phoneme, as in an Arabic, Greek or Latin letter; it is also used to mean any single graphic unit representing a phoneme, syllable or word.

Grapholect A dialect that is associated with acceptable written language and is often a high-status and standard form of language use. It may also have partly evolved from the processes of literacy development and have consequently affected modes of speech.

Great Divide theory Great Divide theory holds that the advent of literacy enhanced our cognitive structures and gave us a new ability to deal with certain conceptual problems. This means we should see literate societies as divided from oral ones by their greater cognitive potential.

Homeostatic A social state that is unchanging and incapable of rapid, creative development.

Human capital theory The skills that the people in a society possess are the key to that society's productivity and thus should be a prime target of investment.

Icon   A type of sign that achieves its meaning by being like or analogous to its meaning. Thus 'blue' can mean sky because it is like the sky, or a map means a city through the process of analogy. Icons that achieve their meaning by being like a very different thing are metaphors, while those that achieve meaning through relational likeness, as in the case of a map, are diagrams.

Ideographic script   A script where the signs do not represent language sounds and language meanings.

Image schema   The mental resources or patterns from which we shape conceptual metaphors. These are generally framed by early physical experience. Thus we use the experience of being 'up' or 'upright' when an infant to express an idea of happiness in the conceptual metaphor 'up is happy' and the metaphor or idiom 'I am on top of the world'.

Immersion (language immersion)   Learning a language through constant exposure and use. Immersion schools teach a second language by getting children to learn all subjects within that language.

Indexical (signs)   Signs that achieve their meaning by indicating it or through some physical connection to it. Thus 'smoke means fire'.

Inflexion   The affix that is added to a word in order to change its grammatical function, in English, for example, the addition of ''s' to indicate possession.

Interpretant   In Peirce's taxonomy of signs, an interpretant is the meaning that the sign represents. An interpretant can be either immediate or dynamic. The immediate interpretant is the meaning of a sign outside a context, or its potential to mean, and the dynamic interpretant is the meaning inside a context.

Language maintenance   Language planning strategies to maintain and foster the use of threatened languages.

Language planning   Planning by a government or other agency to ensure the use of one language or several languages within a given society.

LDC   Less developed country.

Lingua franca   A language composed of two or more other languages, sometimes through interactions arising from trade or commerce.

Literacy framework   A framework of skills involving a strong use of speech and listening to surround the development of literacy.

Logographic script   A script composed of logographs, or signs that represent words.

Meaning potential   In systemic functional linguistics, a text or the words of which it is comprised will mean different things in different contexts. Therefore, outside its context, language has meaning potential rather than meaning.

Mentalist   Theories that emphasise the importance to cognitive development of structures of mind that we carry with us from birth.

Metalanguage (metalinguistic)   Language which is used to describe or comment upon other language.

Metasign A sign which represents another sign. *See also* sign.

Metatext The text in which a text will comment upon itself, the topics it will discuss and the attitudes it will adopt towards them.

Metonymy In rhetoric, a metonymy occurs when we use one part of an item, a sail, for example, to stand for the whole, a ship. In cognitive linguistics it means using a subordinate category to stand for a superordinate one, hoover (a make of vacuum cleaner) for vacuum cleaners for example. It is also a way to manipulate cognitively large and complicated categories through one of their subordinate meanings.

Mind in society *See* mutually constitutive development *and* the socio-historical theory of mind.

Mind style A term coined by Fowler (1996), referring to the world-view, or way of seeing, of the narrator or character in a text.

Mnemonic A linguistic or other device to help one remember a given piece of information through association.

Mode *See* register.

Modernism A movement in art, architecture and thought which sought to make form reflect function.

Morpheme The smallest meaningful unit in language. The English word 'undo', for example, is composed of two morphemes, 'un' and 'do'. Some morphemes such as 'do' are also words, but some such as 'un' are not.

Morphology The study of how morphemes combine to make words.

Morphosyllabary A term associated with DeFrancis's (1989) description of Chinese script. A type of writing system where the signs represent both syllables and morphemes in the language.

Move (text move) A unit of discourse or of genre which performs a given communicative function.

Mutually constitutive development A reference to the socio-historical theory of mind of the Russian psychologist Lev Vygotsky. According to Vygotsky mind and society constructed each other through the medium of technology, language and other forms of sign use. *See also* socio-historical theory of mind.

National literacy strategy The strategy to improve levels of literacy in the UK education system.

Nature–nurture The debate over whether knowledge is largely constituted out of the environment (nurture) or depends on internal structures of mind (nature).

Nominal density The frequency with which nouns and noun-phrases occur in the text. A text with a high nominal density will often use several nouns together and or in close proximity.

Nominal elements Nouns or parts of speech that are used in the same way as a noun, for example, 'broken-hearted', in 'What becomes of the broken-hearted?'

Nominalisation Forming nouns from other parts of speech, normally verbs or adjectives.

Noun-complement clauses Typically 'that' or 'to' clauses which give more information about a noun in a sentence. For example: 'to do' in 'I've nothing to do' or 'that I need to know' in 'I've forgotten the things that I need to know'.

Ontogenesis The development of a phenomenon such as literacy or language within the human individual.

Participatory pedagogy A form of literacy pedagogy associated with Paulo Freire. It involves fostering a dialogue about the language students learn to read and write so that they are helped towards a greater understanding of the world and the circumstances by which they are victimised.

Patient The part of a sentence that has an action performed upon it.

Phoneme The smallest unit of sound in language which can distinguish one meaning from another. 'Bat' and 'hat' both comprise three phonemes and are distinguished by their initial one.

Phonocentricity A view of writing as overly oriented to the representation of speech.

Phonograph/phonogram A sign in a writing system which represents a sound in a language, whether of a word, a syllable or a phoneme.

Phylogenesis The evolution or development of a phenomenon such as literacy or language through historical time within a given community.

Pictograph/pictogram A sign in a writing system that is based upon a pictorial representation of what it represents. Pictographs are iconic.

Post-modernism Post-modernism is a school of thought which reacted to the functional orientation of modernism, emphasising the value of minority interests and cultures, seeing meaning as socially constructed, and hence varying between one society and another.

Pre-reading Tasks that orient students to codes that discriminate one letter from another by engaging them in basic shape discrimination.

Prose literacy The knowledge and skills needed to understand and to use information from such texts as editorials, news stories, poems and fiction.

Quantitative literacy The knowledge and skills required to apply arithmetic operations to numbers embedded in printed materials such as balancing a chequebook, or determining the amount of interest on a loan from an advertisement.

Quipu The quipu is a system of recording information by knotting strings. It was used by the Inca civilisation of South America.

Rebus A process where a sign with a given phonetic value takes on a different meaning because that meaning is normally represented by a sign of equivalent phonetic value. Thus '4' = four, but may come to mean 'for' in a text message: 'it's 4 u'.

Redundancy A description applied to texts that use more words than they strictly need to express their meaning.

Register In systemic functional linguistics, register describes how context configures and is configured by text. The configuration occurs along the variables of field, what the text is about, mode, the medium of the text and the type of activity to which it belongs, and tenor, the type of relationship between the text's producer and its audience.

Reification (metaphor of) The treatment of abstract ideas and actions as if they were things or objects.

Scaffold Creating one social structure in order to build another mental one.

Schema Schemas (Greek plural: schemata) are patterns of mind that store information in a given order. They represent how we arrange the world.

Script (a cognitive script) A cognitive script is a type of schema or mental pattern. It is an internalised procedure or way of doing something. Thus, we can find our way home without conscious thought by making unconscious use of a script of the directions to our house.

Semantic features We can determine what a category is by whether it shares a number of fixed features with other categories. Thus we recognise trees as trees because they have in common a trunk that passes sap up to their leaves.

Semasiographic script A type of writing system that represents meanings and not words. Music and mathematical notation are conventional semasiographic scripts because we understand them only by being party to their conventions or semiotic codes. Iconic systems convey meaning by being similar to what they represent.

Semiosis The process of representing and structuring meanings through sign, and through language (a form of sign).

Semograph/semogram A sign in a writing system that represents the meaning of term.

Senser A term used to describe a grammatical function in systemic functional linguistics. It refers to a mental activity such as 'seeing' or 'hearing'.

Sign Any entity that means something other than itself. Thus a stone can come to mean building material if we treat it as material for building but will mean only stone if do not see it this way. According to Saussure (1974), language is a system of signs.

Signified The concept that the sign represents.

Signifier The part of a sign that stands for a meaning.

Signpost The part of some texts that explains what they are going to say and the conclusions they will reach.

Social construction A process where the meanings that we use are constructed by the society to which we belong and the use to which that society puts these terms. Social construction suggests that meaning does not belong to an object world but is a product of our social needs.

Socio-historical theory of mind A theory of mind associated with the Vygotsky. It sees society as building mind with the knowledge that has been accumulated out of its history, and mind as shaping the nature of society. *See also* mutually constitutive development.

Stem word The stem word is the main meaning-bearing part of a word to which other morphemes may be added in order to modify its meaning. Thus in the word 'hopeless', 'hope' is the stem word and 'less' is an added morpheme.

Subordinate and superordinate categories *See* category.

Subordinative Used here to describe a text that uses subordination or subordinate clauses to elaborate on or explore its central statements: the opposite of aggregative.

Substrata language According to Bickerton (1975), when a Creole forms, one language will graft its lexis onto the syntax and grammar of another language. The substrata language provides the syntax and grammar. *See also* Creole.

Sukûn A sign used in Arabic script to show the absence of a vowel.

Syllabary A type of writing system where individual signs represent syllables.

Syllogism A logical argument that has one conclusion supported by two premises, having the pattern:
A is B, B is C, therefore A is C.

Symbol A type of sign that achieves its meaning through a process of convention or social agreement. Our use of symbol underpins human language and its writing systems allowing us to manipulate meanings outside their context.

Systemic functional linguistics A form of linguistic analysis largely derived form the work of M. A. K. Halliday, which sees each language as an individual system that should be analysed for how it represents the communicative functions and needs of a given society. Language is thus a social semiotic or system of representing meanings in a society.

Tenor *See* register.

Text-frame A pedagogical device where a frame is placed round a section of text that labels its generic moves.

Transformational grammar *See* generative linguistics.

Trigraph The use of three letters to represent one phoneme; 'owe', for example.

Triliteral languages Triliteral languages construct their core meanings from three salient consonants. Thus the consonants k-t-b in Arabic are used to construct the word, *katab*, to write, but also a set of related meanings such as *kitab*, book, or *katib*, writer. Typical examples are the Semitic languages Arabic and Hebrew.

Univocal discourse A discourse which tries to use language as if a given word will refer only to one type of meaning rather as an algebraic sign can be given only one value.

Variable factor *See* diminishing marginal productivity.

Visual literacy The knowledge required to understand pictures and pictographic imagery.

Zone of proximal development (ZPD) A term devised by Vygotsky to describe the maximum amount of cognitive development or learning of which an individual is capable at any one time when assisted by other agents, such as teachers, teaching institutions or caregivers.

References

Al-Sharafah, A. G. M. (2000) Towards a Textual Theory of Metonymy: A Semiotic Approach to the Nature and Role of Metonymy in Text. PhD thesis: University of Durham.

Anghel, F. (1994) Functional Literacy in Romania: Between Myth and Reality. In *Alpha 94: Literacy and Cultural Development Strategies in Rural Areas*. RC 020 235. Http://ericae.net/ericdb/ED386350.htm

Archer, D. (1994) Integration of Literacy With Other Aspects of Development: Practical Innovations Using Participatory Rural Appraisal. In R. Holme (ed.) *Dunford Seminar Report: Functional Literacy for Development. Issues of Language and Method*. Manchester: British Council.

Attali, J. (1982) *Histoire de temps*. Paris: Fayard.

Austen, J. (1972) *Price and Prejudice*. Harmondsworth: Penguin Books.

Bacon, F. (1969) Of Marriage and Single Life. In J. E. George and J. A. Goodson (eds) *Great Essays, from the 16th Century to the Present*. New York: Dell Publishing Company.

Banks, D. (1994) *Writ in Water: Aspects of the Scientific Journal Article*. Université de Bretagne Occidentale: E. R. L. A.

Barber, C. (1993) *The English Language: A Historical Introduction*. Cambridge: Cambridge University Press.

Barber, F. J. W. (1974) *Archaeological Decipherment. A Handbook*. Princeton, NJ: Princeton University Press.

Baron, N. S. (2000) *Alphabet to Email: How Written English Evolved and Where it's Heading*. London and New York: Routledge.

Bartlett, F. C. (1932) *Remembering*. Cambridge: Cambridge University Press.

Barton, D. (1994) *Literacy: An Introduction to the Ecology of the Written Word*. Blackwell: Oxford.

Bauer, P. T. (1971) Dissent on Development: Studies and Debates in Development Economics. London: Weidenfeld and Nicolson.

Benson, N., Gurney, S., Harrison, J. and Rimmershaw, R. (1994) The Place of Academic Writing in Whole Life Writing. In M. Hamilton, D. Barton and R. Ivanic (eds) *Worlds of Literacy*. Clevedon, Philadelphia and Adelaide: Multilingual Matters.

Berk, L. E. (1992) Children's Private Speech: An Overview of Theory and the Status of Research. In R. Díaz and L. E. Berk (eds) *From Social Interaction to Self-Regulation*. Hillsdale, NJ: Lawrence Erlbaum Associates.

Bernstein, B. (1971) *Class, Codes and Control. Vol. 1. Theoretical Studies towards a Sociology of Language.* London: Routledge & Kegan Paul.

Bernstein, B. (1990) *Class, Codes and Control, Vol. 4: The Structuring of Pedagogic Discourse.* London: Routledge.

Bernstein, B. (1996) *Pedagogy, Symbolic Control and Identity: Theory, Research, Critique.* London: Taylor & Francis.

Bhatia, V. K. (1993) *Analysing Genre: Language Use in Professional Settings.* London and New York: Longman.

Biber, D. (1988) *Variations across Speech and Writing.* Cambridge: Cambridge University Press.

Biber, D., Johansson, S., Leech, G., Conrad S. and Finegan, E. (1999) *Longman Grammar of Spoken and Written English.* Harlow: Pearson Education.

Bickerton, D. (1975) *Dynamics of a Creole System.* Cambridge: Cambridge University Press.

Blanck, G. (1990) Vygotsky, the Man and His Cause. In L. C. Moll (ed.) *Vygotsky and Education: Instructional Implications and Applications of Sociohistorical Psychology.* Cambridge: Cambridge University Press, 31–58.

Blunch, N.-H. and Verner, D. (1999) *Is Functional Literacy a Prerequisite for Entering the Labor Market? An Analysis of the Determinants of Adult Literacy and Earnings in Ghana.* Washington: The World Bank.

Bowman, M. J. and Anderson, C. A. (1968) Concerning the Role of Education in Development. In M. J. Bowman and C. A. Anderson (eds) *Readings in the Economics of Education.* Paris: UNESCO.

Breton-Gravereau, S. and Thibault, D. (1998) *L'Aventure des Écritures: matières et formes.* Paris: Bibliothèque Nationale de France.

Brodova, E., Leong, D., Gregory, K. and Edgerton, S. (1999) *Scaffolded Writing – A Successful Strategy for Promoting Children's Writing in Kindergarten.* New Orleans, NAEYC Annual Conference.

Brown, K. (1999) *Developing Critical Literacy.* Macquarie University: National Centre for English Language Teaching and Research.

Bruner, J. (1975) From Communication to Language: A Psychological Perspective. *Cognition,* 3: 233–87.

Bynner, J. (2001) *Outline of the Research, Exploratory Analysis and Summary of the Main Results.* Centre for Longitudinal Studies: Institute of Education.

Carrington, L. (1997) Social Contexts Conducive to the Vernacularisation of Literacy. In A. Tabouret-Keller, R. B. Le Page, P. Gardner-Chloros and G. Varro (eds) *Vernacular Literacy: A Re-evaluation.* Oxford: Clarendon Press, 82–92.

Carter, R. A. (1997) *Investigating English Discourse: Language, Literacy, Literature.* London: Routledge.

Catzel, P. and Roberts, I. (1984) *A Short Text Book of Paediatrics.* London, Sydney, Auckland and Toronto: Hodder and Stoughton.

Chafe, W. L. (1982) Integration and Involvement in Speaking, Writing and Oral Literature. In D. Tannen (ed.) *Spoken and Written Language: Exploring Orality and Literacy.* Norwood, NJ: Ablex, 35–54.

Chaiklin, S. and Lave, J. (eds) (1993) *Understanding Practice: Perspectives on Activity and Context.* Cambridge: Cambridge University Press.

Charbonnier, G. (ed.) (1975) 'Primitive' and 'civilised' peoples: a conversation with Claude Lévi-Strauss. In R. Disch (ed.) *The Future of Literacy.* Englewood Cliffs, NJ: Prentice Hall.

Chomsky, N. (1985) *Knowledge of Language*. New York and London: Praeger.

Christie, F. (1999) The Pedagogic Device and The Teaching of English. In F. Christie (ed.) *Pedagogy and The Shaping of Consciousness*. London and New York: Cassell, 156–84.

Cipolla, C. (1969) *Literacy and Development in the West*. Harmondsworth: Pelican.

Coffin, C. (1997) Constructing and Giving Value to the Past: An Investigation into Secondary School History. In F. Christie and J. R. Martin (eds) *Genre and Institutions: Social Processes in the Workplace and School*. New York: Continuum, 196–230.

Collier, M. and Manley, B. (1998) *How to Read Egyptian Hieroglyphs*. London: The British Museum Press.

Cook-Gumperz, J. (ed.) (1986) *The Social Construction of Literacy*. New York: Cambridge University Press.

Cummings, J. (2001a) The Influence of Bilingualism on Cognitive Growth: A Synthesis of Research Findings and Explanatory Hypotheses. In C. Baker and N. Hornberger (eds) *An Introductory Reader to the Writings of Jim Cummins*. Clevedon: Multilingual Matters, 26–68.

Cummings, J. (2001b) Linguistic Interdependence and the Education Development of Bilingual Children. In C. Baker and N. Hornberger (eds) *An Introductory Reader to the Writings of Jim Cummins*. Clevedon: Multilingual Matters, 63–95.

Cummings, J. (2001c) Learning Difficulties in Immersion Programmes. In C. Baker and N. Hornberger (eds) *An Introductory Reader to the Writings of Jim Cummings*. Clevedon: Multilingual Matters, 148–74.

Dalglish, C. (1982) *Illiteracy and the Offender*. Cambridge: Huntington Publishers.

De Temple, J. M. and Snow, C. E. (2001) Conversations about Literacy: Social Mediation of Psycholinguistic Activity. In C. E. Snow and L. Verhoeven (eds) *Literacy and Motivation*. Mahwah, NJ and London: Lawrence Erlbaum Associates, 55–69.

Deacon, T. (1998) *The Symbolic Species*. Harmondsworth: Penguin Books.

DeFrancis, J. (1989) *Visible Speech: The Diverse Oneness of Writing Systems*. Honolulu: University of Hawai'i Press.

DFEE (Department for Education and Employment) (1998) *The National Literacy Strategy: Framework for Teaching*. London: DFEE.

Denny, K., Harmon, C. and Redmond, S. (2000) *Functional Literacy, Educational Attainment and Earnings – Evidence from the International Adult Literacy Survey*. London: The Institute for Fiscal Studies.

Derrida, J. (1997) *Of Grammatology*. Baltimore: The Johns Hopkins University Press (first Published under the title *De La grammatologie*, 1967).

Díaz, M., Neal, C. J. and Amaya-Williams, M. (1990) Social Origins of Self-Regulation. In L. C. Moll (ed.) *Vygotsky and Education: Instructional Implications and Applications of Sociohistorical Psychology*. Cambridge: Cambridge University Press. 127–54.

Downing, A. and Locke, P. (1992) *A University Course in English Grammar*. Hemel Hempstead: Prentice Hall International.

Drucker, J. (1999) *The Alphabetic Labyrinth: The Letters in History and Imagination*. London: Thames and Hudson.

Egbo, B. (2000) *Gender, Literacy and Life Chances in Sub-Saharan Africa*. Clevendon, Buffalo, Toronto and Sydney: Multilingual Matters.

Eisemon, T. O., Marble, K. and Crawford, M. (1998) *Investing in Adult Literacy: Lessons and Implications*. University of Pennsylvania: International Literacy Institute.

Esteva, G. and Prakash, M. S. (1998) *Grassroots Post-Modernism*. London and New York: Zed Books.

Fairclough, N. (1989) *Language and Power*. Harlow: Longman.

Fairclough, N. (1995) The Technologisation of Discourse. In C. Coulthard and M. Coulthard (eds) *Texts and Practices*. London: Routledge, 71–83.

Fasold, R. W. (1990) Sustainable Vernacular Language Literacy Illustrated by US Vernacular Black English. In *Abstracts 1990*, 34–7.

Fauconnier, G. (1997) *Mappings in Thought and Language*. Cambridge: Cambridge University Press.

Fauconnier, G. and Turner, M. (1998) Conceptual Integration Networks. *Cognitive Science*, Vol. 2 (2): 133–87.

Fauconnier, G. and Turner, M. (2002) *The Way We Think: Conceptual Blending and the Mind's Hidden Complexities*. New York: Basic Books.

Ferguson C. A. (1959) 'Diglossia'. *Word*, 15: 325–40.

Finnegan, R. (1979) Literacy and literature. Mimeo.

Fischer, S. R. (2001) *A History of Writing*. London: Reaktion Books.

Foucault, M. (1974) *The Order of Things*. London: Tavistock.

Foucault, M. (1977) *Discipline and Punish*. Harmondsworth: Penguin Books.

Fowler, R. (1996) *Linguistic Criticism*. Oxford: Oxford University Press.

Fraser, H. (1998) A Place for Critical Literacy in Developing Discussion Skills. In A. Burns and S. Hood (eds) *Teachers Voices 3: Teaching Critical Literacy*. Sydney: National Centre for English Language Teaching and Research.

Freire, A. M. and Macedo, D. (1998) Introduction. In A. M. Freire and D. Macedo (eds) *The Paulo Freire Reader*. New York: Continuum, 1–44.

Freire, P. (1972) *Pedagogy of the Oppressed*. Harmondsworth: Penguin Books.

Freire, P. (1974) *Education of Critical Consciousness*. London: Sheed and Ward.

Freire, P. (1992) *Pedagogy of Hope*. New York: Continuum.

Freire, P. (1998a) Pedagogy of the Oppressed. In A. M. Freire and D. Macedo (eds) *The Paulo Freire Reader*. New York: Continuum, 45–67.

Freire, P. (1998b) Education of Critical Consciousness. In A. M. Freire and D. Macedo (eds) *The Paulo Freire Reader*. New York: Continuum, 68–80.

Gal'perin, P. Y. (1969) Stages in the Development of Mental Acts. In M. Cole and I. Maltzman (eds) *A Handbook of Contemporary Soviet Psychology*. New York: Basic Books, 163–208.

Gaur, A. (1984) *A History of Writing*. London: The British Library.

Gaur, A. (2000) *Literacy and the Politics of Writing*. Bristol: Intellect Books.

Gee, J. P. (1990) *Social Linguistics and Literacies: Ideologies and Discourses*. London, New York and Philadelphia: The Falmer Press.

Gelb, I. J. (1963) *A Study of Writing*. Chicago: University of Chicago Press (second edition).

Gendreau, P. and Ross, R. R. (1983). Success in Corrections: Programs and Principles. In R. R. Corrado (ed.) *Juvenile Justice*. Toronto: Butterworth.

Genosko, G. (1994) *Baudrillard and Signs: Signification Ablaze*. London and New York: Routledge.

Gibbs, R. (1994) *The Poetics of Mind*. Cambridge: Cambridge University Press.

Goody, J. (1977) *The Domestication of the Savage Mind.* Cambridge: Cambridge University Press.

Goody, J. and Watt, I. (1968) The Consequences of Literacy. In J. Goody (ed.) *Literacy in Traditional Societies.* Cambridge: Cambridge University Press, 27–68.

Gough, K. (1968) Literacy in Kerala. In J. Goody (ed.) *Literacy in Traditional Societies.* Cambridge: Cambridge University Press, 132–60.

Graff, H. J. (1981) Literacy, Jobs and Industrialisation: The Nineteenth Century. In H. J. Graff (ed.) *Literacy and Social Development in the West.* Cambridge: Cambridge University Press, 232–60.

Graff, H. J. (1991) *The Legacies of Literacy: Continuities and Contradictions in Western Society and Culture.* Bloomington and Indianapolis: Indiana University Press.

Greenfield, P. M. (1972) Oral and Written Language. The Consequences for Cognitive Development in Africa, the United States and England. *Language and Speech*, 15: 169–78.

Grigsby, K. (1985) Strategies for Mobilisation and Participation of Volunteers in Literacy and Post-literacy Programmes. The Case of Nicaragua. In G. Carron and A. Bordia (eds) *Issues in Planning and Implementing National Literacy Programmes.* Paris: UNESCO, International Institute for Educational Planning, 66–80.

Gropius, W. (1965) *New Architecture and the Bauhaus.* London: Faber and Faber.

Gustafason, M. (1975) *Some Syntactic Properties of English Law Language.* Turku: Department of English, University of Turku.

Gustafason, M. (1984) The Syntactic Features of Binomial Expressions in Legal English. *Text,* 4(1–3): 123–41.

Haenen, J. (1996) Piotr Gal'perin's Criticism and Extension of Lev Vygotsky's Work. *Journal of Russian and East European Psychology*, 34 (2): 54–60.

Hakuta, K. (1986) *Mirror of Language: The Debate on Bilingualism.* New York: Basic Books.

Hall, J. K. (2002) *Teaching and Researching Language and Culture.* London and New York: Pearson Education.

Halliday, M. A. K., (1971) Linguistic Function and Literary Style: An Enquiry into the Language of William Golding's *The Inheritors.* In S. Chatman (ed.) *Literary Style: A Symposium.* New York: Oxford University Press, 330–68.

Halliday, M. A. K. (1978) *Language as a Social Semiotic: The Social Interpretation of Language and Meaning.* London: Edward Arnold.

Halliday, M. A. K. (1979) Differences between Spoken and Written Language: Some Implications for Literacy Teaching. In G. Page, J. Elkins and B. O'Connor (eds) *Communication through Reading: proceedings of the 4th Australian Reading Conference, vol. 2.* Adelaide: Australian Reading Association, 37–52.

Halliday, M. A. K (1985) *An Introduction to Functional Grammar.* London: Edward Arnold.

Halliday, M. A. K (1993) Some Grammatical Problems in Scientific English. In M. Halliday and J. Martin (eds) *Writing Science.* Pittsburg: University of Pittsburg Press, 69–85.

Halliday, M. and Hassan, R. (1976) *Cohesion in English.* London: Longman.

Hansard (1996) The United Kingdom Parliament. http://www.publications.parliament.uk/pa/cm199697/cmhansrd/vo970128/debtext/7012

Harris, R. (1996) *Signs of Writing.* London and New York: Routledge.

Harris, R. (2000) *Rethinking Writing.* London and New York: Continuum.

Havelock, E. A. (1963) *Preface to Plato*. Cambridge, MA: Belknap Press of Harvard University Press.

Heath, S. B. (1983) *Ways with Words: Language Life and Work in Communities and Classrooms*. Cambridge and New York: Cambridge University Press.

Heath, S. B. and Brandscombe, A. (1985) Intelligent Writing in an Audience Community: Teacher Students and Researcher. In S. Freedman (ed.) *The Acquisition of Written Language: Response and Revision*. Norwood, NJ: Ablex, 3–32.

Heine, B. (1997) *Cognitive Foundations of Grammar*. Oxford: Oxford University Press.

Henderson, E. H. (1992) Lexical Competence and Written Words. In S. Templeton and D. R. Bear (eds) *Development of Orthographic Knowledge and the Foundations of Literacy: A Memorial Festschrift for Edmund H. Henderson*. Hillsdale, NJ: Lawrence Erblaum Associates, 1–30.

Hill Boone, E. and Mignolo, W. D. (eds) *Writing without Words*. Durham, NC: Duke University Press.

Hills, A. and Karcz, S. (1990, May). *Literacy Survey*. The Association of State and Federal Directors of Correctional Education and the National Correctional Education Consortium, Inc., Newsletter, special edition.

Hirsch, E. D. (1987) *Cultural Literacy: What Every American Needs to Know*. Boston: Houghton Mifflin.

Hobbes, T. (1983) *Leviathan*. Glasgow: Collins Fount (first edition 1651).

Hodge, R. and Kress, G. (1993) *Language as Ideology*. London: Routledge & Kegan Paul.

Hoggart, R. (1958) *The Uses of Literacy: Aspects of Working-class Life, with Special Reference to Publications and Entertainments*. Harmondsworth: Penguin Books.

Holme, R. (2003a) *Mind, Metaphor and Language Teaching*. Basingstoke: Palgrave Macmillan.

Holme, R. (2003b) Grammatical Metaphor as a Cognitive Construct. In A.-M. Simon-Vanderbergen, M. Taverniers and L. Ravelli (eds) *Grammatical Metaphor*. Amsterdam: J. Benjamins.

Hood, S., Solomon, N. and Burns, A. (1996) *Focus on Reading*. Sydney: National Centre for English Language Teaching and Research.

Hornberger, N. H. (1988) *Bilingual Education and Language Maintenance: A Southern Peruvian Quechua Case*. Dordrecht: Foris.

Hosking, R. F. and Meredith-Owens, G. M. (1966) *A Handbook of Asian Scripts*. London: The Trustees of the British Museum.

Howell, D. R. and Wolff, E. N. (1992) Technical Change and the Demand for Skills by US industries. *Cambridge Journal of Economics*, 16: 127–46.

Huskey, E. (1995) The Politics of Language in Kyrgyzstan. *Nationalities Papers*, 23/3.

Huxley, A. (1937) *Ends and Means*. London: Chatto and Windus.

Hymes, D. (1974) *Foundations in Sociolinguistics*. Philadelphia: University of Pennsylvania Press.

llich, I. and Sanders, B. (1988) *ABC: The Alphabetization of the Popular Mind*. London: Marion Boyars.

International Bureau of Education (1990) *The Struggle against Illiteracy: Policies, Strategies and Emerging Operational Action for the 1990s*. ERIC document: ED 329782.

Jencks, C. (1984) *The Language of Post-Modern Architecture*. London: Academy Editions.

Jensen, H. (1969) *Sign, Symbol and Script.* London: George Allen and Unwin.

Johansen, J. D. and Larsen, S. E. (2002) *Signs in Use: An Introduction to Semiotics.* London: Routledge.

Johansson, E. (1981) The History of Literacy in Sweden. In H. J. Graff (ed.) *Literacy and Social Development in the West.* Cambridge: Cambridge University Press, 151–82.

Johnson, M. (1989) Image-schematic basis of meaning. *RSSI*, 9: 109–18.

Karmiloff-Smith, A., Grant, J., Sims, K., Jones, M.-C. and Cuckle, C. (1996) Rethinking Metalinguistic Awareness and Accessing Knowledge about what Counts as a *Word. Cognition*, 58: 197–219.

Kempa, S. (1993) *The Cost to Industry: The Basic Skills of Different Age Groups.* London: Gallup Poll Ltd, The Basic Skills Agency.

Kuhn, T. S. (1970) *The Structure of Scientific Revolutions.* Chicago: University of Chicago Press.

Kirk, S. (2000) Rights and Routes: Foundations of Text-based Literacy in Pre-lingually Deaf Children. MA dissertation, University of Durham.

Koenig, M. (1999) Social Conditions for the Implementation of Linguistic Human Rights through Multicultural Policies: The Case of the Kyrgyz Republic. In S. Wright (ed.) *Language Policy and Language Issues in the Successor States of the Former USSR.* Clevedon: Multilingual Matters, 57–84.

Kolstoe, P. (1995) *Russians in the Former Soviet Republics.* Bloomington and Indianapolis: Indiana University Press.

Kress, G. (1985) *Linguistic Processes in Sociocultural Practice.* Geelong: Deakin University Press.

Kress, G. (1997) *Before Writing: Rethinking Paths to Literacy.* London: Routledge.

Kymlicka, W. (1995) *Multicultural Citizenship: A Liberal Theory of Minority Rights.* Oxford: Clarendon Press.

Labov, W. (1972) *Language in the Inner City: Studies in the Black English Vernacular.* Philadelphia: University of Pennsylvania Press.

Labov. W. (1982) Objectivity and Commitment in Linguistic Science. The Case of the Black English Trial in Ann Arbor. *Language and Society,* 11: 165–201.

Labor, W. (2001) *Principles of Linguistic Change. Vol. 2. Social Factors.* Oxford: Blackwell.

Lakoff, G. (1987) *Women, Fire and Dangerous Things: What Categories Reveal about the Mind.* Chicago: University of Chicago Press.

Lakoff, G. (1992) Metaphor and War: The Metaphor System Used to Justify War in the Gulf. In B. Hallet (ed.) *Engulfed in War: Just War and the Persian Gulf.* Honolulu: Matsunaga Institute for Peace, 1991.

Lakoff, G. and Johnson, M. (1980) *Metaphors We Live By.* London and Chicago: The University of Chicago Press.

Lakoff, G. and Johnson, M. (1999) *Philosophy in the Flesh.* New York: Basic Books.

Lambert, W. E. (1974) Culture and Language as Factors in Learning and Education. In F. E. Aboude and R. D. Meade (eds) *Cultural Factors in Learning and Education.* Bellingham, WA: Fifth Western Washington Symposium on Learning.

Langacker, R. W. (1990) *Concept, Image and Symbol: The Cognitive Basis of Grammar.* Berlin: Mouton de Gruyter.

Langacker, R. W. (1994) *Foundations of Cognitive Grammar.* Stanford, CA: Stanford University Press.

Labov, W. (1972) *Sociolinguistic Patterns*. Philadelphia: University of Pennsylvania Press.

Lankshear, C. and Lawler, M. (1987) *Literacy Schooling and Revolution*. New York, Philadelphia and London: The Falmer Press.

Lankshear, C. and Mclaren, P. (1993) Introduction. In C. Lankshear and P. Mclaren (eds) *Critical Literacy: Politics, Praxis and the Post-modern*. Albany: State University of New York Press, 1–56.

Laughlin, M. C., Martin, J. R. and Sleeter, C. E. (2001) Liberating Literacy. In P. R. Schmidt and P. B. Mosenthal (eds) *Reconceptualising Literacy in the New Age of Multiculturalism and Pluralism*. Greenwich, CT: Information Age Publishing, 89–109.

Layder, D. (1993) *New Strategies in Social Research: An Introduction and Guide*. Cambridge: Polity Press.

Le Page, R. B. (1997) Political and Economic Aspects of Literacy. In A. Tabouret-Keller, R. B. Le Page, P. Gardner-Chloros and G. Varro, (eds) *Vernacular Literacy: A Re-evaluation*. Oxford: Clarendon Press, 23–81.

Lee, C. (2000) Signifying in the ZPD. In C. D. Lee and P. Smagorinsky (eds) *Vygotskian Perspectives on Literacy Research*. Cambridge: Cambridge University Press, 191–225.

Lemke, J. L. (1995) *Textual Politics, Discourse and Social Dynamics*. London: Taylor and Francis.

Lenin, V. I. (1913) *Collected Works* Vol. 24. Lenin Works Archive. http://www.marxist.org.archive/lenin/works/1913/Jul.

Lenin, V. I. (1918) *Collected Works* Vol. 26. Lenin Works Archive. http://www.marxist.org.archive/lenin/works/1917/oct

Levine, K. (1982) Functional Literacy: Fond Illusions and False Economies. *Harvard Educational Review*, 52: 3.

Levine, K. (1986) *The Social Context of Literacy*. London, Boston and Henley: Routledge & Kegan Paul.

Liberman, I., Schankweiler, D., Fischer. F. and Carter, B. (1974) Explicit Phoneme and Syllable Segmentation in the Young Child. *Journal of Experimental Child Psychology*, 18: 201–12.

Lienhardt, R. G. (1964) *Social Anthropology*. Oxford: Oxford University Press.

Literacy Trust (2001) Adults' Literacy Skills. Literacy Trust: http://www.literacy-trust.org.uk/database/stats/adult.html

Locke, J. (1961) *An Essay Concerning Human Understanding*. London: Dent.

Luke, L. (1994) When Basic Skills and Information Processing Just Aren't Enough: Rethinking Reading in New Times. In P. Freebody, J. P. Gee, A. Luke and B. Street (eds) *Literacies as Critical Social Practices: An Introduction*: London: Falmer Press, 75–92

Luria, A. R. (1976) *Cognitive Development: Its Cultural and Social Foundations*. Cambridge, MA: Harvard University Press.

Magnus, B. (1995) Post Modern Pragmatism. In H. Hollinger and Depew D. (eds) *Pragmatism: From Progressivism to Post-modernism*. Westport, CT and London: Praeger, 256–83.

Mahadeo, S. (2003) Input and Achievement in an Acquisition-Poor Environment: Varying Levels of L2 Proficiency Among Pre-Puberty Mauritian Learners of English. Thesis Submitted for the degree of PhD University of Durham.

Malinowski, B. (1952) The Problem of Meaning in Primitive Languages. In C. K. Ogden and I. A. Richards (eds) *The Meaning of Meaning*. New York: Harcourt.

Martin, J. R. (1997) Analysing Genre: Functional Parameters. In F. Christie and J. R. Martin (eds) *Genre and Institutions: Social Processes in the Workplace and School.* New York: Continuum, 3–39.

Martin, J. R. (1999) Mentoring Semogenesis. In F. Christie (ed.) *Pedagogy and the Shaping of Consciousness.* London and New York: Cassell, 123–55.

Martin-Jones, M. and Bhatt, A. (1998) Literacies in the Lives of Young Gujarati Speakers in Leicester. In L. Verhoeven and A. Y. Dungunoglu (eds) *Literacy Development in a Multilingual Context.* Mahwah, NJ: Lawrence Erlbaum Associates, 37–50.

Marx, K. and Engels, F. (1848) *The Communist Manifesto.* http://csf.colarado.edu/psn/marx/Archive/1848-CM/CM2.txt

May, S. (2001) *Language and Minority Rights: Ethnicity, Nationalism and the Politics of Language.* Harlow: Pearson Education.

Mayabin, J. (ed.) (1993) *Language and Literacy in Social Practice.* Clevedon, Philadelphia and Adelaide: Multilingual Matters.

Mayo, P. (2000) Synthesising Gramsci and Freire: Possibilities for a Theory of Transformative Adult Education. In S. F. Steiner, H. M. Krank, P. Mclaren and R. E. Bahruth (eds) *Freirean Pedagogy, Praxis, and Possibilities.* New York and London: Falmer Press, 249–78.

McLuhan, M. (1964) *Understanding Media: The Extensions of Man.* London and New York: Routledge & Kegan Paul.

McVeigh, T. (2001) Level of Illiteracy among Young is above that of 1912. *The Observer*, 19 August. London: Observer Newspapers.

Mellor, B. and Patterson, A. (2001) Teaching Readings. In B. Comber and A. Simpson (eds) *Negotiating Critical Literacy in Classrooms.* Mahwah, NJ: Lawrence Erlbaum Associates.

Mikulecky, L. (2000) NIFL (National Institute for Literacy) Workplace Discussion List. http://www.nifl.gov/lincs/discussions/nifl-wokplace/mikulecky.html

Mikulecky, L. and Kirkley, J. (1998). Changing Workplaces, Changing Classes: The New Role of Technology in Workplace Literacy. In D. Reinking, M. McKenna, M. Labbo and R. Kieffer (eds) *The Handbook of Literacy and Technology: Transformations in a Post-typographic World.* Mahwah, NJ: Lawrence Erlbaum Associates, 303–20.

Minsky, M. (1975) A Framework for Representing Knowledge. In P. H. Winston (ed.) *The Psychology of Computer Vision.* New York: McGraw-Hill.

Morais, T., Cary, L., Alegria, T. and Bertelson P. (1979) Does awareness of speech as a Sequence of Phones arise Spontaneously? *Cognition*, 7: 323–31.

Morpugo Davies, A. (1984) Forms of Writing in the Ancient Mediterranean World. In G. Gauman (ed.) *The Written Word, Literacy in Transition: Wolfson College Lectures.* Oxford: Clarendon Press, 51–77.

Morris, D. (1992) Concept of Word: A Pivotal Understanding in the Learning-to-Read Process. In S. Templeton and D. R. Bear (eds) *Development of Orthographic Knowledge and the Foundations of Literacy: A Memorial Festschrift for Edmund H. Henderson.* Hillsdale, NJ: Lawrence Erlbaum Associates, 53–77.

The New London Group (2000) A Pedagogy of Multiliteracies. In B. Cope and M. Kalantzis (eds) *Multiliteracies: Literacy, Learning and the Design of Social Futures.* London: Routledge, 9–42.

Nutbeam, D. (1998) Health Promotion Glossary. *Health Promotion International* 13: 349–64.

Nystrand, M. (1997) *Opening Dialogue: Understanding the Dynamics of Language and Learning in the English Classroom.* New York and London: Teachers College Press.

Olson, D. R. (1994) *The World on Paper.* Cambridge: Cambridge University Press.

Olson, D. R. and Astington, J. W. (1990) Talking about Text: How Literacy Contributes to Thought. *Journal of Pragmatics,* 14: 705–21.

Ong, W. J. (1982) *Orality and Literacy: Technologising the Word.* London and New York: Routledge.

Ong, W. J. (1986) Writing Restructures Thought. In G. Bauman (ed.) *The Written Word, Literacy in Transition: Wolfson College Lectures 1985.* Oxford: Clarendon Press.

Organisation for Economic Co-operation and Development, Human Resources Development Canada, Statistics Canada (1997) *Literacy Skills for the Knowledge Society.* Paris: OECD and Canada: Human Resources Development and Ministry for Industry.

Palfrey, C. (1974) Remedial Education and the Adult Offender. *Howard Journal of Penology and Crime Prevention,* 15(1): 78–85.

Parry, M. (1971) L'Epithète traditionelle dans Homère [The Traditional Epithetic in Homer]. In Adam Parry (ed.) *The Collected Papers of Milman Parry. The Making of Homeric Verse.* Oxford: Clarendon Press.

Peirce, C. S. (1931–58) *The Collected Papers of Charles Sanders Peirce.* Vols I–IV, ed. C. Hartshorne and P. Weiss; Vols VII–VIII, ed. A. Burks. Cambridge, MA: Harvard University Press.

Perie, M., Gruner, A. Williams, T. and Kastberg, D. (1999) Literacy in the Labor Force: Examining the Supply and Demand of Literacy in 12 Nations. Montreal: Symposium 19.66. Presented at the Annual Meeting of the American Educational Research Association.

Petterson, J. S. (1996) *Grammatalogical Studies: Writing and its Relation to Speech.* Uppsala: Uppsala University Press.

Phillipson, R. (1992) *Linguistic Imperialism.* Oxford: Oxford University Press.

Piaget, J. (1954) *The Construction of Reality in the Child.* New York: Basic Books.

Plato (1971) *Timaeus and Critias.* Harmondsworth and Baltimore: Penguin Books.

Plato (1974) *The Republic.* Harmondsworth and New York: Penguin Books.

Plato (1986) *Phaedras.* Warminster: Aris and Phillips.

Propp, V. (1968) Morphology of the Folk Tale. *International Journal of American Linguistics,* Part lll, 24: 4.

Quirk, R., Greenbaum, S., Leech, G. and Svartvik, J. (1985) *A Comprehensive Grammar of English.* Harlow: Longman.

Raphael, T. E., Damphousse, K., Highfield, K. and Florio-Ruane, S. (2001) Understanding Culture in Our Lives and Work: Teaching Literature Study in the Book Club Programme. In P. R. Schmidt and P. B. Mosenthal (eds) *Reconceptualising Literacy in the New Age of Multiculturalism and Pluralism.* Greenwich, CT: Information Age Publishing, 367–87.

Rassoul, N. (1999) *Literacy for Sustainable Development in the Age of Information.* Clevedon: Multilingual Matters.

Read, C., Zhang, Y., Nie, H. and Ding, B. (1986) The Ability to Manipulate Sounds Depends on Knowing Alphabetic Transcription. *Cognition,* 24: 31–44.

Rigsby, B. (1987) Indigenous Language Shift and Maintenance in Fourth World Settings. In R. J. Watts (ed.) *Multilingua* (Berlin), 6(4): 359–78.

Roberts, A. R. and Coffey, O. D. (1976) State of the Art Survey for a Correctional Education Network. Washington: US Department of Justice, Law Enforcement Assistance Administration.

Rosch, E. (1975) Cognitive Representations of Semantic Categories. *Journal of Experimental Psychology* (General), 104: 192–233.

Rosch, E. (1978) Principles of Categorisation. In E. Rosch and B. Lloyd (eds) *Cognition and Categorisation*. Hillsdale, NJ: Lawrence Erlbaum Associates, 27–48.

Ross, R. R. (1978) Reading and Rehabilitation. *Crime and Justice* (*Crime et Justice*), 6(4): 207–19.

Ross, R. R. and McKay, H. B. (1976) A Study of Institutionalized Treatment Programs. *International Journal of Offender Therapy and Offender Criminology*, 20(2): 167–73.

Roy, J. D. (1987) The Linguistic and Sociolinguistic Position of Black English and the Issue of Bidialectism in Education. In P. Homel, M. Palij and D. Aaronson (eds) *Childhood Bilingualism. Aspects of Linguistic, Cognitive and Social Development*. Hillsdale, NJ: Lawrence Erlbaum Associates, 231–42.

Saenger P. (1997) *The Space between Words. The Origins of Silent Reading.* Stanford, CA: Stanford University Press.

Sahni, U. (2001) Children Appropriating Literacy: Empowerment Pedagogy from Young Children's Perspective. In B. Comber and A. Simpson (eds) *Negotiating Critical Literacies in Classrooms*. Mahwah, NJ: Lawrence Erlbaum Associates, 19–35.

Sandberg L. G. (1979) The Case of the Impoverished Sophisticate. Human Capital and Swedish Economic Growth before World War I. *Journal of Economic History*, XXXIX: 225–41.

Sandford, A. J. and Garrod, S. C. (1981) *Understanding Written Language: Explorations of Comprehension beyond the Sentence*. Chichester, New York, Brisbane and Toronto: John Wiley and Sons.

Sarashina (Lady) (1972) *The Pillow Book*. Harmondsworth: Penguin Classics.

Saussure, F. de (1974) *Course in General Linguistics*, ed. C. Bally and A. Sechehaye. London: Fontana.

Saxena, M. (1994) Literacies among the Punjabis in Southall. In J. Mayabin (ed.) *Language and Literacy in Social Practice*. Clevedon, Philadelphia and Adelaide: Multilingual Matters, 96–116.

Schank, R. and Abelson, R. (1977) *Scripts, Plans, Goals and Understanding: An Enquiry into Human Knowledge Structures*. Hillsdale, NJ: Lawrence Erlbaum Associates.

Schmandt-Besserat, D. (1992) *Before Writing, from Counting to Cuneiform*. Austin, TX: University of Texas.

Schofield, R. S. (1981) Dimensions of illiteracy in England 1750–1850. In H. J. Graff (ed.) *Literacy and Social Development in the West*. Cambridge: Cambridge University Press: 201–13.

Schön, D. (1963) *The Invention and Evolution of Ideas*. London: Tavistock.

Schön, D. (1993) Generative Metaphor and Social Policy. In A. Ortony (ed.) *Metaphor and Thought*. Cambridge: Cambridge University Press, 137–63.

Scribner, S. and Cole, M. (1981) *The Psychology of Literacy*. Cambridge, MA: Harvard University Press.

Secada, W. and Lightfoot, T. (1993) Symbols and the Political Consequence of Bilingual Education in the United States. In M. Arias and U. Casanova (eds), *Bilingual Education, Politics, Practice and Research*. Chicago: University of Chicago Press, 36–64.

Semino, E. (2002) A Cognitive Stylistic Approach to Mind Style in Narrative Fiction. In E. Semino and J. Culpeper (eds) *Cognitive Stylistics: Language and Cognition in Text Analysis*. Amsterdam: John Benjamins, 95–122.

Shiundu, J. O. (1987) *Primary Education and Self-employment in the Rural Informal Sector in Kenya. A Study of Primary School Leavers in Suna South Nyanza*. Nairobi: Kenyatta University Bureau of Education Research. Montreal: McGill University School of Education, 18.

Shrestha, G. (1997) *Literacy Education at a Distance: Developing Curriculum for Functional Literacy*. INFO21. http://www.undp.org/info21/public/literacy/pb-lite.html.

Shuman, A. (1986) *Story-Telling Rights: The Use of Spoken and Written Texts by Urban Adolescents*. Cambridge: Cambridge University Press.

Sienko, M. J. and Plane R. A. (1976) *Chemistry*. Tokyo: McGraw-Hill (fifth edition).

Skinner, B. F. (1957) *Verbal Behavior*. New York: Appleton-Century-Crofts.

Sorensen, A. P. (1971) Multilingualism in the Northwest Amazon. *American Anthropologist*, 69: 670–84.

Southwell, B. (1987) *Kenneth Burke and Martin Heidegger: With a Note against Deconstruction*. Gainsville, FL: University of Florida Monographs, Humanities No. 60.

Spivak, G. C. Introduction. In J. Derrida (1997) *Of Grammatology*. Baltimore: The Johns Hopkins University Press (first published under the title *De La grammatologie* in 1967).

Stagg, J. (1998) Putting it into Words: An Introductory Study of the Oral and Literate Practices of a West Indian Family Living in Britain. MA dissertation, University of Durham.

Sterq, C. (1993) *Literacy, Socialisation and Employment*. Bristol and Pennsylvania: Jessica Kingsley Publishers.

Street, B. V. (1984) *Literacy in Theory and Practice*. Cambridge: Cambridge University Press.

Street, B. V. (1996) *Social Literacies: Critical Approaches to Literacy in Development, Ethnography and Education*. London and New York: Longman.

Street, B. V. (2001) Literacy Empowerment in Developing Societies. In L. Verhoeven and C. Snow (eds) *Literacy and Motivation*. Mahwah, NJ: Lawrence Erlbaum Associates, 291–300.

Swales, J. (1990) *Genre Analysis: English in Academic and Research Settings*. Cambridge: Cambridge University Press.

Tannen, D. (1982) The Oral/Literate Continuum in Discourse. In D. Tannen (ed.) *Spoken and Written Language: Exploring Orality and Literacy*. Norwood, NJ: Ablex, 1–16.

Tannen, D. (1985) Relative Focus on Involvement in Oral and Written Discourse. In D. R. Olson, N. Torrance and A. Hildyard (eds) *Literacy, Language and Learning: The Nature and Consequences of Reading and Writing*. Cambridge: Cambridge University Press, 124–47.

Tansley, P. (1986) *Community Languages in Primary Education*. Windsor: NFER-Nelson.

Taylor, J. R. (2002) *Cognitive Grammar*. Oxford: Oxford University Press.

The National Literacy Trust (2002) Adults' Literacy Skills. http://www.literacy-trust.org.uk/database/stats/adult.html

Thompson, S. A. (1996) *Introducing Functional Grammar*. London, New York, Sydney and Auckland: Arnold.

Thouvenot, M. (1997) L'Ecriture Nahuatl. In A. Zali and A. Berthier (eds) *L'Aventures des Écritures: naissances*. Paris: Bibliothèque Nationale de France, 73–81.

Todaro, M. P. (2000) *Economic Development*. New York and Harlow: Addison-Wesley-Longman.

Traugött, E. (1987) Literacy and Language Change. The Special Case of Speech-act Verbs. *Interchange* 18 (1/2): 32–47.

Trudgill, P. (1995) *Sociolinguistics: An Introduction to Language and Society*. Harmondsworth: Penguin Books.

Ullman, B. L. (1969) *Ancient Writing and its Influence*. Cambridge, MA and London: MIT Press.

Ullman, S. (1962) *Semantics: An Introduction to the Science of Meaning*. Oxford: Blackwell.

United Nations Educational, Scientific and Cultural Organisation (1957) *World Literacy at Mid-Century*. Paris: UNESCO.

United Nations Educational, Scientific and Cultural Organisation (1972) *Progress Achieved in Literacy throughout the World*. Paris: UNESCO.

United Nations Educational, Scientific and Cultural Organisation (1973) *Practical Guide to Functional Literacy*. Paris: UNESCO.

Uyechi, L. (1996) *The Geometry of Visual Phonology*. Stanford, CA: CSLI.

Vincent, D. (2000) *The Rise of Mass Literacy*. Cambridge: Polity.

Vygotsky, L. S. (1978) *Mind in Society*. Cambridge, MA: Harvard University Press.

Wagner, D. A. and Puchner, L. D. (1992) World Literacy in the Year 2000. *The Annals of the American Academy of Political and Social Science*, Vol. 520.

Wells, G. (2000) Dialogic Enquiry in Education. In C. D. Lee and P. Smagorinsky (eds) *Vygotskian Perspectives on Literacy Research*. Cambridge: Cambridge University Press, 51–85.

Widdowson, H. G. (1979) *Explorations in Applied Linguistics*. Oxford: Oxford University Press.

Wilden, A. (1972) *System and Structure*. London: Tavistock.

Wiley, T. G. (1996) *Literacy and Language Diversity in the United States*. McHenry: Center for Applied Linguistics and Delta Systems.

Williams, S. W. (1991) Classroom Use of African American Language: Educational Tool or Social Weapon? In C. E. Sleeter (ed.) *Empowerment through Multicultural Education*. New York: State University of New York Press, 199–215.

Wittgenstein, L. (1953) *Philosphical Investigations*. New York: Macmillan.

Yates, F. (1984) *The Art of Memory*. London: Routledge & Kegan Paul. Ark Paperbacks.

Zali, A. and Berthier, A. (1997) *L'Aventures des Écritures: naissances*. Paris: Bibliothèque Nationale de France.

Zola, E. (1954) *Germinal*. Harmondsworth: Penguin Books.

Index

Abelson, R., 222
Abstraction and literacy, 172–4
Actionaid, 26
Actor, grammatical function of, 187, 188
Added value, education as, 12, 33
Adjunct, 188
Admixing, 153
Adult Performance Level (APL), 30
Affect and literacy, 31, 78
Africa, Sub-Saharan, 26
African American Language (AAL),
    also African-American Vernacular
    English (AAVE), 86
Agent (in grammar), 44, 154–5, 156,
    183, 193, 194
Agglutinative, 120
Aggregative use of language, 206, 208
Agnate genres, 185–6
Alphabet, the evolution of, 142–3
Alphabet, the nature of, 111–13
Al-Sharafah, A., 108
Amazon, 87
American Sign Language, ASL, 81
Analogical literacies, 1–3
Anaphora, 160
Anderson, C. A., 24
Angola, 25
Arabic language and script, 83, 86–6,
    114–15, 123, 126, 143, 148, 212,
    213, 215
Arabic numerals, 172
Arapho language, 81
Archer, P., 237
Argument and literacy, 6, 156, 159, 164,
    170–2, 208, 210, 214, 225, 230

Aristotle, 104–5, 208
ASL (American Sign Language), 81,
    147
Assimilationists, 89
Astington, J. W., 206
Atlantic, 142
Atlantis, 156
Attali, J., 74
Austen, J., 161–2
Australia, 184
Australian Aboriginal, 102, 130
Aztec, 33, 125, 169, 227

Bacon, F., 157, 158
Banks, D., 154
Barber, C., 171
Barber, F. J. W., 139
Bartlett, F. C., 222
Basic Skills, 12, 18, 19, 27
Basic Skills Agency, 19
Basque, language, 81, 92
Bauer, P., 25
Benson, N., 69
Berk, L. E., 217
Bernstein, B., 55–6, 68
Bhatia, V., 168
Bhatt, A., 70
Biber, D., 155, 160, 166, 167–9, 174,
    178–81, 185, 186, 239
Bickerton, D., 84
Bilingualism, 81, 83, 87–9
Biliteracy, 87–9
Binomial, 168
Birmingham, city of, 19, 160
Blanck, G., 198

Blending, cognitive process of, conceptual blending, 130–3, 193
Blunch, N.-H., 27
Bongili language, 91
Book clubs, 218
Book of Days, the, 74
Bowman, M. J., 24
Brahmi, 113, 114
Brandscombe, A., 217
Breton-Gravereau, S., 74
Bricker, K., 88
British Columbia, Canada, 21
British Sign Language (BSL), 81
Brodova, E., 217–18
Bronze age, 142
Brown, K., 56
Bruner, J., 198
Buddhism, 74, 76
Bush, George, Snr, President of the United States of America, 57
Bynner, J., 19, 24
Byzantine Empire, 3

California state, 88
Canaanite, 141
Canterbury Tales, 85
Captain Corelli's Mandolin, 221
Carrington, L., 93, 94
Carter, R., 175
Cartesian, 170
Case, in grammar, 142
Category theory, 105–6, 108, 144
Catholic Church, 13–14, 22, 146
Catzel, I., 155
Cause and effect, expression of, 108, 155, 185, 186, 188–9, 190, 210, 226, 229
Cawdrey, R., 171
Celtic languages, 81
Centaur, 130
Central Africa, 80
Chafe, W. L., 163
Chaiklin, S., 23
Charbonnier, G., 207
Chaucer, G., 85
Cherokee, Native American nation, script and language, 93
China, 14, 75, 76, 94, 146
Chinese minorities, 82, 83

Chinese, language and script, 113, 114–21, 122, 129, 131, 133, 137, 139, 140, 141, 144, 146, 148
Chomsky, N., 147, 157, 158, 197
Christie, F., 55–6
Churinga (Australian aboriginal text), 102
Cipolla, C., 13
Citizenship literacy, 2
Codes, of signs, 103
Coding competence, 54
Coffey, A. D., 20
Coffin, C., 185–6, 187
Cognitive deficit, in bilingualism, 87, 88
Cognitive linguistics, 125, 158, 211
Cognitive surplus, in bilingualism, 87
Cohesion, 46, 77, 88–9
Cole, E., 171
Cole, M., 65, 207, 210, 212–14, 215, 259
Colonial language, 82
Communist Manifesto, 14, 38
Community languages, 82, 87
Community of practice, 23, 29, 60, 64–5, 66, 198
Compound indicative, 119, 121
Computer desktop, 129
Computerisation and literacy, 23
Conceptual blend, 192
Conceptual metaphor, 50–1, 224–31
Conceptualisation, 50
Confucian, 25
Congruent language, 187–9
Conjunctions, 156
Conscientizacao (consciencisation), 53
Consonantal, 128, 141, 144, 215
Container schema, 225
Contiguity, 136
Conventionalisation, 138
Cook-Gumperz, J., 218
Copernicus, 157
Corpus linguistics, 165–6
Cree, script and language, 81, 93
Creole, 84–5, 86, 93
Crete, 42
Criminality and literacy, 11, 19–21
Criterion referencing, 28
Critical Discourse Analysis, 36, 44–9, 52, 55, 61

Critical literacy, 34, 36–62
Cuban minority, 88
Cultural literacy, 32
Cummings, 88
Cuneiform, 138–9, 140, 146
Cyrillic alphabet, 81, 111, 142

Dalglish, C., 19, 20, 29
De Bernière, L., 221
De Temple, J. M., 2
Deacon, T., 103–4, 109, 239
Deconstruction, 37, 47, 55, 57, 59, 60,
    61, 62, 220
Decontextualisation and written text, 160
Decreolisation, 86
Defrancis, J., 111, 113–22, 139, 146, 147
Delhi, 70
Denny, K., 27
Department for Education and
    Employment (DFEE), 2, 31
Derrida, J., 2, 5, 40–1, 49, 58, 148–9
Descartes, R., 170
Design, in literacy pedagogy, 69–70
Determinative, 119, 121, 129
Devanagari language, 70, 113
Development economics and literacy,
    15–17, 33
Diachronic perspective on writing and
    sign, 125, 133
Diacritic, 112–13
Diagrams as iconic signs, 102
Dialogic construction of text, 156–9
Diaz, M., 199
Dictionaries, 171
Diderot, 171
Diglossia, 85–6
Digraph, 112
Dimension of difference between text
    modes, 178–9
Diminishing marginal productivity, law
    of, 12, 33
Discipline and Punish, 42
Discourse community, 236
Dominant discourse, 68
Double negatives, 171
Downing, A., 188
Drucker, J., 74
Durable nature of written text, 159–60

East Africa, 83
East Asia, 25
Education, banking concept of, 53
Egbo, B., 26
Egyptian language and script, Egypt, 73,
    129, 135, 137, 138, 139–43, 144,
    146, 148
Eisemon, T. O., 17, 26
Ellipsis, 175
Embedded clauses, 166
Emotional literacy, 2
Empiricism, 171
Endophoric, 160–2, 177, 180–1, 190,
    210, 211
Engles, F., 14
Enlightenment philosophy, 13
Epistemic verbs, 169, 209
Ethnic minority language, 82–3
Ethnography and literacy, 77
Etruscan, language and script, 112
Exophoric, 160–2, 177, 180–1, 210
Explicit reference, 180

Fact or opinion exercises, 57
Factor in text difference, 178–82
Fairclough, N., 45, 48
Fauconnier, G., 130–3
Featural writing system, 115
Female adult literacy, 16
Ferguson, C. A., 85
Field, in discourse, 46, 184
Finnegan, R., 206
Finnish language, 81
Fiscal practices, 70
Fischer, S. R., 116, 122, 137, 138, 141
Fog Index, 29
Formality in written language, 170
Foucault, M., 5, 42, 171
Fowler, R., 221
Frame theory, 220–2
Fraser, H., 56
Frazer, J., 60
Freetown, Sierra Leone, 82
Freire, P., 36, 39, 52–5, 57, 60, 61, 164,
    237
French language, 24, 41, 80, 84, 85, 112,
    161, 170, 171, 172
French national curriculum, 2, 3

Fry, E., 20
Full and partial communication systems, 47
Functional literacy, 4, 11–35, 39, 53, 235–6
Functional literacy, problems with, 21–35

Galileo, 157
Gallup, 19
Garrod, S. C., 220
Gaur, A., 76, 102, 122, 130
Gee, J. P., 52, 64, 65, 66, 67
Gelb, I. J., 114, 122, 123
Genosko, G., 100
Genre, 6, 55–6, 59, 60, 61, 62, 65, 66, 76, 86, 157, 164, 172, 174, 176, 178, 179, 180–7, 189, 191, 192, 193, 194, 231, 236, 239
Germanic languages, 215
Germinal, 161
Gibbs, R., 51, 107
Gilgamesh, epic of, 159
Glottic, 126, 127, 133, 134, 192, 193
Glyphs, 125
Goal, grammatical function, 183
Goody, J., 159, 205, 207, 212, 253
Gough, K., 25
Graff, H. J., 12, 13, 20, 22, 23
Grammar and literacy, 171
Grammatical metaphor, 186–90, 193
Grapheme, 45, 101, 112, 116, 143, 148, 163, 192
Grapholect, 5–6, 68, 92
Great Divide, 205–14, 225
Greece, 75, 221
Greek culture and people, 2, 13, 130, 138, 142, 172, 207, 208, 210, 215
Greek philosophy, 172
Greek, language and script, 111, 112, 116, 135, 142, 143, 202–3, 207, 215, 218
Greenfield, P. M., 212
Grigsby, K., 14, 15, 16
Gropius, W., 38
Gross National Product (GNP), impact of literacy upon, 16
Gujarati, 70
Gulf War, 50

Gurmuki, 70
Gustaffason, M., 168
Gutenberg, J., 76

Hakuta, K., 87
Hall, J. K., 60, 91
Halliday, M., 45, 55, 101, 118, 139, 149, 155, 161, 180, 183, 186, 187, 221, 239
Hamilton, Canada, 22
Hangul script, 116
Hansel and Gretel, 57
Harris, R., 101, 104–5, 124–5, 192
Hassan, R., 161
Havelock, E. A., 205, 207, 208
Health literacy, 17–18
Heath, S. B., 216–17
Heine, B., 125
Henderson, E. H., 116
Henry IV of England, 227
Heroditus, 208
Hieroglyphs, 75, 135, 139–41, 143
Hindi, 70, 113
Hiragana, Japanese syllabary, 113–14, 121
Hirsch, E. D., 32–3
Hittite Script, 125
Hoggart, R., 48
Holme, R., 45, 47, 57, 171, 189
Holmes, Sherlock, 60
Holy Spirit, 227
Homeostasis, 205, 207
Homer, 159, 207, 209
Homophone, 112
Hood, S., 56
Hornberger, N., 81, 91, 92
Hosking, R. F., 113, 114
Howell, D. R., 23
Human capital theory and literacy, 12, 27
Huskey, E., 80
Hussein, Saddam, 42, 43, 50
Huxley, A., 52
Hymes, D., 99

Iconic signs, 4, 101–3, 104, 109, 116, 118, 121, 122, 123, 124, 125, 126, 127, 128, 129, 132, 133, 135–7, 139, 140, 144, 148, 192, 193, 225, 238

Ideographic, 111, 117, 119, 120, 134
Illich, I., 205
Image schema, 224–31
Images, as iconic signs, 102
Immersion programmes, 88
Impact on earnings of literacy, 26–7
Inca, 81
Indexical signs, 101–2, 104–5, 106, 108,
    109, 119, 121, 124, 125, 127, 133,
    135, 136, 137–9, 144, 199, 239
India, 25, 82, 90, 113, 142, 143, 164, 168,
    184
Indo-European languages, 142, 143
Indulgences, 73
Inflections, inflected languages, 117,
    120–1, 142, 174
Inner London Education Authority, 87
International Adult Literacy Survey, 29
Internationalisation, of a language, 90
Interpretant, of a sign, 101
Intertextual, 46, 193
Iraq, 42, 50, 57, 71, 158
Iroquois, Native American Nation, 92
Islam, 70, 85, 215

Japan, 75, 146
Japanese people, 90, 106, 146
Japanese, language and script, 113,
    120–1, 141, 148
Jewish minorities, 83
Johannson, E., 14
Johansen, J. D., 3, 103
Johnson, M., 50, 126, 224, 225, 226
Johnson, S., 171

Kana, Japanese syllabaries, 113–14, 121
Kanji, Japanese character script, 121,
    146
Karmiloff-Smith, A., 213
Katakana, Japanese syllabaries, 113–14,
    121
Kempa, S., 19
Kerala state, 25
Kikcongo language, 91
King James' Bible, 209
Kingston, Canada, 22
Knowledge economy, 11–12
Koenig, M., 81

Kolstoe, P., 80
Korean language and script, 120
Kress, G., 47, 124
Kuwait, 50
Kymlicka, W., 81
Kyrgyzstan, 81

Labour market and literacy, 23–4
Labov, W., 68, 86
Lakoff, G., 50–1, 105, 106–7, 109, 126,
    173, 224, 225, 226
Lancaster Spoken Corpus, 166
Language Choice, 80–94
Language Death, 90–1
Language Maintenance, 90–1, 92
Language Rights, 89
Lankshear, C., 30, 32, 53, 164
Larsen, S. E., 3, 103
Latin language, 3, 81, 84, 112, 129, 142,
    143, 174, 208, 225, 227
Laughlin, M. C., 218
Lave, J., 23
Law and literacy, 11, 65–6, 72–3, 78,
    160, 167–8, 176, 188, 193, 208
Lawler, M., 30, 32
Layder, D., 78
Le Corbusier, H., 37, 38
Le Page, R. B., 81
Lee, P., 218
Leibnitz, G., 117
Lemke, J. L., 45
Less Developed Countries (LDCs), 16,
    24, 26, 90
Letter writing and literacy, 74–5
Levant, 142
Levine, K., 24, 32
Lexical variety, 181
Liberman, I., 116
Lienhardt, R. G., 60
Limba, people and language, 206
Linear B, 142
Lingala, language, 91
Lingua Franca, 83
Linguistic imperialism, 89–90
Linnaeus, 171
Literacies, theory of, 65, 66
Literacy campaigns, 14–15, 31, 94
Literacy events, 66–7

Literacy framework, 2
Literacy hour, 31
Literacy practices, 65–79, 92, 94, 99,
    100, 104, 127, 133, 141, 147, 149,
    160, 162, 168, 190, 191–2, 214–31,
    235–6, 238–9
Literacy practices and education, 76–7
Literacy trust, 19
Little Red Riding Hood, 57
Lloyd Wright, F., 37, 38, 39
Locative-subject metaphor, 188
Locke, P., 188
Logographic script, 118, 192
Loma, script and language, 93
London, Canada, 22
Luke, L., 55
Lutheran church, 14

Macdonald's Restaurants, 39, 124
Mckay, H. B., 21
Mclaren, P., 53–4
Mcluan, M., 38
Mcveigh, T., 19
Madagascar, 3
Mahadeo, S., 84
Malinowski, B., 213
Mandarin language, 120
Manuscript illumination, 126
Mapping, cognitive process of, 130–2
Martin, J., 55, 70, 183–5, 239
Martin-Jones, M., 70
Marx, C., Marxism, 14, 38, 39, 89,
    197–8, 200, 203
Materialisation, 217
Mathematics and literacy, 201, 203,
    217
Matsqui Penitentiary, 21
Mauritius, 84, 85
May, S., 88
Maya, 73
Meaning potential, of signs, 101
Mediterranean, 142
Melanesian Creole, 85
Mellor, B., 57
Mental spaces, theory of, 130
Meredith-Ownes, G. M., 113, 114
Metafunction, 184
Metalanguage, 209

Metaphor *see* conceptual metaphor,
    grammatical metaphor, or
    metaphors as iconic signs
Metaphors, as iconic signs, 102
Metatext, 49
Metonymy, 42–3, 107–8, 124, 128, 130,
    133, 137, 140, 141, 170, 197, 239
Microsoft, 129
Milwakee magnet schools, 88
Mind style, 221
Minoan, 142
Minsky, M., 220, 221, 231
Mnemonics, 206
Modality, 170
Mode, in discourse, 46–7, 166, 169, 174,
    180, 181, 184–7, 189, 190
Modernism, 37–8, 39, 40, 59
Monologic construction of text, 157–9
Monumental literacies, 73, 146
Morpheme, 101
Morphological and syntactic
    completeness, 173–6
Morphosyllabic scripts, 117–21
Morpurgo-Davis, A., 125
Morris, D., 116
Moves in discourse, 164
Multinomial, 168
Muslim, 83, 86, 212
Myth and literacy, 168

Nahuatl language, 125
Narrative frames, 223–4
Narrative, 46, 49, 56, 73, 76, 102, 153,
    165, 166, 177, 179–80, 186–7, 194,
    207, 208, 217, 222–3, 224
National literacy strategy (NLS), 2, 31
National minorities, 81
Native American, nations, languages,
    literacies and cultures, 32, 33, 84,
    92, 130, 209, 222, 223, 227
Nature versus nurture, 195
Navaho language, 81
Neo-colonialism, theory of, 89–90
New London Group, 69
Nexus of exchange and literacy, 23
Nicaragua, 14
Nominal density, 178–9
Nominal elements, 160

Nominalisation, 155–6, 178, 188
Norman Conquest, 84
Norm-referencing, 28, 30
Norse Sagas, 158
Noun compliment clauses, 173–4
Novaya Zembla, 211
Number systems, 125–6
Nutbeam, D., 17
Nyerere, J., 16
Nystrand, M., 55, 217

Object, of a sign, 101
Objectivisim, in pedagogy, 53
Observer newspaper, 19
Occupational status and literacy, 22
Old Testament, 206
Olson, D. R., 170, 202, 205, 206, 207, 209
Ong, W. J., 168, 205–10, 211, 212, 213
Ontogenesis, 136, 143, 186, 200, 201–3
Organisation for Economic Co-operation and Development (OECD), 13, 30
Ottoman Empire, 215

Palfrey, C., 20
Paper, invention of, 75
Papua New Guinea, 85, 92
Papyrus, 141, 146
Parry, M., 207
Participatory Pedagogy, 36, 37, 52–4, 61
Participatory rural appraisal, 237–8
Passive, in grammar, 44, 47, 154–5, 156, 193, 194
Past tense, 169
Path image schema, 225–6
Patient, in grammar, 154–5
Patterson, A., 57
Pedagogic device, 55–6
Peirce, C. S., 100, 101–3, 121, 239
Perie, M., 23, 24, 30
Periodic appraisal, 185, 186
Persian, 126
Peru, 81, 92, 93
Petterson, S. S., 5, 149
Phaedra, of Plato, 52
Phillipson, R., 89–90
Phoenician, 141, 142–3

Phoneme, 45, 54, 58, 101, 105, 111, 112–13, 114, 116, 118, 142, 144, 146, 163, 173, 175
Phonetic, 56, 106, 112, 117–18, 121, 122, 128, 131, 132, 133, 139, 141, 145, 147, 148, 215
Phonocentric, 148–9
Phonograph, 120, 121, 122, 123, 128, 131, 133, 138, 139, 140
Phonology, 75, 105, 120, 144, 147
Phylogenesis, 136, 143, 186, 200–3
Piaget, I., 199, 201
Pictograph, 4, 119, 121, 122, 126, 127, 133, 137, 138, 139, 141, 143, 144, 192
Pidgins, 84
Pillow Book, the, 75
Plato, 2, 12, 52, 53, 104, 154, 156, 208, 209
Post-Modernism, 36–44, 45, 46, 47, 48, 49, 50, 52, 53, 55, 58, 59, 61
Pragmatic competence, in critical literacy, 54
Pragmatics, 45–6
Praxis, in participatory pedagogy, 53
Prayer and literacy, 73–4
Pre-reading (Prélecture), 3
Present tense, 169
Primary discourse, 68
Private speech, 217
Private verbs, 178
Process, grammatical function, 183
Progeneration metaphor, 226
Promissory notes, 71
Prosodic appraisal, genre of, 185–6
Proto-Indo-European, language, 81
Prototype theory, 106
Proto-writing, 137
Puchner, L. D., 16
Punjabi, 70

Quantitative literacy, 27
Quechua, language, 81, 92
Quipu, 138
Quirk, R., 154, 179
Quran, 86, 213, 214, 215

Raphael, T. E., 218
Rassoul, N., 14, 15, 16

Read, C., 116
Rebus, 118, 119, 121, 122, 128, 131–2, 139, 140, 143, 144
Recidivism and literacy, 20–1
Recreational literacies, 76, 77
Redundancy in discourse, 298
Reformation, protestant reformation, 13–14, 22, 94, 146
Register, 6, 55, 61, 66, 71, 160, 165, 166, 174, 176, 178, 181, 182, 183–90, 193, 194
Reification, metaphor of, 73
Relative clause, 166, 167, 180, 181
Restricted code, 68
Richardson, S., 76
Roberts, A. R., 20
Roberts, P., 155
Roman alphabet, 103, 105–6, 111, 112, 115, 116, 135, 142, 143, 146, 215
Roman empire, 112
Roman numerals, 126
Rosch, E., 106, 173
Ross, R. R., 20, 21
Roy, J. D., 86
Runes, runic alphabets, 112, 146
Russia, 211
Russian, language, 80–1
Ryerson, E., 13

Saenger, P., 76, 99
Sahni, U., 165
Sandanista National Liberation Front, 14
Sandberg, L. G., 23
Sanders, B., 205
Sandford, A. J., 220
Sarashina, Lady, 75
Saussure, F., 40, 100, 173
Saxena, M., 70
Scaffolding, 198, 216–18, 262
Scannable nature of text, 163
Schank, R., 222
Schema, 46, 175, 222–4, 238, 239; *see also* image schema
Schmandt-Besserat, D., 138
Schofield, R. S., 22
Schön, D., 49
Schuman, A., 69

Science and literacy, 31, 40, 55, 67, 72–3, 154, 155, 167, 172, 177, 190, 201, 203, 215
Scotland, 94
Scribner, S., 65, 207, 210, 212–14, 215, 259
Scripts, schema, 222
Scriptura continua, 75
Seals, 104
Secondary discourse, 68
Seeker, grammatical function, 188
Semantic competence, in critical literacy, 54
Semantic features, in category formation, 105
Semantics, 45–6, 75, 105, 170
Semasiographic, 121–33, 145, 147, 148, 149, 192, 193
Semino, E., 221
Semiosis, 126, 127, 136, 138, 148–9, 164, 191, 193, 199, 201
Semitic languages and scripts, 114, 116, 139, 140–1, 143
Semograph, 124, 125, 128, 138, 139, 141, 144, 164, 192–3
Senser, grammatical function, 187
Shakespeare, W., 84, 207
Shared activity, 217–18
Shrestha, G., 16
Sienko, M. J., 154
Sierra Leone, 25, 82, 206
Sign Language, 81, 117, 120, 147–8, 262; *see also* ASL and BSL
Signified, 40, 100
Signifier, 40, 100
Signs, 3, 4–5, 31, 38, 40, 41, 43, 45, 51, 58, 71, 72, 74, 76, 100–10, 113, 114, 115, 116, 117, 118, 119, 121, 122, 123, 124, 125, 132, 133, 135, 136, 137, 138, 139, 192, 199–200, 201, 202, 213, 239
Sikh, 70
Silent Reading, 75–6, 99
Situated, speech as, 169
Situation-dependent reference, 180
Skinner, B. F., 197
Smith, Adam, 13
Snow, C. E., 2

Social construction, 41–2, 44, 58–60
Social exclusion and literacy, 19–21
Social function of literacy, 4
Social practices, 4, 7, 31, 64–6, 67, 70,
    77, 78, 99, 109, 145, 146, 165, 172,
    185, 197, 201, 214, 215–16, 219,
    225, 231, 235, 236, 239
Social semiotic, language as a, 183
Socio-historical construction of mind,
    198–201, 238
Socrates, 52–4, 74, 104, 156, 208, 211
Sorensen, A. P., 87
South America, 81
South Asia, 25
Southwell, A., 59
SOV (Subject Object Verb) language, 120
Soviet Union, the former, 80–1
Spain, 94
Spanish language, 80, 81, 88, 91, 92, 113,
    227
Spivak, G. C., 149
Stagg, J., 165
Starr, D., 120
Stem word, 120
Strauss, L., 207
Street, B., 31, 48, 55, 60, 65, 66, 70, 94,
    102, 145
Subculture and text, 128
Subjectivism, 53
Subordinative use of language, 206, 208
Substrata languages, 84
Subtext, 43
Sukŭn, Arabic diacritic, 115
Sumeria, Sumerian language and script,
    72, 104, 129, 135, 137–8, 139
Sunday Times newspaper, 42
SVO (Subject Word Object) language,
    120
Swahili, language, 83
Swales, J., 181, 236
Sweden, 14, 22
Syllabary, 111, 113–17, 118, 121, 133,
    142, 213
Syllabic alphabet, 116
Syllogism, 210–11, 225
Symbolic Signs, 101–2, 103–8, 109, 121,
    125, 126, 132, 133, 135, 137, 143,
    173, 192, 194, 199, 225, 238, 239

Syncretism, 192
Syntax, 75, 82, 84, 117, 120, 174, 208, 227
Systemic Functional Linguistics (SFL),
    36, 44, 45–9, 183–90, 239

*Tabula Regum Anglie ab Adamo usque ad
    Henricum IV*, 227
Tajikistan, 81
Tamil, 113
Tannen, D., 154, 169–70, 177
Tansely, P., 87
Tanzania, 16
Taxonomies, 171
Taylor, J. R., 158
Technologisation of discourse, 48–9
Tenor, in discourse, 46, 193
Text Box, 129
Text frame, 164–5
Text-messaging, 5, 127, 131, 164, 170
Thesis appraisal, 185, 186
Thibault, D., 74
Thompson, S. A., 45, 186, 188
Thouvenot, M., 125
Tibet, 74
Tigris-Euphrates valley, 71
Timaeus and Critias, 156
Time and literacy, 74, 168–9
Todaro, M. P., 12, 16, 24, 26
Tok Pisin, language, 85, 93
Tokens, 138
Totem pole, 144, 227
Transformational Grammar, 44, 227
Traugott, E., 208
Tree diagrams, 227
Trigraph, 112
Triliteral language, 114, 115, 140, 141
Troilus and Cressyde, 85
Trudgill, P., 85
Tukano people, 87
Turner, M., 130–3
Twelfth Night, 171
Type-token ratios, 171

Uganda, 83
United Nations (UN), 26
United Nations Educational, Scientific
    and Cultural Organisation
    (UNESCO), 3, 11, 14, 15, 16, 29, 38

United States Army, 13, 17
United States Bureau of Census, 29
United States Office of Education, 30
Universal Grammar (UG), 197
Universal writing systems, 117
University of Texas, 30
Univocal discourse, 171
Uyechi, 147

Vai, people, script and language, 93,
    212–14
Vedas, 158
Vermeer, J., 207
Vernacular literacy, 93–4
Verner, D., 27
Vincent, D., 23, 75, 77
Visual literacy, 2–3, 18, 124, 237
Vygotsky, L., 136–7, 198–203, 206–7,
    210, 213, 214, 215, 217–19, 238

Wagner, D. A., 16
Washington, DC, 42

Watt, I., 159, 205, 207, 212
Webster, N., 172
Wells, G., 198, 200, 261
Welsh, language, 88, 92
West Africa, 80, 82, 93
West Indian, 165
Western Europe, 18, 82, 112, 126
Wiley, T. G., 1, 83, 86, 87
Williams, S. W., 86
Wolf, E. N., 23
Writing history, 5, 135–43
Writing, nature of, 145–50
Written and spoken language,
    differences between, 154

Yemen, 74

Zimbabwe, 25
Zola, E., 161
Zone of Proximal Development (ZPD),
    201–3, 216, 218